To my de

Love all your encouragement

Margarette

BEEN THERE, DONE THAT

Lived to Tell

Magarette Boutillette

PAGE PUBLISHING, INC.
New York, NY

First originally published by Page Publishing, Inc. 2016

ISBN 978-1-68409-645-9 (Paperback)
ISBN 978-1-68409-646-6 (Digital)

Printed in the United States of America

DEDICATION

Okay, so here I go again, trying to start writing my book that everyone keeps telling me to. I finally decided for my husband, Chris, who has been my solid rock for so many years.

CHAPTER 1

I grew up under the terror and love of my older brother whom I called Bruce. He sabotaged my every move, from trying to walk to wanting the attention of one of our parents—or anything for that matter. Yet I adored him beyond measure.

When I was about five years old, I thought he was dead when I saw him fall off his horse Dotty. When the ambulance arrived and they carried him off in a stretcher, I went hysterical as I watched this scenario unfold. Hours later, I calmed down when he walked through the door, wearing his trophy—a cast on his arm. He survived!

As he was catwalking along the roofline of our two-story Cape Cod style house, I was frantic that he would fall. I could never relax; I was always stressed whenever my brother was out of my sight. I even hated when he went into the first grade and I did not get to see him for hours. All the while, he was so mean and rough with me.

I did catch a break when my brother Dave was born two years later. But not much of a break—at least not until Dave got big enough to throw around. By that time, three more siblings came into the fold. I loved my baby siblings so much—until they got big enough to not do what I wanted.

I did manage to survive, though, in spite of Bruce's sneaky tricks to sabotage my every move, and as time went by and we tangled, screamed, and teased one another, I yet still managed to be in awe of my big brother.

One day, I was invited to stay for the weekend with my cousins Pam Bunny and Paige Putnam who lived about two hours away from us. My parents drove me out there and then left. I was so happy to be getting a break from the torturous daily routines. I really loved spending time with them, and I adored the girls' parents, who were my mother's cousins that we saw quite often. I was not in a space unfamiliar to me, yet that evening when we were going out for ice cream, I began to get weepy and began to cry for my mom. Nothing any of them could do made me feel better, so they decided to just take me home.

I had a terrible cold, which had turned worse daily; all the while, Mom thought I was just being a crybaby. I was always sad about something, so she thought it was just me being me—crying, sulking, depressed, and lonely. I hardly ever smiled. So here it was almost a week of me being whiny and cranky, making everyone miserable. When it was getting hard for me to breathe, Mom would bring me down into the cellar and put the dryer on, which moistened the air, helping me to breathe enough to sleep for a while. Finally, the day when I was lying on the couch and struggling to catch a breath, I slowly started to drift off, floating down a long dark yet not scary tunnel, and yes, there was white misty light at the other end. While I was slowly spiraling up and down and all around, quite enjoyable, I did not feel the discomfort of not being able to breathe anymore, then I heard my grandmother say, "Betty, she is turning blue." I thought, *So what? I like the color blue.* Next thing I knew, the paramedics showed up, and I had this ugly black rubber thing on my face. Next was the trip to the hospital, where a nurse took me out of my dad's arms and backed through the doors of the emergency room. I ended up staying in the hospital for a while—at least two weeks in an oxygen tent. I had to get injected twice daily with something painful and had to drink some foul fake-cherry liquid, which I always proceeded to throw up. I still can't stand the taste of cherry medicine.

Another instance I went through which was kind of traumatic was when I saw an angel outside the window. The first thought I had was that he had come to take Bruce back to heaven. I screamed, I cried, I thrashed around until someone came to see what all the commotion was. As I was explaining to my mother, she carried me to the window to show there was no angel outside waiting to take Bruce away. I continued to cry, sobbing that the angel was on the other side of the house, waiting for her and Daddy to leave for the Fireman's

Ball. After what seemed like forever, I finally calmed down, and my parents were able to leave. My favorite babysitter was with us, so it was not a ruse to get them to stay home. Even at my young years, I knew the ball meant a lot to my mother as she hardly ever got to go out for anything special with my dad. I thought she looked beautiful; I wanted her to go. Well, that angel never took him (even though sometimes I should have wished him that). Nothing could shake my devotion to him.

My younger brother David was born May 6, 1954. He and I were best buds. He would do and help and be with me whatever I asked him too. Kim-Laurie was born January 22, 1957, and I couldn't wait for her to grow up a little so she and I could play together instead of me changing her diapers or feeding her, although I didn't mind carrying her around while I waited.

I began first grade the fall of that year. On the first day, we all had to show our vaccinations; I was the only one who did not have it on my arm. I had to go outside of the classroom and wait for the teacher to come out and have me pull up my skirt to show where it was on my leg. I was mortified. I was the odd ball. Not only that, but there was no desk for me. I was the only one not having a desk or chair. I did not understand that then, nor do I now for that matter. I did not even know how to spell my name or count from one to ten. I could not even write my ABCs. I was so ashamed because all the other kids in my class knew how.

Over that first year of school, I was painfully shy. If the bell to line up for marching into the school had rung before I had reached the playground, I would wait and hide behind the town hall, which was next to the Center School there in Bellingham. I would wait till almost the last kid was through the doors and then run to get in before those doors shut, causing me to be considered late for school. As the year progressed, I didn't. I could not grasp anything the teacher tried to tell me. I just couldn't get it. Nothing really registered. Because of that, I had a tendency to daydream and stare out the windows. When the teacher wanted to have me repeat the first grade, my grandmother said no, and because Mom did not dare to cross her and the teachers were afraid of my grandmother as well, she passed me.

My mother brought me to a child psychologist for evaluation on what my problem could be. After a series of Q and A, as well as some pictures shown to me and what I could do in writing skills, I was told to sit in the waiting room while Mom was given the results of the testing. I actually heard her say, "Well, Betty, she isn't exactly retarded, but she is slow." After hearing that, I thought, *Of course I am not retarded, and I will show you I am not slow. I will be fine.* Whatever that meant to me at the time.

Then I was off to the second grade to continue my struggle. I eventually got some things right, and I did love reading. I did not read fast. Once I figured out things, I could really get going. One day, as I sat in the classroom, listening to the substitute teacher talk, I made my nose wrinkle as it was a continuous habit I had and always tried to hide it, but this one time as I could not control the urge to do it, my former first grade teacher walking past saw me through the window in the door. Immediately she stuck her head in and said I was to see her after class. She happened to be the principle then as well as first-grade teacher.

When the bell for lunch rang and my classmates and all the other four grades were enjoying their free time, I was in the principal's office. I will never forget the feeling of defeat as I knew she would not believe me. I tried to explain that Mrs. Ambler was my 4-H teacher as well as one of my Sunday school teachers and I really liked her. She was kind to me and patient. I would never make a face at her, and there was no reason for me to make a face at her. I was told to go tell Mrs. Ambler I was sorry and then to report to the principal's office after school. No way was she understanding that I could not help it when the twinge struck. Till this day, it is hard for me to curb the urge. So off I went to the restroom where Mrs. Ambler was washing her hands, and I went over to her and explained the situation. I told her through my tears that I would never do that to her. She in return smiled at me and said "I know." But why did she not defend me to the principal? Back in those days, no one wanted to rock the boat in any situation, I guess. I was lucky that I did not get the over-the-knee spanking that time. I did get one later on in the year. The regular teacher told me to take off the money belt I had on, but I did not. I don't know why I was so obstinate over that as I knew I was going to be reprimanded. I never thought she would spank me. I was told to come to the front of the class, and she pulled her chair to the front of her desk. Taking my belt away from me, she proceeded to make me lie across her lap and began wailing on my butt. Mortified does not even cover it. Not only that, but I knew everyone would be telling Bruce, and for sure, he would make fun of me as well. Plus I knew the teacher would be calling Mom to tell her what went down, and that meant another scolding when I got home. I just could not win.

July 19, 1959, Jimmy was born. I was so happy to have another baby to play with again. I will never forget Uncle Howard, upon first look at him, said, "That is the ugliest baby I ever saw!" I was so mad at him I countered, "No! He is beautiful!" That sticks in my mind even to this day. Then Ross showed up, born on Father's Day June 1960. After that, things in life began to take a terrible turn. Ross would be our only joy during that time.

I knew my mother was not really happy because she was always making little comments about Grandma (my dad's mother), who lived not one hundred yards away. The gripe was how she always criticized everything Mom did. My father was always an angel in Gram's eyes. The local townspeople (mostly the women) were jealous of my mother because she was so beautiful. Even after having all us kids, she still looked awesome, plus having a great personality. Why my father treated her as a brood mare and housekeeper was beyond me. I knew things were getting sticky. I could tell my mother needed more than just her children. Dad never tried to help her with anything. He never took her out, and rarely would he go on vacation with her or us. All the while, Grandma was harping on my mother about this or that she was not doing right.

CHAPTER 2

One day, I guess they had a discussion, and Mom told Dad that she was not feeling happy or fulfilled as a wife and partner. My father decided that all the marriage needed was a little bit of house renovation to make her happy, and along came the Boyer Brothers Carpentry to do the work. They were two older men, brothers working as a team.

The first thing they built was a picnic table and benches for our kitchen. We loved that. Then they went on to work on other rooms. The kitchen was the last room they worked on, and it was during that time the drama quietly began. That day, my mother was very sick with tonsillitis, which anyone who has had that as an adult (or youth) knows how painful and feverish you get. We had never seen Mom so sick before, but being kids, we thought it was a vacation from her scolding and yelling at us all the time. She did not even care that we never got out of our PJs or as we ran throughout the house. By noon, my father came home, and the first thing he did was ask Mom how come us kids were not dressed. Seeing how sick she was, he told her that he would go eat at his mother's. He did not even offer her any help; instead, upon seeing that the cat had pooped on the floor, he then told her to clean up the mess. All the while, Vern Boyer, overhearing all this, finally could not stand all that he had witnessed over the past few months, and that little episode just sent him over the edge. He picked up the cat poop and tossed it out the window, just missing Dad as he walked past on his way to his mother's lunch. Being the wimp that he was, he never said anything about it; he just kept walking. After that, Vern turned to us and ordered us to get dressed and go outside and play. Giving us gum kind of sealed the deal to listen to him. The next day, Vern brought Mom some ice cream and sat with her before going to work on the kitchen. My mother was so starved for some compassion and thoughtfulness that this kind older gentleman was showing her, and over the next few days, he saw to it that we got fed and dressed and left Mom alone stressing how badly she felt and that we all had to help her. Mom was falling in love with him. The life as we knew it was about to change drastically.

Remember, this is in the early 1960s, and extramarital affairs were highly frowned upon. So the times Mom hooked up with him was very clandestine, until she started nursing school—something she always wanted to do but got married instead because her mother insisted that Donald R. Thayer was a good catch. So to please her mother and father, she did. You would think that getting a broken nose and blackened eyes from her hitting a tree after getting stung by a wasp while driving home the day before her wedding, then she and bridesmaid being forgotten to be picked up for the wedding, then having her trousseau stolen would give pause to the justification of said marriage, yet on she plodded.

Now that she has enrolled in nursing school and setting up residence in the dorm, Mom set out to carve her own niche in the world. We were too young to be allowed to care for ourselves, so Dad had to hire a live-in nanny for us as he was gone from dusk till dawn. Blanche was absolutely disgusting but the only one willing to take the job. I guess we were a handful. Blanche was short and fat, and her hygiene was nonexistent. She was afraid of water, and she never washed up, showered, or bathed. She stunk like sewer, and she had no teeth. She would sit by the telephone and dunk her toast in her coffee, then mash it in her toothless mouth—gross. When she would use the bathroom, we would have to spray room deodorizer just to walk past. I thank God we had a second bathroom.

Mom would come home for the weekend, and we would be happy for a couple of days. Then I had to have my tonsils removed because the crazy doctor thought that was what was making my knee swell. Really. My dad was in charge of that one. On the day of my surgery, I was admitted then put in a room with another young lady.

Someone dressed in scrubs (or whatever) who looked like a doctor pulled the curtain around my bed, saying he had to do a routine check on me before surgery (I wondered why, but in those days, kids kept their mouths shut). This person proceeded to do a vaginal check on me! I wondered what that had to do with my tonsils but allowed him to do what I thought was protocol even though he was not my doctor. I never mentioned it to anyone. Now I know that the young lady and myself that day in that room were violated. Thank God I never gave it much thought till later in my life.

That night after my surgery, I was crying quietly in my bed; my throat hurt like crazy, and I missed my mom. This was the first time ever she was not with me when I felt bad. I must have fallen asleep, because in the quiet of the night who should be standing there next to my bed but my mom! I was okay, then the world was all right. She was even dressed in her nurse's student uniform. I will never forget the burgundy color of it. Till this day, it is one of my most favorite colors. She had driven straight from her classes in Westborough, Massachusetts, to the hospital in Cranston, Rhode Island, so she could be with me. She was allowed in so late after visiting hours because she was a student nurse and my mother. She too wondered what the heck my swollen knee had to do with my tonsils. Seeing as she had so much trouble with hers her whole life, she thought it was better to get rid of them anyway.

Weeks after the tonsil thing, we noticed and I felt my knee was no different and still painfully swollen. During the weekends when Mom was home, she would forfeit sleep so she could sit up with me while I cried from the pain. Finally, she made an appointment with an orthopedic surgeon in Worcester Memorial Hospital, where she was doing some more training as a student nurse. Dr. Eddy took fluid out of my knee and noticed it crunched after that procedure. He made provisions for me to be admitted the next day for surgery to remove cartilage from my kneecap. I was in the hospital for three weeks, and it was summer. Mom was able to come see me a lot during the day whenever she could. She would bring me doughnuts or other sweet stuff. That made it tolerable to be in the hospital so long. Of course, Bruce had to poke fun at me because I could not go swimming for the rest of the summer. I was on crutches for a couple of months. Nowadays, it is such a minor and easy fix with no scars! I have a huge earthworm-shaped scar around half my knee. Ugly.

When my father brought me home, I remember asking where my duck Gretel was. My dad had to tell me that the mountain lion that had escaped the zoo had gotten her and my dog had a gash across her face from it as well. At least she survived, thank God. I also noticed that my clarinet was gone from the closet as well. The school took it back. I was not happy. I loved playing that thing, but we did not have the money to continue my lessons.

That was about the time my mother could no longer hide the fact that she was pregnant, and it was not by my father. My mom had been in the relationship with Vern now for a year or so. I will never ever forget the day she came home with all kinds of baby presents. The girls in her nursing class threw her a baby shower, never knowing the whole truth. I recall walking all around the dining room table, touching all the precious things. I could not wait to hold this new baby.

Mom was still only coming home for the weekends but then didn't come home for two weeks, and those couple of weeks dragged on without any news of where she was or what was happening until one evening in the dead of winter, as I sat in a chair, looking out the window while silent tears fell down my face. I did not think anyone even noticed, nor did I care. That was the only time I had a warm feeling toward Blanche as she gently touched my head and softly said, "You miss your mother, don't you?" I only nodded and wiped the tears off. As I sat there, staring out the window, I saw through the snow that was falling Vern's long white car slowly pull up to the edge of the driveway, and I saw my mother all bundled up with a hood over her head as she made her way slowly through the snow to the basement door. I flew down the stairs, and upon seeing her, I expected to see a baby in her arms, but I saw nothing—nothing but a sad-looking woman as she walked past me toward the stairs. I called after her, "Where's the baby?" Her reply was short and cold: "She died."

My first thought was, *Noooo! It was a girl? Nooo, she is not dead!* I refused to believe it. I would not believe it! I *knew* that baby girl was not dead! So where was she, and why was she not here with her sisters and brothers?

I went to bed shortly after, but sleep would not come till very late. I was devastated.

When I woke up early the next morning, I couldn't help but overhear my father talking to Mom. He was telling her he would adopt the little girl and never tell anyone she was not his. I was aghast! I was right. The baby was not dead, but alive—alive and well somewhere. I did not understand the rest of what they talked about. All I cared about was that I had a baby sister and I was sure I would get to hold her and watch her grow up—until I heard my mom say, "No, I cannot stay. I want a divorce."

My world vanished from under me. I went to school that day, feeling nothing. I could not pay attention to what the teacher was even saying. Thankfully, she was so gentle and kind to me. Somehow she knew. She put a gentle hand on my shoulder and said, "I know what you are going through." With that, she did not call on me for answers on lessons.

After a few days of heavy hearts, I was sitting in the den when I heard a soft weeping coming out of the bathroom. I knew it was Mom, so I just opened the door and saw her sitting there on the closed toilet seat with my little brother Jimmy sitting on her lap with his little arms around her neck and with a big smile, telling me that we have a new baby sister. So I wondered why my mother was still crying. I was overjoyed, and I said with a huge grin on my face that I just knew the baby was not dead. Mom said, no, she was not dead but very much alive and beautiful. Her name was Sheila Verna Boyer. So okay let's go get her and bring her home. Mom began crying again and explained that we could not do that. She had given her up for adoption, and that was a done deal. It would be better for the baby to go to a good home with two parents and not have to worry about growing up being illegitimate, which would cause society to treat her badly and all the crap that went with the territory.

My mother went on to explain how Sheila was being fostered by a wonderful woman and her husband until the right family was found. That was the demand she made in exchange for signing the baby away. Mom and Vern paid in full for the birth so she had the right to choose who and what criteria were to be found.

Every other day, Mom would go to Springfield to spend time holding Sheila and feeding her. She did this for a few weeks until the family for the baby was found. The last time my mother was going to see Sheila, she took us kids along for the ride so we could see her, albeit through the window. I will never forget seeing a woman holding this beautiful baby girl, my baby sister. She was holding her right up to the window, and I will always remember seeing a tiny dark-haired baby, and all I wanted to do was go grab her and run, just run to where no one would ever find us. Of course, I could not, so I just stood there and stared at that beautiful child, whom I would never get to hold or know. I cried. I cried for her over the years, wondering if she was all right and if she ever knew about us. As the years passed, I wondered if she even knew she was adopted and that her birth mother along with her other siblings loved her so much. Until we were actually reunited with Sheila many years later, there was always this heavy darkness that hovered over our hearts. Every sixth of March and at holidays, we would each in our own silent way think about our little sister and prayed she was happy and healthy.

That winter went by unremarkably. Mom went back to her nursing school and her dorm. When asked about the baby, Mom told them what she had initially told me. The baby died.

Then summer finally came, and the edges of sorrow abated, a little for me anyway. My mother now was putting in her time working at a mental hospital (no longer called that). When she would be with us, she would tell us some pretty graphic and pitiful things. Sometimes it would take hours for me to get my mouth shut from shock and disbelief!

Like any life situation, things at the start go strange, different, and a bit scary at first but then gradually morph into the norm, and that was how our lives went. We now had to make our own breakfast and then lunch for school, and because Blanche—that old bat—

would make lunch for my father, he never believed us when we told him she never made us anything. The money my father would give her for food shopping she turned around and gave us a list of what was needed for the next week, and we would go to the grocery / feed store, which incidentally was owned by dad's cousin Vinny. There we would go up and down the aisles as we filled the basket. This activity would become a habit, and we complained each time because we wanted to play and not have those extra chores that were not part of the deal. That is when I began to shoplift; cousin Vinny knew and told Dad, who turned around and just paid him. It was during that time of our lives that we as siblings pulled together more than fight— although we still had them, just not as severe.

Blanche would pick on my little sister Kim a lot, and I never could figure out why. One time, for no apparent reason, she made Kim go down to the basement and closed the door. Oh, and she neglected to turn on the lights for the little girl. As Kim sat on the top step just on the other side of the door, I sat on the floor, talking to her for company, all the while continuously asking the old crow the cause of the punishment. No good reason ever came forth.

As the weeks and months rolled on and we would see Mom on the weekends, Blanche would go back to her house in Franklin. We would tell Mom about everything, and she would go to my father and tell him, but he would just say Blanche was doing a fine job.

I have to say, we would get back at stinky Blanche by making the rocking chair rock on its own, which would send the old stink pile into a fit of superstitious fear, bingo! We had found our fun of getting even. Not only did she think her dead sister was in that rocking chair but that anything else she perceived as supernatural to be real, so one day, we devised a plan to scare the living daylights out of her. Bruce dressed up in his disguise as the Albino. He would cover his entire body with a white sheet, cutting holes for the eyes, of course, topping it off with a cowboy hat. He also had a birch branch stick horse, which he would ride around on. So one day, we decided to give Blanche a good scare. Putting on his disguise and going into the woods at the furthest distance from the house, which was bordering a big field, the plan was for us to scream and run all through the house that the Albino was coming and going to steal all of us and kill us! Blanche was beside herself and screaming as well, especially when Dave said, "I'll go out and try to stop him!" Now Blanche was hysterically begging him not to, but "Go get your father!" Her toothless spittle all over her terrified face was too much, and it was all we could do to keep up the ruse. After Dave ran out of the house, we were all standing in the doorway and windows, looking out into the back field where the Albino was riding back and forth, yelling and waving his white handkerchief like a madman. All of a sudden, David came running out of the woods to capture the apparition, and Blanche was now beyond herself, screaming. Bruce then grabbed Dave and pretended to kill him. As Dave was falling to the ground, feigning death, Blanche was so far gone that we had to try calming her down. We tried to tell her that it was only a game and not real. It took a *long* time to convince her. That night, after telling my father what we had done to her, well, I can't really recall. It was so worth it though. Payback is a ——.

It was not long after that when Mom was told by her lawyer that if she did not come back to the house to live during the week and not the part-time parent she had become, then the courts would have to separate us among the family and close friends of my father's until the divorce was complete and that we would no longer be together as a family. Actually, that is exactly what happened at first. Bruce and I had been put in my paternal grandparents' care while David and Kim went to Aunt Jeans. Jimmy and Ross were placed with Aunt Eunice, who lived in Westborough, Massachusetts. And baby Sheila had been relinquished for adoption. All seven of us were no longer together.

When Mom had made her decision, which did not take but a few seconds, she packed up her things from her dorm room and moved back to Bellingham. When my grandmother told me that she was now back, I was given an ultimatum. If I was to choose my mother, then I would have to return all the pretty dresses she (my grandmother) bought for me. I could not believe that she would do that! If anything, that showed me what a mean thing she was capable of being, plus the fact that Mom had lived next door for so many years and dealt with it for so long.

Gradually, all my siblings (except for Sheila) and I had been brought home, and once more, we were together again.

After giving back all the dresses (some I had even worn) Gram turned around and gave them to my cousin Diane. I was so sad because they were so pretty and I had been the one to pick them out, but I did not blame Diane, although I was jealous that she had a nice family life and even got my dresses on top of it all. That is how it appeared to my twelve-year-old brain. Crying as I told my mother about the Indian giver Gram turned out to be, Mom promised to buy me a new dress to replace those I had forfeited. It was a bummer that I was to get only one dress when I had given up four. Ah, well, my mom meant more to me than the dresses.

That Christmas, my father gave me a present all nicely wrapped. Excited to have a gift from my pop, I carefully opened the perfectly wrapped package only to find that he had given me the one dress I favored most out of the four (the tiny stain was still on it)! I was crushed as I knew then that he did not even pick out something himself but had probably not even known what was in the prettily wrapped box anyway. *Crushed* would be a more accurate way to put it.

That summer arrived, and as soon as we were all out of school, Mom packed up what necessities we would need to camp. My mother's sister Eunice had come to help her pack up our dilapidated square green Rambler, which even had the back doors held on by nylons. The gas pedal was no more than a stub of metal, but onward we rolled.

Our first stop was at a campground in Connecticut, where we stayed for two weeks. Then on we went to camp for about a month on a hill behind my maternal grandparents' house and in the same block of homes owned by aunts, uncles, and cousins. We had a fun time for the most part with our cousins but were told not to bother the grandparents as they did not want us running all over the place, wreaking havoc on their lives.

It was a very rainy summer and rather raw and chilly, which made for miserable camping on those days. We had an old leaky tent that would get a terrible musty smell, not to mention the dampness that penetrated everything.

I got invited to stay with a cousin of my mother's with his wife (also a cousin) and their daughter. I was in heaven seeing as I now had a warm, dry bed and real shower to enjoy, plus being able to play with my cousin Debby.

The fact that they lived on the grounds of the Baptist Youth Camp in Groton Mass, where it was so beautiful and had a lake to go swimming in, was truly a wonderful time for me to say the least. At the end of the second week, I had to return to my camping life. I was so very sad; I cried for days. My Aunt Ginny teased me, saying I had met a boy while there and was now pining away for him. She couldn't be more wrong! I fell in love with a home!

We finally overstayed our welcome in the family compound and packed up yet again to find another campground. We ended up going back to that first campground in Connecticut. After being settled in there for a week or so, my brother Bruce, along with a friend he had made while there, decided to break into the concession stand down at the lake. Of course, he got caught, and when my mother was told to pack up and leave, she had a fit. She stormed down to find my brother, who was hanging out at the lake, and upon finding him, she proceeded to chase him all the way back to our site, all the while whipping his legs with a willow branch. As he tried to outrun her, his legs were bleeding from the maniacal rage of Mom's strikes. I tried to make her stop but to no avail. So onward we rolled—mattress back on top of our little green car with kids hanging out the windows, crying because we had to move again!

We ended up staying at one in Sutton, Massachusetts. It was not nearly as nice (in my childish opinion) as the one we were kicked out of. We stayed there for a couple of weeks until we had to move on due to a time limit at the campsite. I think we ended up camping for the last weeks of the summer when my Aunt Eunice found a house for us in Webster, Massachusetts. It was an old mansion that was rumored to be haunted. We thought that was kind of cool and looked forward to moving in. This house was perfect as it was set about one thousand feet off the road with a wooded area behind. No houses near enough to us to be bothered with all the noise six kids could make, as well as a mother screaming at us all the time. Plus, she was hired as a nurse at Hubbard Regional, which was only a half mile from our doorstep, making her able to walk to work.

We were getting used to living in a house big enough to allow us all to have our own rooms, until a doctor at Hubbard Regional told my mother he had looked at it to buy but did not like the fact it was so far from town, where he would have to bring his kids for activities all the time. Upon asking how Mom liked living there, she began to sing its praises on how she did not have to worry about us making noise and bothering neighbors, and best of all, we were so far away from getting into the road. The next day, the creep bought it right out from under her. He knew she was renting to buy.

We found a house on Poland Street, which was closer to town, and in the end, it worked out for us kids as we were getting into our teens and could walk to town and not bother anyone for a ride.

During the famous blackout and while Mom was bathing by candlelight, I worked up the courage to ask her if I could go back to Bellingham to live with my father and his new family. That was when she told me he didn't want me. From that moment on, my life spiraled totally out of control. I had always thought that my dad loved me. Amazing how nowadays it is a daily thing that parents walk out of their children's lives. It makes for a thick skin.

I was never accepted as a friend unless it was to get close to my brother who was now going by his first name Donni and not by Bruce (his middle name). Donni was considered by all the girls as a handsome star, especially seeing as he was now playing in rock bands, and he was the only one in the high school with long hair.

Thanks to "a talking to" by my mother's boyfriend (and the father of two of her children), Donni now was my hero and best friend for real. He and I would hang out and hitchhike to Oxford for his band practice or whatever was the plan of the day.

Mom would get pregnant again, only this time we all said she was not to give the baby up. She assured us she would never do that again.

Lorne was born November 2, 1966. We were inseparable for the next three years.

I think it was in the late spring of '69 that I had had a terrible experience of having a bad trip. I had gone to the beach with a friend Don "Bird" Bertrand, and we took Mescaline. By the time we got there an hour later, I was tripping. Don had never hallucinated so did not understand where I was in my head. By the end of the day and heading home, Bird was already crashed and back to normal while I was only just peaking. Long story short, by the time we got back, I was in no shape to be taken home and stand in front of my mother. Ohhhh noooo! So this "friend" took me to a diner called the New Yorker, which was in Shrewsbury, Massachusetts, thinking something to eat might bring me down enough to get past my mother. Well, that was not the case, as I tried to walk and act normal even as the floor was an undulating ribbon, and I had to work on keeping my balance while listing to and fro as I somehow made it to the back of the diner to where the payphone was. I can just imagine what the other diners must have thought as they watched me do the balancing act for no apparent reason. I called my mother to tell her we were at the New Yorker Diner and that I would be home when finished eating. After what seemed like hours, I could not take any more of the rising colors and bright lights of the place, so the Bird (brain decided he had had enough of me) drove me home to my waiting mother. As soon as I walked in the door, she confronted me with the query of "Are you high?" Well, with her being a nurse and having had training in the rising epidemic of teens taking drugs, she looked deeply into my eyes, and upon seeing that they no longer had any color (instead completely black, all pupil, nothing else), I believed she wanted me to deny that I was high and delving deeply into my subconscious of truth or nontruth. I was always terrified of lying to her as she would discover the truth as well as not, and the punishment was *not* worth it. Usually.

This time, I had to do it! I had to tell her a straight-out bold-faced lie! Yes, I dared to chance it for the first time. I answered her with a resounding "No!"

With that said, I was making it (trying) up to my bedroom, but she stopped me and said I had called to tell her I was in New York, so where was I really? Damn it, she was looking at me again, and all the while, her face was like a sponge pulsating and changing colors like a light show or lava lamp. As steady and normal as I could muster, I was able to tell her that the phone must have had a bad connection because I was only in the diner. At that, she let me go on to my room.

After reaching my room, where I hoped and prayed I'd come down even a little (I had to), I was going crazy now. Not only did I not come down, but I hallucinated more. And as the night crawled on, I was not being able to relax even a second without some hallucination knocking me back down. I could not handle it anymore by myself, so I went into my brother Dave's room; I woke him up and told him he had to please get up and help me. Poor guy, he was trying to stay awake for me, but he kept falling asleep. As I watched him sleep, I saw silver balls of fire spinning around where his eyeballs should have been. Oh man, that lasted for a few minutes till I could not take it anymore. I had to wake him up before I screamed!

I don't know how much longer it was before I saw an Indian with feathers in his hair and a buckskin around his waist climbing up the tree that was just outside the bedroom balcony! I had to sketch this scene. It came out pretty good too. I had that sketch for a long time just as a reminder of the hell I wanted to avoid in the future, hoping I even had one—future that is. Plus, I wanted to show myself I could actually draw. LOL. Although I never want to go through that again just for some artistic skills!

By now, it was getting to be dawn, and I was still not coming down from that horrible trip. I went downstairs to go sit in the backyard, thinking some fresh air might help. Instead, it sent me even higher! I was just waiting for the top of my head to blow off. It was now almost twenty-four hours of hallucinating, and how much more could my mind and heart take? I was getting so frightened I was in some deep trouble. Would I ever come down?

I sat on one of the big rocks in our backyard, and I looked at the apple tree in front of me, and suddenly, as I was sitting on that rock, I realized I was now in the middle of the sea. And as I watched, the tree turned into a big Christmas tree with all kinds of toys on it with lollipops, candy canes, and dolls all hanging and glittering sparkling like thousands of diamonds! I think that one was the only one I enjoyed. I know it was not possible, but there it was, plain as day and as real as anything in my life.

I went back inside to try to figure something out. I called Bird, but he said he couldn't help me out. What an ass. I was beginning to panic; I didn't want my mother to see me, because I knew she would take me to the hospital and then have me put in a reformatory. I had to avoid her at all cost. I decided to call my friend Earl "Boob" Holmberg, knowing he could help me. He was a few years older and knew a thing or two about rough patches. He straight away said he would be right over. What an angel, kind and gentle giant he was (still is). Dave was relieved of sister-sitting. Plus, he knew Boob would take care of me and I would be safe in his care.

Being agitated and antsy, I could not wait for him to get to my house, so I began to walk to whenever he would get to where I was. I had made it around the corner when he pulled his hearse over to pick me up. All I was wearing was jeans, a T-shirt, desert boots, and an army blanket wrapped around me. Earl said I looked a mess. My hair was not brushed in two days, and I had not slept nor had I any real color in my face, except for two large dark circles to go with my gigantic pupils.

I think I was crying too. From that point on, I began for the first time to feel safe. He was so wonderful and patient with my stupid hallucinations and not making fun of me or even trying to talk me down. He just took me to some quiet section in the woods and let me be and, all the while, keeping a sharp eye out. I don't know how long we stayed there, but when I heard gunshots, I was almost out of my mind, so he quickly got us out of there. Hunters, I guess, or target practice. I never found out. We then went to the Burg-O-Rama, an Oxford local after-school hangout for the teens. Almost every town had one. As a matter of fact, that old place is still there, only a bit changed after all these years, but it is a landmark to us baby boomers.

So by now, Boob could tell by my body language that it was safe enough to bring me over to my brother's place, where he and I hung out, and by this time, I thought I would be this way for the rest of my life and would only be able to weave baskets while living in a nut house. This thought made me cry in such sorrow that I didn't know what to do anymore. At some point, someone gave me a joint to smoke and or some downers, perhaps both, I can't remember, but it worked! I finally realized I was no longer hallucinating. Hallelujah! By now, it was after four in the afternoon and I got home in time to keep my mother off my case.

Of course, being a typical teenager, I just had to push the envelope of getting busted by Mom, but being with my brother, I felt safe enough. Sure as shooting, who should drive by the minute I stuck my thumb out to hitch hike but my mom and Vern as they were heading out to a restaurant in Worcester. I knew she would not just keep going, so I had to watch as it appeared to me in slow motion as Vern made a U-turn, pulling up next to us, and as I looked into the face of what would make a marine drill instructor shake in his boots, I saw my summer vacation fizzle. Being sixteen years old, that was a death sentence.

So my summer went. I was able to take my younger siblings to the beach, and I did enjoy those times.

CHAPTER 3

In August, Michelle Cloutier asked if I wanted to go to a concert in Woodstock, New York, where a lot of really cool bands were playing for an entire weekend. We would be going with Boob. I knew it would be great to go with these guys, but I knew my mother would not let me go since my grounding two months prior. I asked her anyway. Lo and behold, she said I could. It was nothing short of a miracle! Although she did ask if she could go too. Ahhhhhh, noooo! No way would it be fun to go to a three-day concert with my mother! Arrrrgh! I later realized that she thought I was going to the Woodstock in Connecticut, which incidentally I did not know existed at that time of my life. Anyway, she did say, "If Michelle's mother lets her go, then I think it will be okay, so she had me call Mrs. Cloutier, and Mom spoke to her. It was then she said I could go! I had a shock but didn't waste any time in packing my duffle bag and having Boob pick me up. I don't think we went in the hearse. I will have to ask Boob when I see him again. I saw him about four years ago for the first time since then. That is a story for later.

We drove to Woodstock, New York, that afternoon, and when we got there, we were told it was moved to Bethel further upstate, so off we went on another excursion to locate this concert. Before we left the town of Woodstock, we went to a restaurant for some sandwiches. Like a dolt, I asked the waiter if they served Alice B. Toklas brownies, as I chuckled thinking I was being cute and clever. After all, this town was such a hippie community. I figured he'd get a little ha-ha out of it and see that I was not just a dumb little kid, but cool like him and everyone else that lived in that awesome place.

Well, you'd think I'd insulted him as he gave me a scowl and, very blank and blah as possible said, "I don't know what you are talking about," as if he had no clues. Yeah, right. So I ended up feeling like an idiot. I was so small that if I sat on tissue paper my feet would dangle. That was one of the first of life's worldly lessons I learned that day.

We finished our sandwiches and left this place, where we were clearly not wanted. Even the other patrons in the restaurant were giving us the stink eye. As it turned out, we were not the only ones to have made that same mistake of where the actual location of the concert was. At least they did let us know where it was so we could quickly get out of dodge.

Everyone now knows how Woodstock said no to the concert, therefore sending it somewhere else. The rest became history.

It was amazing as we got closer to the site. I never saw such a traffic jam. Hippies all over the place were doing everything you'd expect to find in a hippie utopia. I was enthralled, all the while wondering where and when we were going to stop to buy tickets. Most of us didn't have one. We came all the way up, expecting to be able to purchase them. Who knew this concert was to attract so many from so wide and far? Finally, we had to just park the car on the side of the road as we could not go any farther anyway. We then proceeded to carry our gear to wherever we were to set up camp. As we trod along the road, I saw people in the ponds and lake naked. Whoa! That was a first for me seeing anything like that. Oh, wow, I could not believe anyone would feel comfortable, but okay, so this is what is meant by free spirit. Whoa, that part of freedom was not for me; it took another year for me to get educated in such things.

People were smoking pot right there in the open or passing tabs of acid Mescaline or just a bottle of wine. Maybe even a container filled with goofy grape, which is grape Kool-Aid laced with acid. Oh, and don't forget the bottles of Ripple or Boone's Farm being passed around. I steered clear of that! I didn't even smoke any pot while I was there. All I wanted to do was have a great time and listen to all those awesome bands. I had not gotten to see any of them play in concert before and was so excited to be there, and that was a high for me—plus the fact that I was free, free, free from my mother for three whole days! Yee-haw!

We finally ended up in a spot we thought perfect for pitching our tent, which was an old army issue belonging to Michelle's dad. We shoved our stuff into the tent then proceeded to walk around the place, which was called the Hog Farm. I always wondered why no other section had a name. I eventually did learn why and who those cool funky people were. There were children and tweeners and dogs running around the farm as well. They stayed there and did not try wandering in the Hog Farm. The only nude ones were the children. They were so cute and unencumbered. They were, by all observations, so free and happy. I was glad to be a part of it even for a little while. I was not crazy about the food they ate. I was not into eating what looked like tree bark and dandelions. I have to say they were very generous in the sharing of what they had. I also thought it quite cool and groovy to eat that stuff. I was going to try by god. Just not now. Ha ha ha ha. Wait till I was really hungry. I don't remember what we brought for food, but I am sure we must have brought something, even Twinkies and maybe a Coke. We had been so sure that there would be food stands there, and there were, except they ran out of food by the second day. Hog Farm food looked pretty good then.

When we had first gotten to Yasgur's Farm, Joan Baez was playing. So beautiful she was, voice straight out of heaven. I was overcome with all the crowd, yet I was not feeling the anxiety being in a swelling of humanity. Maybe it was due to the fact that almost everyone was so high and mellow. There was no fear emitting from any soul I came in contact with, and that was huge! Five hundred thousand in all had eventually arrived from the entire continent of USA. From the coast of Maine through to the coast of California they came. No threats or arrests of a single one in those three days. A couple of times when an officer would try to arrest someone, the crowd would make a wave leaning to the right then to the left to engulf the individual being arrested for smoking a joint. After doing that maneuver a few times, the police got the picture. Not today, not this weekend. The police were actually very nice and mellow themselves.

I can't express how free I felt that entire time. I had my first taste of freedom, of being out in the world on my own. Well, I was with trusted friends. But still.

So the first day went smoothly. Michelle and I walked around for a while and went to watch the bands playing. I don't remember who was on, but I was enjoying myself anyway. At some point, a joint came down the line, but I passed it on to the next person as I did not want to take a chance of taking a hit off of something that would cause me to flip out. Sometimes people would lace their pot with other drugs. I had had enough of that, and not too long ago either. After a while, a wine bottle came down the line, but I passed on that as well. Whatever came my way, I just passed it on or just refused politely. I did that all weekend. I was so not going to take any chances. I definitely did not trust the Kool-Aid either, no matter what the color of it was!

The next day, as Michelle and I were walking around with, at that time, only three hundred thousand other folks, who did we see come walking toward us with his full beard and big bushy hair but the Surfer Dude! He was (still is) our friend that we hung out with back in our town of Oxford, Massachusetts. As he approached and recognized us, he began his crazy antic of kicking one leg out high in the air, all the while saying, "Hey, groovy psychedelic! A-okay!" Whatever came after that, I forgot as I was astounded as was Michelle that we even ran into anyone we knew! We only caught up with Boob at night back at the tent! We never saw him otherwise in the crowd. This was amazing. I am in awe even to this day. There are more Surfer stories as we go on in life.

Hooking up with us, we became the three musketeers. Surfer (Kenny Beaudry) and Michelle became, shall we say, "close" for the next three days. The only time I got a bit out of sorts with them is when they were under the covers instead of watching Ten Years After or Sly and the Family Stone or even Led Zeppelin! I wanted them to dance and get the powerful vibes of everyone having fun. But no, they just rocked and rolled to their own music! Oh well, I had a groovy time all by my onesie. You really could not feel alone with so many fellow rock and rollers digging on the same music all at the same time!

Everyone knows that it rained pretty much the entire weekend, creating a mud bath for all, and because there were so many people, the food ran out and the water. We ended up getting food dropped in by helicopter. What an amazing sight and sound the army helicopters made. The bullhorns they used made it sound as if we were in a war zone. I guess it had to be treated that way, seeing as there was no more food for anyone. The Hog Farm came to the rescue in so many ways. They were, I discovered later actually, called in before the concert was to begin for helping people who might have a bad trip. They were brought in for their experience with all sorts of drug-related mishaps. These folks were worth their weight in gold as there was a lot of it going on. I remember thinking how glad I was at my decision to avoid taking anything from anyone, even the people I came with. Then we all heard the announcement repeated over the intercoms that there was some bad acid going around and was repeated by Wavy Gravy (head of the Hog Farm cat) from the stage between groups. Oh, how glad I was that I was straight, as I would have for sure been a patient in the Hog Farm's tent with other fear-filled trippers. I am also grateful beyond words at how quiet they were able to keep those incidents. Knowing and seeing folks freaking out would have sent me into a frenzy as well. But that did not happen. I wanted to enjoy the music, not the drugs.

That night, when we all turned in, it was still raining. I shared a sleeping bag with the Boob because I was the smallest and him being the biggest. Sometime during the night as we all—me Boob, Michelle, and Surfer—snug in our sleeping bags in this old army tent, we heard the sudden roar and whirring of a chopper and someone yelling into a bullhorn, telling us all that food and water were being dropped. You could not really tell what they were saying, but the garbled words along with the sounds of chopper blades and the pounding rain must have caused Earl to have a nightmare that he was back in Vietnam. We saw him as he towered at a whopping six feet five at least and had been on the front lines over there, where he told me at some point in the past, "My back felt as broad as a barn." It had to be a frightening experience to live to tell about. So this night-mare caused him to catapult up and almost (but not quite) out of the sleeping bag, which he, in his panic, dragged me outside the tent and into the rain with him. My heart broke for him and his unwelcome memories and nightmares. We were finally able to settle down and go back to sleep.

Speaking of sleeping bags, I was lying in one outside the tent, taking a warm nap when all of a sudden someone stepped on me, hard. When I yelled, the person doing the stepping replied, "Oh, damn, I thought that was just an empty bag! I never even saw you!" The sleeping bag was very big and, well, baggy, so I guess my little self could not be discerned in the pile of material. I don't know why that incident sticks out in my memory, but I thought it was funny anyway.

Earlier that day, when it really began to look ominous with the winds picking up and the dark clouds were getting closer, Michelle, Surfer, and I went to join the crowd for the day. As we were walking from the Hog Farm, we could hear Joe Cocker with the *Mad Dogs & Englishmen* starting their set. We did not want to miss that concert. As we were walking, the wind really kicked up so hard and furious that it tore my scarf that I had tied into a blouse, actually got ripped right out of their knots, which I had tied around my belt loops so that it was flapping in the wind, leaving me practically shirtless for the seconds it took me to grab a hold of it as it flew like a flag at full mast from my neck. Not that anyone noticed due to the fact that, by then, so many folks were half, if not completely, naked from being soaked. I tied it back in place anyway and laughed at myself as we three continued on to catch the show. He was singing, "With a Little Help from My Friends." Great performance. What a wonderful time we had.

Now we are in the final day; it is Sunday, and by now, we are all hungry and tired and dirty beyond words.

We packed up our dirty, wet gear and hauled our wet, dirty selves to hunt down the car, which we found what seemed at least to be two miles down the road.

About an hour later, we stopped at a restaurant for some real food. Michelle and I went into the ladies' room to do our business and wash our feet and face. There was a sign on the bathroom wall that said, "No washing of feet in the sink." There must have been a lot of that happening and making a terrible mess of the place. We were desperate and so went ahead anyway, washing three days' worth of caked-on-red-dirt mud. We did clean up after ourselves at least. I will never forget the wonderful feeling of being clean for the first time in three days—well, our feet and face at least.

Finally, we got home where my mother was a little bit upset but not really at me but at the fact she didn't know it was a three-day festival and that it was not in the next-door town of Woodstock, Connecticut, which was only twenty-five minutes away from where we lived, which was why she asked if she could come too. When she was watching the news after I had left already (phew), she saw how big and long it was to go on as well as all the major roads being backed up so badly, and not to mention that it was over a four-hour drive away. I think maybe even longer. Little did I know what a huge piece of history Michelle, Surfer, Boob, and I had become a part of. I don't even remember the others we went with. The only ones I remember were Michelle, myself, and Earl, but I do know there was at least one more.

Little did I know that in a few short months, I would truly be living on my own—being my own boss, paying my own way, and learning life the only way left for me to (and that was with freedom and all the wonders and terrors of it). It would be a couple of years later when a movie/documentary would come out about Woodstock, and I would go to see it, of course. I was then living, working, and enjoying myself and making my own decisions—oh, and paying my own bills, which was a learning curve in itself.

I had to learn life's values and lessons. I had to find and discover for myself that what you see isn't always what you get. It took me half my life to figure that out. I wasn't a slow learner. I just wanted to make sure I tested all the waters. Whether swimming freestyle or diving headfirst, I tried as much as I could.

CHAPTER 4

Chris reminded me just recently about the day I ran away from home; it was October 30, 1969. He had just driven me home in his multicolored Buick. He was the only one my brother Donni would allow me to go anywhere with. I thought he was pretty cool.

I was one month into my seventeenth year of life, and I could not take any more of my mother's rules, so I packed an army duffle bag and gave my baby brother Lorne a big kiss and hug, telling him that I'd be around and see him soon and that I would always love him so very much. That broke my heart to leave him unprotected in that house of rigid rules, but I could not back down now. I knew our neighbor Terry Koslowskl would look after him. She and I both always fought (in fun) over who would have him for the day.

My mother had come home that evening to find I had run away. She was angry, hurt, and saddened that I had chosen her birthday to do it. It broke my heart as well, but it was a now-or-never moment. I knew if I had waited, I might have chickened out. My mother had told me earlier that day that I could leave home for all she cared as she had tried for sixteen years to teach me to be a lady and that, whatever I did in my life, just don't disrespect myself. That conversation she later denied. Those words rang in my ears every day of my free life, and I wish I could have thought to tell her how much those words helped me in so many decisions.

I stayed with my brother Donni for a while—he and his girl-friend Diane "Spooky" Paradise. I loved staying there as I loved both of them dearly and still do, even when they went on to separate lives.

On the first day of my emancipation, I woke up to a lovely sunny day, and the sight and scents that enveloped me were bittersweet. I knew I would never look back. I was feeling sad about my mother and how she would feel at my sudden disappearance, especially on her birthday, which still haunts me to this day.

It was about seven thirty in the morning when there was a knock on the door and, upon opening it, finding our younger brother Jimmy standing there with a box of my things. As he handed it to me, he said, "Mom said to take these things, because if you didn't want her, then she didn't want you." I understood he himself did not mean a word of it, but knowing Mom and how you did not cross her ever, my poor little brother had no choice but to say such cruel words. After taking the box, I hugged him, and he went back to the car where our mother was waiting, seething.

About an hour or so, another person came to the door, looking for me. It was the truant officer telling me I had to return to school. I told him, "I quit!" The school had thrown me out two weeks prior, and I had had enough of their dictatorial ways as well. That particular school the next year was told by state authorities to fix the deplorable condition of the school or get closed down. Condemned. To this day, it has a level 1 (out of 10 being the best) rating!

I had wanted all throughout my high school years to go to Oxford High with the people I liked, as well as knowing that the teachers there were fantastic. The only way I could have gone was if I had testified in court that my home life was horrible and that I wanted to live with Meg and Dick Gould. If I had indeed done that, it would have resulted in all the kids getting taken away from my mother, and I really did love her; therefore, I would not, could not, do that to her. Deep down, I knew my mother loved us. As aforementioned, she loved us with a fear that only a mother could know. I decided to leave by myself.

And so there I was, making decisions for myself for the first time in my life—life-changing decisions. "Look out, world. Here I come!" Or should I say, "Look out, self. The world is about to hit you!"

Sometimes I used to go downstairs to hang out and smoke pot, do speed or acid—whatever. The druggies always shared their stuff with me. One day, they were shooting up heroin and asked if

I wanted to try shooting some instead of always snorting it. I didn't think one time would make me addicted, but I did want to see what the high really felt like. As I was being tied off (getting my veins nice and bulging), someone else was making the drug in a spoon. It was almost time for the needle to suck up the dope and shot into my waiting vein when all of a sudden Chuck Kalenowski, the drummer for the band my brother Donni was in, walked into the apartment and saw what was about to happen. He got furious and told them to never ever try to do that to me again, and he sent me back upstairs to my brother's apartment. When I think about that moment in time of my life, even though it was only a moment, it separated me from God knows what kind of destiny. Heavy addiction? Life on the street? Jail? Death? The sky is the limit on the disasters that awaited me if that moment had taken place. Chuck (a.k.a. the Rude Dude) was my angel that day even though he was one of the drug users himself (which was why he was there in the first place) and not expecting me to be there, awaiting to be shot up full of an evil drug.

I continued to hang out with those people and was always aware of the unmarked police cars that constantly sat across the street. I also was aware of the fact that they were not local cops but narcs waiting—for what, I was not sure of. Nonetheless, my hairs stood on end whenever I saw them. And if they were not bad enough to scare me out of my wits, then the rumor of one of the dudes we would hang out with on the downtown common should have. The story was that this cat, who showed up in town selling lots of dope and was supposed to keep a low profile so as not to gain the attention of the police, was anything but. He would brag about all the places he would get to go and all the things he would buy, plus the fancy car he drove around. Until one day he disappeared. Rumor had it that he got bumped off by the mob. Well, yeah, that kind a spooked me.

I was still hanging with the same crowd when one of them asked if I wanted to go to the Boston Tea Party that night. Everyone else was going to the Rolling Stones concert at the Boston Gardens. We would see Joe Cocker and Fleetwood Mac. Of course, I wanted to go. I think I was loaned the money to get in.

The day before, I had dropped some acid; I know I had not planned on doing that anymore, but this was not Mescaline, and I wanted to see if I could handle the trip this time. None of the people I hung out with ever hallucinated and could not understand how or what I was going through. I was determined to enjoy tripping like they did at least once. I was such an idiot. Anyway, I dropped the acid and had a fairly nice time. I just cannot relax to really dig the high. I did crash on a timely schedule.

So now it is the morning of the concert, and I was given some speed. When the time came to drive into Boston, I was crashing from the drug so then partook of the pot being passed around. No big deal. I could handle that then.

I actually don't remember getting in or where I had wandered off from those I came with. My memory picks up at the point where I was swaying to the music playing in this beautiful scene in my head when all of a sudden I realized that the music had stopped, but I kept on like a Hawaiian palm tree in a gentle breeze back and forth as it felt so good. All of a sudden, I had the feeling I was being stared at, just a sense I had, and I just needed to turn and look (an instinct). What I saw was really funny to be sure as I saw a man with long shoulder-length curly black hair staring at me, so my inner self was correct. There was indeed someone staring at me. I had a small startling in my guts as I thought I had stopped tripping, yet there was a pole growing out of this man's back along with those black eyes. I was not sure if what I was looking at was real even. Then he began weaving his way through the crowd and reaching his hand out to mine. I felt hypnotized into taking hold of it. He introduced himself (in a British accent) as Peter Green (his guitar was slung across his back). In what seemed surreal, he led me off back further into the crowd until we came to a door in the wall, which he opened and led me into a dark hallway, and as we stepped into the hall, we came face-to-face with Joe Cocker as he waited to go onstage. This person I was with introduced me to him. They were friends. Whoa! I was just amazed at what interesting fortune I had fallen into. I had heard of him. I was up for the adventure.

Next thing I knew, I was being invited to go to the Rolling Stones concert. These guys were friends as well! I did not get to see Joe Cocker though. So what? I was getting to go backstage with the Stones and maybe get to meet them as well. Oh man! I was going to have a field day with this tomorrow!

I can't recall what transportation we took to the garden, but when we got there, we were escorted to the stage left. I was too small to see over the other people standing there, so Peter got me an apple crate to stand on. So there I was, standing not twenty feet from the band. Mick kept looking over at me as if he thought I was someone he did not expect to see. I was a little nervous and overwhelmed. I was mistaken for so many other girls all my life, why not him too?

When the concert was over, we (Mick Peter and I) headed to the hotel where the Stones were staying. Being that they were changing out of their stage clothes, Peter asked if I would be all right to wait for him in the hallway outside their rooms. I was fine and so sat for the next thirty minutes or so until Mick and Peter came out. From there, we went on to their hotel. I was not feeling nervous about going to their room. I did not suspect anything was going to be demanded of me as they made me feel so comfortable and safe.

When we got to the room, Mick went off to shower and then flopped on his bed, and we all proceeded to chat, starting off with asking why I wanted to take drugs and why I should not. This conversation helped me to make better decisions. As the evening wore on, Peter wanted to show me the new book of Salvador Dali's famous artwork he purchased earlier that day. I was amazed at the style of art it was. All the dripping clocks and things hanging like melted wax or plastic over the edge of tables and other flat surfaces. I felt like I was looking at someone who was painting while on Mescaline!

After a while, we went to crash on the other bed. Peter was a gentleman and did not try to do anything with me. He was a good man. Honorable.

The next morning, we all headed for the lobby, where the band was getting ready to leave for a gig in NYC. Peter gave me the phone number to the hotel where they were staying and asked me to call him at six o'clock so he could make sure I got home all right. I was surprised that he would care.

I guess I did have some money to take a bus back to Webster. I was just excited to tell the gang back home about my adventure. I was walking on air at the moment. To have a famous English rock star care about me was over the top.

That evening at the appointed time, I made the call Peter asked me to, and to my amazement, he was waiting for my call!

He wanted me to go back to the Tea Party and hook up with some friends of his that were playing there. He gave me the name of the person to ask for, and he would take care of me. I did not exactly know just what he was planning for me, but I was curious enough to go back to the club. The band was called the Nice. I told my name at the "will call" window, and the friend of Peter's came to get me in. Once inside, he told me that he did not have a place for me to stay as the wives were coming in so there would be no extra room for me. I did not expect to stay anyway, so it was no biggie to me, although I did not expect to not have a place to crash for the night. Oh well, I would figure that out later. Man was I brave then.

While I was there, I just enjoyed the band playing. I was not interested in the American band that was booked to play with them, so I did not really watch or listen for that matter to them. The British band the Nice featured the keyboardist Keith Emerson, who was so mesmerizing to watch I didn't even notice the other guys in that band.

I hung out with Neil till I can recall. Anyway, Neil and I rapped the evening away until it was time for him with the Nice to head back to their hotel. Now I was getting somewhat nervous as it was very late and I still had not figured out where or what I was going to do about getting home or a place to crash there in Boston. I did not know anyone there. As I was wandering around upstairs where the dressing rooms were, I noticed this man sitting on a table, picking at a guitar that I assumed belonged to one of the musicians, and I thought it was so rude for this person to be messing with someone else's instrument. What made me think that is still a mystery to me. This fellow looked up and saw me there, and so asked if I had a place to stay that night. I said "No." He said, "Y'all can stay with me if you want." My first thought was relief and the fact that he was not much bigger than me, so if he got "funny" with me, I could take him—at least enough to get away, that is. I figured I'd crash till early morning then hitchhike back home. I was thinking I would be spending the night in some little fourth-floor flat somewhere in the ghetto part of Boston.

He led me to the van he was traveling in, and as I entered behind with him, I noticed that I had climbed into a vehicle full of men! Oh my god! What had I just gotten myself into? I was near panicking, then I realized that these were southern men and that must be why this guy was wearing a cowboy hat! I figured I'd act unafraid so they would not think I was a dork, or if they were weirdoes, I would not let them see any fear, which I knew would be my undoing. As we were rolling along, they were talking to me in a normal fashion, nothing threatening or sleazy; I began to feel a little less anxious. When we pulled into the Fenway Hotel, I was thinking, *What the...?* It was then that I realized they were the band that played that night. Okay, then I felt I was safe enough. At least I was not in the dregs of the city.

I came to realize that this nice guy who offered me a place to stay was Dickey Betts, and he had every right to be playing on his own guitar!

As we walked on down to his room and upon entering, the first thing I noticed was the other bed was occupied with a guy and a girl, and they never even took notice of the two of us walking right in on them while they were having sex. I was so shocked that I did not know what to do, so I acted as if I never noticed a thing, until Dickey right then and there introduced me to the guy under the girl as Kim Payne, who was one of their roadies and friend. Kim politely said hi and then resumed his playtime.

Dickey and I went on to prepare for sleep. I am sure he took a shower, but I had no desire to take any of my clothes off (just in case). After we were in bed, Dickey asked if I would take off my trousers that were made of wool. They were making him itch. He said he would not touch me. I removed my trousers but left my underpants and shirt on. We slept that way for the rest of the night, and it was a single bed too. True to his word, he never put a hand on me. When I woke up, he was gone, but another guy came in and proceeded to sit on the bed next to me before I was able to get my britches on. Why he sat there and not on the other unoccupied bed baffled me, but it was more his right to be there than I did, so I just figured I'd wait and see what he was going to do. After making a phone call, he turned to me and asked, "What's your name, little one?" After I told him, he then introduced himself as Duane and asked if I'd like to come have some breakfast. I was hungry, and so gladly accepted.

Duane led me to where the hotel restaurant was and onto the booth where the other guys I had met the night before were already eating. During breakfast, I was introduced to them. There was the Roadie Red Dog, whom they also called Oggie Doggie, and Jai Johnny Johnson, one of the drummers whom they called Jaimo, and the road manager Twiggs Milton Lyndon. They were so kind and nice to me; I loved them straight away.

After breakfast, Duane took me with him as he and some of the other guys went out to do some shopping. I had a wonderful time as we went into some of the coolest shops and boutiques where they bought shirts and other things. I was having so much fun with them that I did not realize the time. It was getting on in the day, and when they were piling into the van to go on to the next gig, Duane just led me into the van, and I ended up in NYC with them. I didn't have a change of clothes, just some of my makeup and a hairbrush. Maybe I did at least have my toothbrush.

Upon arriving in the city, Twiggs checked the guys in, and because no females were expected to be checking into the hotel with them, Duane had Dickey loan me his cowboy hat and jacket. Tucking my hair up under the hat, I put my face down and just walked in and into the elevator with Duane. Once we got safely in the room, laughing that I had just impersonated a guy, I gave Dickey back his belongings. We all thought it was funny. Once checked in, it was easier getting in and out unnoticed.

It was then that Duane had told one of the guys that I was a steak. I later realized that was a compliment. Sometimes he would call me a stizake. That play on the word was so funny I never forgot it.

The President Hotel was a dump compared to the Fenway Hotel, but it was the most reasonable and safe one to be had in those early days.

That night we all just hung out around the city and took in the atmosphere. I think it must have been the next night that they played at Ungano's, a small intimate nightclub. The dressing room was large enough to fit us all fairly comfortably, and when they went to play, I too came out to watch. This time, I paid more attention to their style of music. I was enthralled. The talent of each and every one of them just astounded me. I was to become so familiar with their personal style of playing, facial expressions, foot tapping, head and shoulder positions. All became so dear to me. Dickey always seemed to be standing back so quietly and what looked to me as trying to blend into the back. All the while, his amazing guitar licks playing back and forth with Duane were enchanting.

The New York crowds were and still are notorious for being very hard to please, so when by the end of the first song the audience gave a thunderous applause, I knew they were going to be big, and real soon.

The next night, of course, the crowd was even bigger, so I did not tempt fate by being out in the front. Being only seventeen and underage, I did not want them to get in trouble for having me there, so I remained for the most part in the dressing room. This night, there were more people that showed up in the dressing rooms, so I had a lot to look at. For some reason, I kept looking at one of the ladies there who had on the coolest pair of boots I had ever seen and promised myself I would have a pair someday.

As I hung out in the dressing room, some guy came strolling in, acting like he was king of the hill and promptly introduced himself as David Clayton Thomas, lead singer for the band Blood, Sweat, and Tears. After a few minutes, he decided that I should come outside with him to his limo to smoke some pot with him. I did not care who he was and had no intention of obliging him (in any way). He kept demanding I join him. I finally told Duane about this rude character, and he said he better leave me alone because he would have to "kick his ass, I don't care who he is." Well, I did not want to see that happen, so I stayed out in the front with Duane. That evening ended with no incidents, and everybody was happy. Even the NYC crowd was really digging the Allman Brothers Band, and "If you make it there, you can make it anywhere" holds true.

CHAPTER 5

One of those days while in NYC, I was out walking with the Red Dog, and we saw an old man lying on the sidewalk. I immediately went over to see if there was anything we could do for him, but Red Dog stopped me, saying, "That is a common sight here, and no matter what you do for him, he will end up here again." So I had to walk on even though it was upsetting to me to just walk away.

Before we headed back to Massachusetts, we took a side trip to the Village where the Fillmore East was, and we wanted to see their poster on the wall of bands to come. The guys were so proud to see that they were getting more and more gigs that would elevate their status as a rock band worthy of such places as the Fillmore. They were indeed worthy and then some.

We headed back to Massachusetts to Amherst College. It was now getting colder by the day as we were getting into the middle of November, and I was not sure how long I was going to be with the Brothers. One thing I did know, and that was I was going to need some warmer clothing and soon!

By the time we pulled into the college town, we were so ready to get out of the van that we were all crammed into together like the proverbial sardine can, with Twiggs driving. We checked into the hotel, then went off to check out the place they were to play. It was on the basketball court. After that, we went back to the hotel. Later as we heading into the gym, I heard my name called. It was my friend Mary from Webster. I tried to hang out with her until her mother told me that I could not hang out with her anymore because I was such a ragamuffin and she did not want her daughter to be associating with someone like me. That was a couple of years prior. I was glad to see Mary, because I always did like her and did not blame her for how her mother felt. I introduced her to the guys, and they went ahead and got Mary a free pass! I never even asked for them to. She was my friend, and that was all they needed to know. That was the last time I had seen her until my brother's reunion concert with Mad Angel in 2012. I have not seen her since, but I still think of her.

As usual, the show was an incredible hit with everyone, and more fans were made. They were playing two sets, so the guys were relaxing in the adjoining area. Duane was so tired that he fell asleep while sitting on the floor with his head against the wall. While he slept, one of the guys was making paper airplanes. I think it was Butch. He was tossing these missiles, and one of them flew straight across the room and landed perfectly wedged behind Duane's head. It was such a fluke landing, not to mention how funny it looked. We all burst out laughing, waking Duane up. Seeing his mood, we all stopped our guffawing immediately. I felt so bad I should have just shushed everyone and took the thing away nice and quietly. I don't think he was feeling well anyway.

By the time the gig was over and we were on our way back to the motel, we stopped by a liquor store for a bottle of wine or whatever the amount of money that could be scrounged up. I was able to toss in fifty cents, leaving me one silver dollar, which was worth more than one dollar as it was very old. We had scraped up enough for a cheap something, anything. Greg went in for the purchase and soon came out with the brown paper bag along with a smile on his face. As he stepped out of view and as he went to open the van door, all we heard was a crash and a screech curse that turned the air green, and we finally saw the carnage of a smashed gallon wine bottle in a wet mess of glass. So into the van Greg climbed, still cursing and angrier than I had ever seen him, bummed out as all the guys were. It was still hard for us not to keep laughing. I guess making him even angrier. Recalling that still makes me laugh. It is one of those "freeze frame" moments we get in life.

The next stop on their tour of New England was in an old theater, and Spooky Tooth was the featured band. I sat up in the upper level with their wives and watched from the farthest distance yet.

I don't remember where we went to next, but it was to be one of the last days of my time traveling freely with them with nothing to worry about—no deadlines, dates, or mother to deal with. I guess this was to be my last fling of carefree traveling and getting to see so many shows. Mainly, I loved being on the road with these kind and talented southern men and being considered their little sister.

The day came when it was time for the guys to head back down to Georgia, and therefore, I had to head back to Webster, where I was staying with my brother. It was only a couple of days before. Before the guys were to head back down to Macon, Georgia, they had a couple more gigs to play, so onward we rolled to the next one. For the past couple of days, we all had been feeling junky, and finally, Twiggs decided that we needed to go to the emergency room. We sat all in a row, each one of us in our own misery. Duane and I were sitting next to each other in the first seats, so when someone came out and called for a Howard Allman, I thought it was a mistake, but then Duane stood up and followed them into the examining room. Later when I would ask him about the name thing, Duane explained to me that was his first name. Duane was his middle name. Well, that sure surprised me! He did not strike me as a Howard.

I did not want to go get checked out as Twiggs kept insisting, but I held firm and reminding him I was underage.

By the time they were to head back to Georgia, I had learned their mannerisms, quirks, moves, and sounds. Watching Duane play and memorizing his facial expressions, whether he was playing while sitting on the bed or on stage, became so dear to me. Sometimes I still have dreams where I see him and hear his voice. Playing with those special bottles that he would get delivered to him from a pharmacy was so magical. When he would exchange licks with Dickey was nothing short of enchanting. Dickey always seemed to keep his head down, never at the audience, in those days, and I loved the exchange of guitar licks. The way I saw it, it was poetry spoken between guitars. I loved to watch Berry Oakley with that beautiful shoulder-length wavy hair and the way he would turn his foot inward while tapping to the beat he was playing on bass guitar, and Butch Trucks, my dear friend, with his tall hat, and just the way he sat at his drum kit and his hair sticking out and arms flying like a windmill while Jaimo, who looked so amazing while he exchanged those precision drum riffs in perfect unison with Butch. How they could always do that was nothing short of miraculous to me! Oh, and let's not forget pretty-boy rough-voiced ladies' man Greg Allman, Duane's younger brother. He was the most gorgeous man I ever saw! Tall with long silky, shiny blond hair and with the sexiest voice I have ever heard in my life, even to this day (next to my husband, that is). I would get awestruck just looking at this beautiful man sitting behind his Hammond organ, swaying with his eyes closed as he sang with that righteous old black man's craggy voice. I loved them all.

The day when they were heading back down south, I had to head back to Webster. Red Dog was going to call a cab to take me to the bus stop, and he gave me some money to buy the ticket with. I was grateful. To his dismay, I told him I would rather hitchhike.

I ended up being propositioned by the first ride I got. Thank God, he let me out without a problem. After dropping me off, I reluctantly had to stick my thumb out again. Not long later, a nice gentleman picked me up and insisted on taking me to the bus station. I did not argue that. When I was safely on the bus headed to Worcester, I was able to relax and recall the past few weeks.

When I finally got to Webster, I wanted to see my mother and siblings before heading back to the apartment I stayed in with my brother.

My brother Dave was home at the time, and I immediately played the *Allman Brothers Band* LP the band gave me. Dave was so impressed he could not wait for his friends to hear them. This was truly the start of something new in rock and roll.

CHAPTER 6

Thanksgiving and Christmas came and went, and the family was all together. Life was looking pretty good. I went back to Boston to meet up with Peter Green, who invited me to hang with him at a friend's flat for a couple of days. At night, Peter and I slept in a hammock—very hippie. Very cool.

Before he went back to England, Peter gave me his linen robe and a 45 rpm record of "Rattlesnake Shake." My sister Kim has held on to them all these years for me.

I found the number of the two sisters, Agnes and Paula Hewitt, whom I had met in the lobby of the hotel that Fleetwood Mac was staying in the first time I met Peter and Mick. Finding a payphone, I called and asked if I could stay with them for a little while. They said, "Of course." I was so excited as it would be the biggest step away from home yet.

I wish I could remember the actual move into Boston, but I can't. All I remember is living there and having to get a job, which I did straight away, and it happened to be just down the stairs from where we were living. It was a cute little diner, and I worked the breakfast shift. I remember being nervous and excited at the same time.

I went back to Webster to visit my family, and Mom was happy that I had a job and even a uniform, and was not a bum on the streets of Boston. It was nice knowing that my mom and I were able to be together and no more fighting or her ruling me with that iron fist of hers. Yes, I was very happy. Life was now opening up and revealing the world, and I was full of questions and wonder at all that lay ahead of me. I was no longer afraid. Having my mother as a friend now was a sweet change.

I went back to Boston a couple of days later and back to work at the coffee shop / diner. Life went on daily in a normal routine—if you could call living with someone who had a morbid fear of vampires normal! I was fascinated to say the least, especially when she would line the windows, the mirrors, and the bed frame with garlic and crosses. I did not laugh, as she was truly afraid!

The girls were friends with a brother who was a former resident at the St. Joseph's Abby in Spencer, Massachusetts. This dear man would talk to us about God and Jesus. I would feel blessed. One day, he brought me to a psychiatrist for an emotional evaluation. This doctor, after an hour of interviewing me, said I needed more therapy, but I had other ideas. I would look to God for my healing and understanding. Besides, I like evaluating situations no matter who or what they are and didn't need to see someone else for that.

One weekend, we all went to Spencer to the Trappist Monastery, where Agnes and Paula would sometimes visit. I fell in love with the place, and the Father John, who was the only one with the freedom to speak, was the sweetest, gentlest person, and we kept in touch over the next few years. I wish I had those cute letters he sent me, even the little book he had published. We spent the next day and a half visiting and discussing God and Jesus. We had dinner with them and got to visit the gift shop where their handmade jams and jellies along with religious items were for sale. I bought a pewter cross with Christ crucified. It was on a leather strip. Father John blessed it for me. I held that cross close to my heart for a long time.

I know it was the earnest prayers that were said on my behalf by that dear man that really helped in my safekeeping. Many times I should have not gotten away from incidents that were a threat to my life and well-being. It was in those times that I truly began my search for the true God and his purpose.

Okay, so now we are back in Boston, and one of the evenings, we girls went to some friend's penthouse apartment on Beacon Street. It was a beautiful large place, and we were drinking cola (I still had not begun to drink any alcohol). We smoked some pot and just hung out. At one point in the conversation, I was asked if I wanted to make a lot of money. I was told that I would be able to buy anything and could shop all over the world, which meant flying places and having fun—all for just "carrying" things that had to be smuggled. Oh well, that put a damper on my initial excitement, but I sat and listened to the spiel of the glamorous lifestyle that could be mine until he was finished. After that, he told me I would be a perfect mule, as I looked only about twelve years old and incredibly innocent. I would be able to waltz right on through customs and such. That was all it would take to earn a fortune. Well, I tell ya I was tempted, but when I asked what would happen if caught, the answer he gave me was the deciding factor in my decision, not to mention thinking about something my mom said to me before I left home, and that was "Don't disrespect yourself." The reply I got was, "If you can't do the time, don't do the crime."

So I chose wisely in saying "No, thank you." That was one of the pivotal points in my life. Not knowing exactly what that was; I just knew it would serve me well over the course of my life.

One day, Agnes and Paula told me they were going to NYC for the weekend to make some money. I was informed that they did this every few months to make the rent. They asked if I wanted to come with. I thought it would be exciting to get to see NYC again and see what they did for work. All I needed for the weekend was only my toothbrush and my makeup (I went nowhere without my makeup). I did not take all of it though, and that was enough to cause morbid speculation that something bad had happened. I had expected to return with the girls in a couple of days.

We hitchhiked and luckily got a lift all the way there and were dropped off on the corner of Times Square. I had seen New York City just a couple of months earlier with the Brothers, so it did not have the impact as it did then; nonetheless, I was excited to see more of the city.

We walked a couple of blocks to a building that had an agency on one of the upper floors, and on the door was the sign that read "Milton's talent agency." Ha, little did I know what kind of talent he represented. He seemed genuinely happy to see them. When he saw me, he asked if I wanted to work as well and how old I was. I said, "Seventeen, why?" He said he would find me fake ID, but when I realized it was dancing in cages or on stages with skimpy tiny costumes, which were actually bars filled with dirty old men, no thanks!

Paula and Agnes got their gigs set and told me that they would come back for me, and I waited for them where we were dropped off earlier. Okay, so I waited for a few hours then proceeded to the designated spot. It was cold and dark by this time, but I truly believed they would not leave me there for long. Quite some time had passed, and I was cold, hungry, and tired, not to mention getting a little scared. Where were they, and why were they leaving me stranded? So there I stood with my maroon army blanket with a hole cut out for my head, knee socks, and my suede chukka boots, which were well-worn. I was wearing a well-worn purple corduroy dress with a nice burn hole from a cigarette, and I don't think it was mine but came with the dress which came down to my ankles. Needless to say, I must have been a sight to behold, a little lost girl in the big city.

Finally, I was so cold and hungry I decided to go back to Milton's office in hopes he could tell me if they called to tell me what to do instead. Nope. Nothing. I was getting really scared as I had no place to go! This is when I believe Father John's prayer was first heard. There was a beautiful tiny Spanish woman Anna Banana in the office, and just before the office was to be closed, she invited me to come stay with her till the next day when my friends would most surely be at the office to get me. Oh, I was so grateful I almost cried. I could not believe my situation, and why was I abandoned?

Anna lived in a security building with a twenty-four-hour doorman. I was very impressed. She had a cute one bedroom with a tiny kitchenette. I can't remember what floor she was on, but it was higher than I had ever been. Again, I was impressed. Anna set up the couch for me to sleep, and I was finally able to relax for that night.

The next day, we went for breakfast and then back to Milton's office. The girls never showed up or called. I was getting nervous all over again, but at least it was now early in the day, and I had time to figure out what I was going to do.

I spent the day doing errands with her, and I think she really trusted me, which was a gift, especially from this tiny beautiful Puerto Rican woman who had been burnt so often by friends in her life. For her to extend a trusting hand of help to me was such a blessing. And I was grateful. After a about a week, Anna and I went out to get an errand done, which was where she was going to make a quick $50, and I was instructed to wait for her on the corner of the building, which ended up being only about fifteen to twenty minutes. I saw her walking out of the building and toward me all the while wiping something off her mouth. *What could that have been?* I wondered. Before I could say anything, she told me what she had done. Oooooohh mmyyyyy ggggooooddd! But I had to flush that information out of my brain, or else I was to be sick. I could not allow Anna to see how grossed out I was. Then we went on to the rest of the day.

It was that night that she asked if I wanted to come to her dancing job, at which I thought might be very interesting. As I was only seventeen and underage, I would have to remain in another part of the club. I could not believe it when the club owner, knowing how old I was, asked if I wanted to dance as well! I was mortified. Anna danced topless! I will never forget the song "Venus" that she danced/ground the stage floor to. I was more than happy to stay hidden in the back room till the end of the job.

After a few more days, I knew Agnes and Paula were not coming back for me, so I had to figure out what to do with my time until the Allman Brothers were coming back to town in a couple of weeks. If I could just hang in there till then, I knew they would take me with them. By now, I was officially labeled a runaway, seeing as I had been incommunicado with my family back in Massachusetts. Even my brother Donni I could not call to let him know, because I knew he would let my mother know, and the consequences to me were not even in the equation. The result would be the reform school. Not happening!

So I continued to stay and go everywhere with Anna Banana, from Milton's office to work to shop, but when it got to her private time, I was beginning to get in the way. Finally, she asked a friend if

I could stay with him for the remainder of the time till the Brothers got in town.

I stayed in Queens for a little over a week, and the gentleman who was kind enough to allow me to stay there was a dear heart. He never once tried to do anything inappropriate. I am still so grateful for that (another example of angels watching over me).

When the day for the guys to be in town arrived, I was so excited I couldn't wait. I knew they would be staying at the Chelsea Hotel on 23rd Street, so that was where I called. When I got connected and heard who I think was Red Dog's familiar voice, I could almost cry. I told him where I was, and he said to get in a cab and come straight to the hotel and that he would cover the cost of the ride. I immediately did, and when I got there, sure enough, the Oggie Doggie was out there, waiting for me. I stayed with Duane, and while waiting for the day of the Fillmore East gig, we tooled around town, shopping or sightseeing. We went to check out the marquee to see their names up there big and bold, which was the first time they were to play there, and that meant, *yes*, we made it! The Fillmore East was a Bill Graham production show as well as one out in San Francisco known as the Fillmore West, where all the top of the top bands played, and now the Allman Brothers were about to get some serious recognition.

While Duane was introducing me to people, there was one particular guy they called Bear, and he had a flat down in the Village. Duane wanted me to stay there when the band was out of town, and Bear was going with them so I would have a place for the time being. I had met a girl in Milton's office who was from Topanga Canyon in Southern California. Jojo also happened to live at the Chelsea so had offered for me to stay with her, which I had already accepted as I did not want to stay alone down in the Village. Duane was not happy with that answer. He said she was trouble and would get me into trouble with her, but I remained steadfast in my decision. I often wonder how different my life would have been if I did what Duane wanted me to.

I knew I had to work, and I needed to make good money legally. I had decided the only way to accomplish this was to try dancing. Jojo told me I did not have to dance the way Anna Banana did and that there were clubs in New Jersey where the dancers wore costumes that were no more than sequined and beaded bathing suits, and under the bottoms were two layers of stockings, of which the top pair was of fishnet, and the shoes had to be high-heeled silver or gold. Jojo had a friend's birth certificate which she used until she made eighteen (the legal age in NYC), so she gave it to me to use. I studied that thing till it was second nature to answer if I ever had to. Even if I were asked any part of it, I knew it better than by heart. I can still tell you what was on that birth certificate.

I asked why she was able to have it, and she informed me that the owner was not in need of it because she was in a mental institution, and I believed her! As I write this, I am getting a more mature insight to the things that happened to me. Although it did not take a brain surgeon to realize, most situations were blatant displays of ignorance and naivety; even my palette was uneducated.

When the Brothers left the city to go back across state line to head back down to Georgia, I stayed behind and became a go-go dancer.

Milton loaned me my first costume, which I paid for with the first two dancing jobs I did, and after that, it was all mine minus, 10 percent commission, which was $5 out of $50 each time I went off to dance for eight hours. We did half hour with fifteen-minute breaks or forty-five-minute sets with half hour break. The clubs were, for the most part, grungy and funky-smelling (old booze and cigarette smoke), but I got to dance on stages away from touchy, feely people. The money was awesome for a seventeen-year-old runaway. For the most part, the agents already knew the style of dancing each one of us did, therefore booking us appropriately. There would be times when we would get booked to work in a not-so-nice club, in which case if it was really bad, I would leave. No compromising my self-respect. No matter where I was—whether it was upscale or not—I would respect everyone, and they respected me for the most part.

After having worked for a few months, I had met someone who said they had a movie I would be perfect for. I thought I was getting my big break, and so I went to the place of filming only to walk in and be given the instructions for my part, which was to dance in a cage. My costume was what I worked in, so that part was easy. I stepped into the cage hanging up high above the floor, and upon looking down, I saw naked bodies having sex on the mattresses strewn everywhere. I thought I was going to cry. As the filming went on, I tried to ignore the sounds coming from those people. Alas, I had been really hoodwinked. I was doing a porn. As soon as that scene was finished, I could not get out of there fast enough. I used a fake name in case someone recognized me. Because I had a look common to many women, I planned on saying "No, that was not me!" Yet another lesson. Truly, my life was indeed the School of Hard Knocks. I think it was University of Hard Knocks!

At least over the years I could warn other young actors to be so aware of things like that. We are so eager to believe someone thinks we are the cat's ass.

So my days went as such. Whenever the guys were in town, I would not get booked. I would spend all my time with Duane and the others. They all were so much fun to be around. Butch Trucks was so dear to me. I could squeeze him and Berry, and I had a real brother-sister feeling that I will forever treasure. Jai Johnny (Jaimo) was an enigma to me, and I was ever so fascinated by him. And Greg. Well, he is another story altogether. The girls loved him, and I do venture to say he really liked them too. Sometimes he would ask me to tell them some really personal intimate things so that he would not have to, and I am not speaking of "feelings" he might have had.

I would always go through a grief when they would leave but look to when they would be back. Even though they always invited me to come down to Georgia and stay saying "We got plenty of room," I was reluctant only because I knew drugs were a huge part of their life down there and I could not risk being a part of that. I truly did want to go with them, but I was still underage. I honestly thought someday I would end up going with Duane to stay there. Just not at that time. I don't know what I was thinking—that they would stop doing the drug scene in the near future. Another thing I knew was that Duane was still in the beginnings of being famous and having many ladies wanting to share their drugs with him. I understood this, and of course, it hurt very much when he would just take off and leave me alone while he was doing dope somewhere, and naturally, being female, I knew he was doing other things as well. I wanted him to get all that out of his system before I could allow myself to think he was ready for what I needed. I also needed to be free to live my life single, subconsciously knowing this. I believe it was that angel of mine.

Now that I was making money and paying my own way, I was able to do more and keep myself occupied. There were two or three days of acting school and HB Studios on Bank Street down in the Village that kept me busy either with learning a script and learning the personality of character or working with another actor for a scene we had been assigned. We had to bring all our own props, and that was so clumsy to do, hauling things on and off the subways. I eventually decided to just take a cab on those days.

I also studied tap dance with Henry Le Tang, who was one of the best in the city at that time. There were professional headshots to be taken and agencies to sign with and go-sees to do. I was auditioning for commercials, films, or stage productions. When I think of all the opportunities, when I had an "in," something would happen to quash it, so much so that I had to start looking heavenward. It happened too many times to be just coincidences. These many years later, I see the part of the big picture.

I have no regrets.

One of the ins I had was when I was living in the Chelsea and two of the residents were the authors of *Hair*. We were neighbors, and they became my good friends. One day they told me there was an opening for a part. They convinced me to go to the playhouse to meet with the director. They brought me down to the backstage door themselves to introduce me, but upon reaching to open it, I chickened out! I did not want to perform nude! Jerry and Jimmy both assured me it was no big deal. I would be on a swing the entire play, and all I had to do was sing from there. Also, everyone else was naked, even a pregnant woman. I said I didn't care and did not want to do it, so we all went back to the hotel. That is one of the first of many opportunities, or the situation I was in took care of the rest. Some I will share as they appear in my timeline.

CHAPTER 7

One day I somehow I found out that my fourteen-year-old brother Dave had run away. Dave had been living with our dad and his second wife and her two daughters Wendy and Pam. We loved the girls and accepted them, but their mother, Norma, was two-faced. When we were not in her presence, she would go back to her real self.

When I had first met this woman, I was happy for my dad that he was able to get on with his life (after Mom) even though she was downright homely with rotten teeth! A one-eighty from my mother! All I cared about was that she would accept us as hers, as well seeing that we were officially her stepchildren. Norma was a brilliant pianist, and so she taught her daughters. Plus she put them in ballet classes, both lessons of which I too wanted to take. I was sure she would love to do this for me. What was I thinking? Not only did she not want to teach me piano, but she did not want me to be any part of *her* family. I have to say one thing in her favor, and that was that she gave me weekly singing lessons, my first of many to come over the years. But alas, Norma ruled my dad, and that was enough to keep me at arm's length until he would be free of us *or* they moved so far away. And they did.

Back to brother Dave's story. He was supposed to live with them, and all was supposed to be well, until Norma convinced herself that Dave and Wendy (who was a free, wild spirit herself) were getting too cozy. She did whatever it took to get rid of her perceived problem. In so doing, she got Dave kicked out of *her* house, causing Dave to run away. When he was caught, he was sent to live in the New Hampshire Mountains with our Great-Uncle Fred and Aunt Carrie. Now he is living in an old house with a couple of pack rat hoarders like you see on the TV these days. What hillbillies they were. You had to use the outhouse no matter what time of year, ick! They were both college educated, so one would think they would be a little more intelligent in their hygiene. Dave stayed with them for a little while before giving up such a stupid way of living, not to mention secluded. One day, Dave jumped on the old sled and went all the way to the bottom of the mountain where he left the sled for Uncle Fred to find and proceeded to hitchhike to anywhere.

I think he ended up in Boston, where he met a girl a couple of years his senior, Darcy. She took him by the—ahem—hand and taught him how to survive the jungle of life, whether it was playing a con or downright theft.

When he called me from Danbury, Connecticut, I immediately made plans to go meet up with him. Our reunion was so emotional for me as I missed him so much. We spent the day together, and when I had to get back to the city, we planned to get back together for an upcoming weekend. When that time came, I took the train again to Danbury. Dave, Darcy, and I drove all around the area, talking, planning, and such. I had taken my "ID" and, as carefully as I could, altered it to say I was a twin so that we could say Dave was at least eighteen and not fourteen.

We (Dave) drove a van around like he was born to drive (he was), and at one point, we had an issue causing us to pull off the highway. Lo and behold, a police officer came by and began questioning us. We were able to stay strong and focused making the man believe we were not trouble. He just let us be! My angel again?

I went back to NYC and resumed my life, feeling a little better knowing I could see and call Dave when I wanted to. Not too long down the road, they came by to stay for a couple of weeks with me while they planned their trip across country in the van. I quite enjoyed them being with me. Off they went into the wild blue yonder, leaving me alone again. Ah, well. None of us knew when they would be returning, if at all. About three weeks later, I got a call from Dave saying that they were trying to get back to the East Coast but had run into van trouble and needed money to get it fixed. Another issue they were facing was the fact that he had long hair and was now a full-blown hippie, and they were stuck in good-ole-boy country. His life had been threatened, and he was scared, causing him to hide in the van. That was all I needed to hear and wired him about $300 to get him out of there. They finally arrived back in NYC and stayed with me, which was for me a great thing. I worked while they hung out at the hotel. We had made friends with a family from Jamaica. Valerie was from there, but Paul, her husband, was from the States. They were part of the Black Panther Party. Val and Paul had a beautiful little girl Camille, about four years old; we became close all of us.

During the time, Dave and Darcy stayed with me. I was hanging out with others living in the hotel. One British fellow was packaging some custom-made acid that was imported from England. This friend was the one to distribute this new version of LSD. It got to the point where he was getting trippy just from touching the stuff. I watched this nice level-headed man go from just that to a crazy person. Not using my head, I asked him for some speed, which he gave me.

That afternoon, I took the pill, but instead of speeding up my metabolism, it was making me hallucinate. I knew then that he had either made a mistake or did the switch-up on purpose; all I know is that I was getting higher and higher. At one point, I ran a bath for myself, thinking that would help me to come down a little. I climbed in with all my clothes on, which I was not intending to do but could not help myself. No sooner had I gotten into the water when I felt like I was being strangled by everything I had on—jewelry, clothes, right down to my underwear. I had to get out of the water as it was making me feel strangled by it as well. I do remember thinking, *What a waste of wonderful warm water.* But I had to get out before it killed me. Of course, as soon as I was out of the water, I removed my clothes. I am amazed I did not rip them off. Perhaps I tried, but have you ever tried to rip a wet garment? It is not easy. Never mind, just trying to get it off!

All the while, my brother and Darcy were in Val and Paul's apartment, hanging out.

After tearing my clothing off, I felt as if my room was now closing in on me and just ran out naked as a newly hatched jaybird! Up and down the hall I ran, trying to get free from the grip of the drug that was trying to kill me.

Yeah, by that time the entire floor of the Chelsea Hotel caught wind of a naked girl running up and down the hallway with wild eyes and hair, and oh, by the way, she was also dripping wet! Naturally, Dave heard the commotion in the hallways and came out to see what the deal was when he saw it was *his sister*! He grabbed a blanket and threw it around me and proceeded to take me to the hotel doctor on one of the upper floors.

The doc took one look at me and immediately put together an injection of Thorazine (a powerful depressant).

One of the guys from a California band was in the room, hanging out with the doc at the time of my crisis, and he offered to stay with me as he had been through that drug overdose (and so had many of his friends), therefore being the best person to help calm me down while waiting for the shot to work.

Oh, I wish I could remember the sweet dear heart that so gently tried to help me. I know his band was called PG&E. I know West Coast folks know that name well, Pacific Gas and Electric. I recall that he was a white guy with a huge soft Afro, which was in during the late '60s and on through most of the '70s. When after half an hour and the drug was still not working one iota, the doc gave me another dose of Thorazine. Actually, I think he doubled the dose this time. At that point, I think my brother took over my care, and while walking with me back to our apartment, I was getting even higher and more crazed with fear, so Dave brought me back up to the doctor, and he gave me yet one more large dose of the drug. This was the last one he could give me. Doc decided to walk with us back to my room, and when I went to step over the threshold, my entire body turned into a steel flower that was growing out of the concrete (the floor had carpeting). I was not even in the hotel in my mind. I could hear the mechanical creak and squeaking of my metal body as it grew out of the crack in that concrete. I was so very frightened because I could hear and feel all that was happening to my mind and body; I was aware all along throughout every moment of horror I was living. As I was describing this to the guys, suddenly my steel body turned into a cube of butter, and I began to melt right there on the spot! As I was relating this to them, I was becoming nothing more than a pool of the most yellow butter. All that was left of me was my eyeballs looking out of the pool of butter. I did manage to relate this as well. I heard the doctor say, "I gave her enough Thorazine to knock out half of Brooklyn! I can't do anything more. We will just have to watch her."

As I lay writhing on my bed, I was so incredibly scared, out of my mind. I could not go to the hospital because I knew (still I was pretty cognizant of my situation) where both my brother and I would end up! Reform school. I knew I had to suffer through it and hoped that I could find some peace while my brain and imagination had a vice grip on my entire psyche. We had a friend who drove a taxi, and when he said he had leave for work, I asked if I could go with him because I knew vehicle motion would calm me somewhat, and he agreed to take me on his shift. Off I went for my experience of riding around the city. I have to say that was an experience I will always remember with a laugh. The nuts and the eccentrics, the hippies, and God knows what other characters got in and out of that cab! I can tell you one thing, and that is the drive sure did help in calming me down quite a bit. I also think perhaps that being aware of all that went on that evening was helping to get my mind off myself.

When we got done with his shift and it was now nearly twenty-four hours later, I realized I was exhausted and wanted to go to sleep, which I did the moment I lay down. I don't even remember how long I slept. I just know and will never forget the relief that flooded over me as I became aware of the fact that I was no longer tripping. Sweet exhaustion took me over and away to dreamless deepest sleep. When I finally woke up, I was so incredibly happy to be just really stoned on a serious depressant (but happy). That lasted for a few days. I was so groggy, but at least not hallucinating! I did not realize how messed up my muscle coordination was until I went to the Horn and Hardart (a cafeteria-style restaurant) on the corner of 23rd and 7th; I was having a difficult time trying not to drop, spill, or break anything. I had fun with it though. A few days later, I was back to normal and could resume dancing.

I worked all over Long Island, New Jersey, as well as upstate New York. I took trains, planes, and automobiles. Once, I even took a ferry. The jobs I was booked for were all the tamest and nicer clubs that did not want any raunchy actions. I was always perfect for those gigs.

There were a few clubs where I had to show my (fake) ID and sometimes even to the cops. Knowing that information as well as I did was extremely helpful, especially when they would ask something, something at random, to try catching me in a lie. They never did, and there were some interesting spelling of the middle name. I aced those tests until one day. Milton booked me one gig out of desperation as there were no ladies available (all booked). Not realizing the magnitude of the situation I walked into, I was suddenly faced with what could have turned into a life-threatening position!

This club was located somewhere far out on the island. This particular club had been raided in the past from what I heard quite a few times, and the next time would be the last and then the place would be shut down. There had been many underage drinkers and such goings on—I guess drug dealing. I walked into the club, and as soon as the owner saw me, he came right over and proceeded to grill me on who I was and how old I was. This character was big and ugly; he looked like he had been in a lot of fights in his life, and he looked like he never ever smiled. Okay, that was scary enough, but as soon as he opened his mouth, I knew I was in trouble—real trouble. "Quick prayer up to God Almighty" scared! In his deep Brooklyn Bronx accent (oh, and the Italian flair to top it off), he asked me for my ID then proceeded to peruse it. Then he asked me to spell my middle name (it was a Spanish name, hard to pronounce), and I did without batting an eyelash. Then he went on to throw in rapid fire more questions on that birth certificate, which I answered in perfect time. After he put me through the third degree, he went on to tell me, and I quote "If this ain't you kid and I get busted again, they will close me down, and I won't be able to open ever again, so if this ain't you for real, then tell me now and you can get outta here. But if this ain't you and you chose to stay and the cops come in and find out this piece of paper ain't real and they shut me down, I will hunt you down and break your fucking legs! I don't care where you try to hide, I will hunt you down no matter how long it takes, and I'll break your fucking legs! So dis bettah be you!" unquote. I think that had to be one of the few things said to me that I will never, never forget in my life.

Oh god! I knew in a single flash moment that if I did indeed admit the truth I would not only be in big trouble anyway with that big beluga, but Milton would also be up the creek without a paddle. Who knows, he probably would have killed him. I could not take that chance, so I did another quick prayer to the Almighty to help me get through the next three hours safely, and you know the "I promise I'll do whatever you want me to" prayer song? Only I meant it!

My search has now led me to study with Jehovah's Witnesses. So I made it through those long torturous three hours, constantly looking out the window every time I saw even a resemblance to a cruiser or uniform. I was sweating like crazy and silently praying the whole time.

I think the guy bought me a drink and acted like I was an okay person. I had to keep up the facade of a tough girl that happened to look underage.

When the gig was over, I collected my pay then ran out the door into a taxi and made off for the train station. I could not get out of that town fast enough.

When I got back to the city and in my own digs, I collapsed and cried from relief and mental exhaustion.

When I went to Milton's to get my next job assignment, I had to tell him the story and to never send me back there or anyone else he even suspects to be underage.

I went on to many more new places, and most of them were really very nice, and the owners could care less that I looked twelve! Some of them I think enjoyed the intrigue. In those days, I had never heard of pedophiles. I'm sure there were some then. I just worked and got paid really well, and the tips were phenomenal for a seventeen-year-old kid that never had enough money to buy any of the nice clothes, shoes, purses, or whatever I wanted. I could afford that now. Many people told me I should get a place out on the island or Queens, even New Jersey! Ugh, no way would I live in New Jersey. I was a New Yorker, and that was all important to me for some strange reason. When I look back and think of all the money I pretty much tossed into the wind, I feel a wee bit of regret—not too much but enough. Anyway, I paid by the week for a room at the Chelsea. That was quite a bit of money in '69, and I was making good money, and living from day to day was all I could handle at that time. I was still a babe in the concrete jungle. The Chelsea, as I said earlier, was a haven for me.

One day, the Brothers came and parked in front of the hotel in the biggest thing I had ever seen. It was one of the new motor homes that had just begun arriving on the camping/traveling scene. They were in town for a few days, and when the business they had to do was finished (studio stuff), the plan was to go on to Buffalo, upstate New York, for a one-night gig at Alliota's, and for the next day, Duane said he wanted to take me to Niagara Falls. Neither of us had ever seen it. Who knows, I might have just gone on back to Georgia with him after—that is if everything went according to plan.

On the way up, they had a stop to play Stony Brook. It was a beautiful college town, and the campus was exquisite. It was one of the most peaceful and lovely times for me. Duane was very sweet and attentive to me and kept near me. I think I now just realized why.

Go back a month or so. I realized I was gaining weight and noticed that I had not gotten my cycle for a couple of months. I was irregular, which is why it took me so long to figure it out. When I began to get feeling tired and sick, I had to find a doctor. I had never been to an ob-gyn and did not know where or who I could trust not to turn me in.

I was friends with Johnny Winter and his lady (I think her name was Barbara); she took me to her doctor, and that is when I found out that I was pregnant! I was out of my mind scared (again). What would I do? I would not be able to dance for very long, and where would I be able to earn enough money to pay for myself and baby? The doctor told me I would give birth in September a little before my eighteenth birthday; that meant I would most likely get the baby taken away from me, and I could not bear that. So what do I do? I did not want Duane to find out because I was afraid he would think I did it on purpose. I would never trap someone like that or in any other way! When I got back to the hotel, I had to tell Jojo and swore her to secrecy, but alas, she could not keep it and immediately called Greg to tell him, and of course, it got to Duane unbeknownst to me at the time. It was while Duane was walking into the lobby of the Chelsea with me that he came out with the statement of "I know about the thing." Naturally, I asked what thing, and his response was, "You know, the kid." I had a moment of nervousness, not knowing what he was going to feel about me, but he immediately said we would discuss it later. I was relieved for the time being.

Back to the story. After they got finished playing, we piled into the Winnebago (the windbag) and headed out for the long drive to Buffalo. Upon arriving in Buffalo, we drove by the club where the band name was on the marquee and, for the next night, was billed the Small Faces with Rod Stewart. We checked into a really nice hotel which was the best one I had stayed in with them to date. Duane and I had our own room as did the rest of the band. As we checked in, it felt good not to have to try looking like a roadie. It felt great to know the guys had made it enough so far as to be able to have a room to themselves, no more doubling up! That night, we headed to the club. I pretty much had to stay in the Winnebago because I was underage and did not want to give any reason for problems.

I listened to them from outside the open door, and they sounded awesome as usual. During their break, I wandered in with Red Dog at one point, and Duane was bellied up to the bar, which was on the left side just as you walked into the place. I had put on his boots and trudged on in, looking like a dork, a little stupid kid; I am sure Duane was embarrassed to acknowledge knowing me (and I still feel mortified). What was I thinking? I immediately walked back out and holed up in the bag. During the evening, Duane wandered in and out of the camper with girls whom he brought up into the over-cab bed, where he was doing drugs with them and laughing the whole while. I was overcome with hurt and anger. I think I might have even said something to him at which he just ignored me. These many years later, I can see and understand the power of drugs over any kind of love and care one may have for those in their lives. I was going to have to ignore those unbearable quiet moments as he and the females he was entertaining (or they him). I had to bury my head and heart. At least until the gig was over and we were on our way back to the hotel, which wasn't getting there soon enough. At some point during the night, I started getting terrible cramps and suddenly began spotting blood. I got a bit nervous, wondering what was happening. I asked Red Dog, and he told me to just stop standing and sit or lay down as much as possible. So I did as he said.

Finally, everyone and a few others climbed into the Winnebago, at last heading back to the hotel. While on the way, Twiggs was telling us how the owner of the club didn't want to pay them until they performed the next night, which was not on the schedule. Small Faces cancelled, which meant there would be no one to play. Twiggs argued that they were not going to stay and wanted to get paid now. Throughout the entire ride, he ranted and raved about how he was going to wave a knife in his face, and if he accidentally stabbed the guy, then he would be in court explaining to the judge why he did that. Twiggs ran back and forth, acting as if he was a lawyer asking questions, and he would then act like he was sitting in the box and gave his answer. Then he would jump up and act like the prosecutor and so on. He went on like this for at least ten minutes until we reached the hotel. Duane and I went off to our room and enjoyed our solitude.

The next day, while I was alone in the room, Twiggs knocks on the door, and of course, I let him in. As he very excitedly paced around the room as if looking for something, he asked me where Duane's bowie knife was, which happened to be a special gift with Duane's name on it. It was in his briefcase in the closet, so I (feeling a bit uneasy) told him where it was and that it was locked. He asked me if I knew the combination, but I (was happy about this) did not. I can't actually remember how he got that knife unless Duane actually told him.

I was in the process of gathering Duane's clothes that needed washing and went to collect more from the other guys who needed theirs done as well. One of the new roadies, Joe Dan Petty, who was a real sweetheart, and I were done filling up pillowcases with laundry.

We called a cab, and while waiting for it, Twiggs asked if he could catch a ride with us to the club where he was planning on making the owner pay up or else. We dropped him off, and we went on to the local Laundromat, where we hung out for a few hours, washing, drying, folding, waiting for machines to become available. It took a while as usual. I never was lucky enough to just walk into one of those places and have a nice machine all empty and ready for use. Then we had to wait for the dryers to become available. We must have been there for three hours.

When we were finally able to pack up all the nicely cleaned and folded clothes and call for a cab back to the hotel, we were looking forward to getting back on the road to enjoy some R & R, especially me, because Duane and I were going to do something really cool together. Well, that was not to be. No sooner did we pull up to the hotel and were getting the laundry out when I saw Duane come walking very quickly toward me. At the same time, he was pulling a wad of cash out of his pocket, and as he was stripping off a bunch of bills, he quite anxiously proceeded to tell me that I had to hurry up and get out of town.

He said, "Little one, here is enough money for you to fly or take a bus, whichever is faster getting out of town. Twiggs just stabbed the guy, and I think he killed him. If they find you with us seeing that you are only seventeen, they will skin us alive!" But he did, however, tell me it would be a huge help if I joined in with the rest of the guys in cleaning the RV. That was how I waited for the cab to arrive.

It did not take me long to figure out that I wanted and should go to the airport for the fastest means of escape, not to mention it would be my very first airplane ride—the first of many to come. Everything was happening so fast and furious that I did not have time to panic myself. I knew that if they found out who and where I was, they would call me to testify against Twiggs. I was mortified at what my friend had done! I knew it was all the meth he was on. As a road manager, he had to be so many things for so many and do most of the driving, which meant staying awake and alert. Well, this was his breaking point when the guy refused to pay up and then proceeded to laugh at him.

Yes, and the district attorney was looking for the kid that had been with them, but luckily, I had many friends that were in the business of keeping their friends safe from harm, especially if they were just little girls. That was how my bosses at all the clubs I worked in felt about me. They all respected me as one of their kids. I was so young and naive, and that was how they wanted me to remain.

I really felt like I had now really gone underground, hiding out from my mother and now the authorities in Buffalo. When I had returned to the Chelsea and upon entering my room, I noticed many things were missing. One of the items gone missing was a really cool pair of handmade leather pants. I was so upset that someone had ripped me off! Later, I found out that the junky down the hall had broken into my room and took them. Someone had seen them on him. When I approached him on the subject, he vehemently denied it. I wanted to believe him as I thought we were friends. I should have known better, because I knew one thing about those people and I knew they would steal from their grandmother for dope money.

Anyway I, could not prove it so, I had to just let it go. It was not from being careless that I got robbed; it was the amazing resolve of the junky. (A few months later while walking down Times Square, I noticed that guy whose name was January (yeah, right) was standing in front of a table filled with used items, and he was selling them. I had seen from the distance that he had on my leather pants. When I told him that he did in fact take them out of my room, he said he had bought them from someone. I knew he was lying but, of course, could not prove it, and so I had to give it up—but at least I had a closure of sorts about it. So life and lessons learned go on.

Anyway, a couple of days after I had gotten back to the city, I knew why Duane had not called me. I knew that all the phone calls and any communication between us would be noticed by the people in Buffalo.

I was so scared and worried as this was truly one for the rock and roll records. I had to stay quiet about even being there. I had to tell my bosses from the clubs I worked (as stated earlier) so they would help me stay hidden as it were. After the trial, which took over a year and a half, somehow Twiggs got let out of jail, and the only thing he had to do was never come back to New York. I was amazed at the incredible lawyer he had! He got him off from being convicted of stabbing and killing a man in the back! Wow!

A couple of years later, Twiggs would get a waiver so he could come back to NYC for a special gig the guys were doing. I think it was Carnegie Hall. It was over breakfast in some diner that Twiggs told me how his lawyer had used so many clever approaches to the witnesses in making them look like they could not remember what they had seen, heard, or anything at all. He was brilliant. I was also told how the DA was searching all over the place for me. Whoa, that gave me a stab of fear, even after the fact! All said and done, I just couldn't feel the same warm fuzzy about my friend anymore, and that broke my heart. I still considered him my friend, but it was different now that he was a murderer even though the victim was an absolute jerk. It was then that I realized never just threaten because more than likely it will come to pass.

Now getting back to the time I had returned to the city and returning to life as usual, not a week later, I miscarried. The doctor couldn't figure out what happened. I think it was all the anxiety and fear that did it. In a way, I was relieved, but sad. About a year later, I would realize I had a problem, and so the doctor figured out that I needed a DNC (scraping of the uterine wall). I hadn't had one when I miscarried, and that is one of the things that has to be done after those situations.

I think it was during this time in my life that my brother and Darcy headed out to the West Coast in their van. So all that just happened in the Buffalo scenario was, I think, during that time, because I was still living in room 300 and it was after I moved into a bigger room that had a balcony overlooking 23rd Street that my brother came to stay with me for a couple of months.

I went back to work about a week or so after my procedure, and life continued on. I had gotten booked at a summer resort in the Poconos, upstate New York. It was a beautiful place, and my style of dance was acceptable. I worked in that place for about a week and made awesome money. That was just one of the cool places I worked during the summer. I was glad to be on my own, but I was missing my family terribly, especially my older brother Donni and my young-est brother Lorne. I missed my mom. I still loved her and wished that there was no fear of what she would do if she knew where I was.

Now that I think of it, it was after one of the guys who worked as an engineer for the Allman Brothers was in town to do some busi-ness on their behalf. Of course, he stayed at the hotel as well and knew me. He was in my room, hanging out and listening to music when he told me that they got a call down in Georgia at the studio from the police looking for me, and they told him there was an APB (all-points bulletin) out for me. Oh no, that is not what I wanted to hear! So my mother was really seriously looking for me, and I inter-preted that to mean *reform school*. If I was captured.

Well, that put a whammy on my anthill for a while. The intense paranoia had softened a little for me over the past months, but now it was back with a vengeance.

My work kept me busy, traveling all over upstate New York. In some places, I would stay on with new friends I would have made, and they would then take me back to the city later on. I was doing a lot of downers in those days (no more acid or anything else). I would go to work while feeling quite mellow, and in those days, it made me feel my sadness all the more intensely.

There was one place I worked in, and I was so mellow that I kept kicking accidentally all the racks of pretzels and potato chips off the end of the stage. It was a long stage, but I managed to keep on losing the place of where I was supposed to stay, and it was plenty of room. No one seemed to care as they just kept picking it all up.

I remember when the song "He Ain't Heavy, He's My Brother" would play, and I could not help the tears that threatened to fall. I would think of my brother Donni and my other brothers. Ah, well, it was getting through those times that made me stronger for later trials that would appear in my life.

CHAPTER 8

One of the jobs that I had been booked will always be ever strong in my memory, even though I wish I could forget, but it was a learning curve for me, teaching me a huge lesson. It was somewhere out on the island, of course, in a nice little club, and everyone was polite, even the big ugly pock-marked-face man that was the bar manager, but when I think back on his subject of conversation, I learned something valuable at a great cost. I know it was my angel(s) keeping a watch over me.

It is hard for me to put this down in writing (which makes it seem more palatable)—the return of the fear, disgust, and horror that I felt at that time.

I tell this story because I need to make a point again how I was helped by the Almighty Creator Jehovah, and just as it is written in his Word, his angels have assignments; they (I know of at least one for sure) have been able to get out of or at least through all my crises.

The one I am about to tell here is definitely one of them. I had done my first set (half hour) of dancing with a half hour off. Most of the clubs wanted us ladies to sit with the customers (just like in the movies), and I managed to be booked in clubs where you either were not allowed to drink or you didn't have to. All that was expected of us was to just sit and hang out with the men or women, which there were plenty of, and I expect in hindsight to get them to believe they had a shot at being with us. Ha! Not in my book.

Anyway, this ugly man who happened to be the bar manager didn't make me sit with anyone, but he wanted me to hang with him as he described to me what he thought was sexy in women. Here I thought I was exactly *not* what he liked as he was looking at the dancer on stage. That time he was comparing how womanly she looked as compared to someone who had a boyish strong athletic body with boobs. Gee, who could that be? I could even figure that one out. Me. I had a body with no hips but a bubble butt, small waist, and decent-sized boobs. Thinking I was in no danger, I accepted a ride to the train station when the gig was over. So off we went. Now I did not know the lay of the land there, but I did know approximately where I had gotten off the train, and we just drove on past it! It was then I absolutely had that intense gut feeling that something was going very wrong. When I mentioned about him missing the street to the station, he told me I was wrong. I had to make myself believe he was being honest with me; after all he had just gotten out of prison from doing six years. What in the world made me think he could be trusted? I knew in those moments that I should have taken a cab. He drove longer than it should have taken to get to my destination, and I mentioned it to him again, and at this point, he began to tell me that he decided to drive me back to the city. Oh noooooo! That horrible feeling of dread washed over me. It was when he told me he wanted me to touch him on his crotch that I got sick to my stomach and began to get weepy and told him to please let me out and I would find my way home, but he said not until I did what he wanted me to do.

At that point, he had to stop at a red light, and when I looked over seeing a police cruiser, I did a scenario in my head (isn't it interesting how much length of thought can pass in a nanosecond?). That is I waved and screamed at the cop right next to us. I knew he would have seen me, and I could have gotten away from that uglier-than-evil person. Alas, I already knew (in that nanosecond) that I would only end up in the dreaded reform school! I was still only seventeen. So off we went when the light turned green and into a night of perversion and degradation, and let's not forget the sheer terror of thinking I would never make it out of his grip alive.

At this point of just driving around all the back roads of who knows where at 3 a.m., this creep after telling me that he had a gun in his glove compartment and he was not afraid to use it on me told me to unzip his pants. I again tried to get him to let me out of the car, and when I just tried to make a break of it, he just reached out and grabbed me by my waist-length hair and pulled me over beside him and repeated his threat and to unzip his pants. Slowly I did as he ordered, and with shaking hands and tears rolling down my face, I proceeded to do the task. It was when he made me pull out his disgusting part that again I tried to refuse and beg him not to make me do this thing, at which point he told me that if I didn't shut up and jerk him off, he would pull over and make me do more than that. I had not a choice; I had to agree to his demands. God only knows what he would have done to me if he did indeed pull over. While I was trying not to make a sound, I had to keep up the action he demanded of me. I had to keep up a rhythm steady and strong, all the while trying not to gag at feeling such grossness. The saying is true, when something horrible is happening, that minutes turn into hours, and I was living through some long unending hours. I still was not sure if he was going to kill me or do more with me; I had no clue, so my fear was not able to subside until he was finished with his business, and that was even something I nearly threw up at. I had to summon up all the mind-over-matter tricks I could muster to keep my stomach under control.

Lo and behold, when he was indeed finished, he was also finished with me and proceeded to pull over to the curb and let me out. There was a subway, and I don't know if that was a coincidence or he already knew of it. Before letting me get out, he stuffed a $50 in my pocket, and when I tried to throw it back at him, he told me in no uncertain terms to take it. Again, after putting this down in writing, I have gotten hindsight in figuring out why he made me take that money. It was not because he felt badly; it was so he could say I was a hooker and that was my payment for services rendered. Fine, so I took the money. I couldn't get away from him fast enough. Shooting down the stairs, I looked to see what train would get me back to the city. Finding the one I thought was correct, I don't need to look for a seat at that time of the morning. Druggies, alcoholics, dealers, pimps, and any other lowlife you can imagine was usually on them, but this morning, there was only one young black man sitting across from me. I had gotten dropped off in Harlem. Again, hindsight kicks in.

I'll bet he thought I'd be eliminated at some point between there and 23rd Street, Manhattan. After looking at me and the state I was obviously in, that young man asked me if I knew where I was and where I was going. I answered with a crack in my voice that I did not and told him where I was trying to get to. With that, he came over and sat next to me. After what I had just gone through, I was desperate for a kind word, a kind face, a kind anything. This man had a kind face and eyes; something made me trust him. The Almighty moved in my heart to realize this person meant me no harm. Amazing isn't it that I should even allow a male figure to get within five feet of me. He was truly different.

I don't even remember his name. I was in a state of shock at that point. Messed-up hair, ghost-white face, and to finish off the portrait, there were black circles under my eyes which were themselves wide and horror-struck still. I am surprised I didn't scare him. The way I see it, you can't scare an angel. Truly he was one.

He guided me to the right train to transfer to. He came all the way to the stop I needed to get home. Mr. Angel walked with me all the way to the front of the Chelsea Hotel and waited till he saw me get into the elevator. He never even asked if he could come in; he just told me to get to my room and feel safe. I can't even remember what we might have even talked about that entire time. Two hours it had to be because by the time I got back up to the room that I was sharing with Jojo, it was after 5 a.m. Jojo was so surprised at how I looked upon entering the room. She immediately knew I was in a state of shock. She was great in helping me calm down and helping me get through all the vomiting that lasted for at least an hour. My stomach was bruised; I swear for a week. I could not sleep much with the nightmare replaying in my head. Jojo said we would go straight to Milton and tell him as soon as the office opened.

Upon arriving at the office, Jojo proceeded to tell Milton my story. All the while, he just kept writing something while sitting behind his desk. He did not seem to care one way or another. All he said was that I should take a few days off and get myself back as much as I could to normal and that he would look into the situation. I so had hoped he would not think I did the hooker thing that jerk planned on accusing me with. Who knows, maybe he really did expect me not to have made it out of Harlem.

I did take a few days off to recuperate as much as I could. The next gigs Milton gave me were places he was sure of my safety. It would be many months later when that place was mentioned by someone. I told them about what kind of dangerous people that worked there. This individual then went on to tell me that around, that time someone fitting that exact description went missing and no one knows what happened to him. It was then it all came back to me as I remembered how Milton never looked at me but kept writing something as my story was being told to him. Even I could put two and two together then. I knew who we all ultimately worked for. Somehow, both Jojo and I knew that waste-of-skin person was probably sleeping with the fish. Hmmmm, do I feel bad? Take a guess.

That last story I told is out of sequence and actually happened not to long after I began dancing.

Where was I? Oh, I think we were at the time frame when Dave and Darcy came back from being holed up in Wyoming or one of those cowboy states. I used my rent money to send money via Western Union for fixing the van and getting outta Dodge (no pun intended). Dave later told me the men out there hated hippies and were going to hurt him, which is why he was hiding out in the van.

Within about a month they made it back to NYC. And I think I left off earlier in the story to relate that period of time.

The whole time I was living at the Chelsea, which was about eight months, I had some crazy things happen. I am putting them down as I recall the incidents.

There was the time Janis Joplin came to stay with her band. Some residents that had been living in the hotel for years told me of the time she tried staying there a few years back, but because she was loud and nasty, as well as allegedly doing some hooking on the premises (she wasn't famous yet), plus she allegedly was wrecking rooms, she was kicked out. She was allowed back now because she was famous. The person telling me this thought it was weird that she should ever want to come back, unless it was to make a statement. One day while a friend of mine Beth Van Blerkome (I had met while she was being a groupie with the Grateful Dead) was visiting me, and we were walking down the hallway to the stairs when all of a sudden Ms. Joplin stopped in her tracks to stare at Beth and, in all her feathered finery, proceeded to bend down as if addressing a dog and began making the "come here" whistle and snapping her fingers and slapping her leg, all the while saying, "Come here, Binky. Come here, Binky. Here, Binky," then walked off laughing. What an ugly face and heart she had in that moment. That is another "frozen in time" moment in my memory. What a mean woman she was. Talented but mean. Seeing as she was not even close to attractive. I guess she was jealous of anyone that looked better then herself. Beth wore much of the same style as Janis. Maybe she was angry because Beth looked better in it than she. Who will ever know?

Beth and I became good friends. She was so funny I was laughing all-the time with her. The only thing that made me nervous while with Beth was that while with the Grateful Dead, she would do whatever drug they were handing out, and they did quite a bit. The Bear, as they called this guy traveling around with them, used to make acid and sometimes lined unopened Coke cans with the stuff. I even heard a rumor that he was thinking about putting some in the water tanks of the hotel. Whoa, that scared the crap out of me. I started getting jugs of water from other places so I could drink that while the Dead were in town. One time, Beth and I were invited to a friend of the band's birthday party. She owned the entire top floor of a building in Manhattan, and it was awesome. There must have been six birthday cakes all laced with something. As much as I love cake, especially birthday cake, I would not even touch the plate, never mind the frosting. Beth, on the other hand, had fistfuls of cake. Within the hour, she was tripping her brains out. All I could remember was when I was in that same position. She could not get a grip on reality in any shape or form. Beth was so high even she was getting scared. At one point, she did not know who I was. It was then that I knew we were in for a long haul.

Beth stayed with me, although not knowing who I was. We had tickets to see Ten Years After, which was an English band I loved. Because she was so far gone, I had to take care of her like a little kid.

When we got to the concert, no sooner than the band got one song played, Beth didn't know who *she* was anymore. By now, many hours had passed, and she was not coming down at all. If I did not have a similar situation happen to me, I would have had to drop her off at the hospital emergency room. I knew that was not going to happen. I did not want to see my friend in trouble. Seeing that the music was not helping but causing her to trip more, I was getting nervous, so I made the decision to get her back to my place.

When Beth finally returned to normal, she agreed to never do that again. For myself, I had already decided not to experiment with my mind. Downers were still something I needed to get away from my depression.

Milton booked me in a club at Sylvan Beach, again upstate New York. They told me the movie *One Flew over the Cuckoo's Nest* had been filmed there, fascinating. I was to work for about three weeks there, and I would be given a room in the hotel I would be working at. Upon arriving, it was a pleasant surprise to see it was such an extra nice place, and the people were excellent folk. They saw to my every need and comfort. They became my friends.

After working there for over a week or so, someone whom I thought my boss and his wife knew had asked me out for breakfast. My boss said he was okay and we would all go to the diner together, so that was more appealing to me. After a nice pleasant visit, this "friend" asked if he could drive me back to the motel. By now, I thought he would be fine, so I said okay as it was only five minutes' drive away, so when the guy went the wrong way, I mentioned it, and his reply was, "I just wanted to take a little drive." With that I knew something was going to go wrong. I knew if I were to tell him to let me out he would not, so I prayed that he would not try to kill me after I had figured out what his intentions were. My instincts were to just act my way out alive and unharmed, with protection from the Almighty. I knew that I was about to be attacked. On and on, he drove, and I was doing my best not to panic. He finally got far enough from civilization and turned down along dark dirt road where he pulled over and slid across the seat to me. I cried and tried to act as crazy as I could, hoping that would change his mind, but he was already in his own selfish filthy mode, and his reply to my tears and begging was to shut up and get in the back seat. I kept begging him to stop and please take me home but to no avail. His only remark at that was that he had a knife under his seat and would not hesitate to use it. Okay, that did it for me. I had to reconsider my attitude. I was not a bar of soap, so I would not wear out, and maybe, just maybe, I could get away from him after. When he had gotten his jollies, he climbed over to the front seat and started driving away. That was a good sign at least. He was acting like nothing happened at all out of the ordinary. When we got back to the motel and before dropping me off, he had the audacity to ask if he could see me again! I was shocked! What the…? What was wrong with him? Of course, he had not stopped the car yet, so I said okay. Tomorrow night after work to meet me. He believed me and let me out the door. Oh man, I ran to my room and locked the door. I first gave thanks to God for my angels. Again.

All I could think of was how to get even. I called one of the other ladies who bartended there and told her what happened and by who. She and I agreed that I should go to the police. A few minutes later, a couple of officers came over to take my statement. I was able to describe the route we went and where I was sure he had pulled over. When we took the drive, sure enough, I had recalled correctly and the tire marks were still in the dirt even. That is when they believed me completely.

I told them of the "date" we made for the next night. It was decided that the police would come at the time. He was to show and arrest him for kidnapping and rape. When they left, I took a hot shower. Of course, the creep made bail and denied the charges. I knew I was in for a fight. As it is today, it took forever to have a pretrial meeting with the judge. I had to get back to the city, so I was to wait for many months before summoned back.

Upon returning to the city, I got on with life. It was to be one of the last gigs I would be doing out of Milton's agency. By then, I had turned eighteen and had been reunited with my family. I joined Mambo Hye's team of ladies, and it was not long before I became a set employee at the Metropole Cafe in Times Square.

Off and on, I would get a call from the Bureau of Investigation to see how I was doing and to tell me that the pretrial was set by the defense strategically a few days before Christmas, counting on me not appearing.

Well, they were in for a shock when informed of my arrival. Bill and Cathy, a family I had become close to, were the ones picking me up and bringing me to stay with them in their home during the time I was to be there. I had a return ticket to fly back to NYC on the 23rd of December, which would allow me to get back to my mother's house in time. That evening it began to snow quite hard, and in upstate New York, the snow is intense and heavy. By the time I was to be at the judge's quarters, it had been snowing all day long, making it almost waist high and driving difficult. However, my friend got me there with time to spare, as she was used to maneuvering through such conditions. We trudged through the snow and were amazed at how much had actually fallen as we waded through it to the front door. The judge's wife showed me to his office, where Cathy and I sat and waited for the opposing side to show up. As we waited, the snow kept falling and piling up. After waiting over an hour, the judge informed me that we had to postpone to a later date because the weather was keeping the other side from showing up. I was also told by him that I had done wonders for my case just by showing up. Still, I know they could have made it just as I had. Adding insult to injury, my return flight the next day had been indefinitely cancelled. When I tried to get a train or bus ticket, I was told all forms of transportation had been cancelled. My heart was broken as this would mean I would miss, for the first time, Christmas with my family. The family I was staying with were wonderful as they did all they could to share their holidays with me with a lot of love, but I cried constantly anyway.

I also knew that I would most likely not be returning for another fiasco, so I had to be content knowing that my rapist was now known as such and that his wife obviously believed he was indeed capable of such an act, therefore leaving him. That had to be enough retribution for me to let it go, not to mention that I was believed by the Bureau of Criminal Investigations, or the BCI. I was told he had other accusations on record, which meant that my testimony, in addition to the character references against him, all but proved my truth. I had another problem, as I was undergoing medical procedures at the time that required me to be on some serious pain medication, which had run out while I was trapped there. Because I was unable to pick my prescription up on time, I ended up having to take my last pill days before I could get home. The pain that I no longer had meds for was unbearable, so my friends sought to find anyone who could get me something to provide relief. By that evening, we had found someone with codeine, but I learned an important detail upon taking a codeine pill from a man over three hundred pounds! Not only did I take an entire pill but before that, I had taken four Demerol and four Excedrin. By the time the codeine kicked in, I was so high that I was very scared. For the second time in my life, I would think a nice warm bath would help, only to get in and get right out again. I was not only floating in the bath, but my head was floating in a haze of whirls and colors. My friend and I had been hanging out at the club, and for some extra cash (I was broke by then), the club owner hired me to dance. It was during my last set that I began realizing how high I was getting, and that was when the owner of the club gave me the key to a room to take that bath that I had in mind. Everyone was so helpful and kind, and those are the memories I choose to take away from that town.

When I had gotten myself together enough to head back to where I was staying, my friend had secured a ride for us back to her home where her husband was with their daughter. Upon arriving at the trailer, which was a good way off the road, I did not want to remain in the car where my friend and her friend were chatting away, so I began the short walk toward the trailer, but about halfway there, I became so weak and exhausted from trudging through the snow, which by then was past my waist, making my trek seem like miles. I decided to lie down for a few minutes of rest. As I lay down in the soft snow, I felt so comfortable and actually warm. I thought I would just stay in that wonderfully warm and pain-free environment. The next thing I realized was Cathy yanking my arm, pulling me out of my warm white cocoon. She happened to look out the window as I was lying down and jumped out of the car to get me into the trailer. Again, I have to give the credit of my ever-present angel making my friend look in my direction. Upon getting safely inside, both Cathy and Bill realized I had seriously overdosed and went into action. Being a former police officer, Bill knew what to do. He put ice cubes on my wrists and neck while walking me around, sometimes having to slap my face to keep me awake. Finally, enough time had passed to allow me to go to sleep. I must give them so many thanks as they did not get sleep either until I was out of the woods, so I want to say it here.

The next day, when I finally woke up, they told me if I had been allowed to fall asleep, I would never have woken up because I had taken so much codeine. I weighed only one hundred ten pounds back then, and the man who had given me his codeine pills weighed over three hundred pounds. I did not know medicine was made according to weight. We sliced and diced the pills into smaller doses. It held me over nicely until I got back home.

CHAPTER 9

One of the places I had been booked for a couple of weeks was again upstate in Albany, New York. That time I was booked with another lady. One day, she and I decided to hitchhike into town when an unmarked police car went past, and we knew we were busted. I had the crushing feeling of "this is it, I'm doomed!" I thought for sure they would discover my real identity. As we were headed to the police station, we were informed that we were picked up because I fit the description of a girl who had shot her father. At that, it was a relief in the sense that I knew my innocence of that crime, but would they find the APB for me? I prayed yet again for deliverance from being discovered. After a torturous amount of time, we were free to go. The officers drove us back to where we were staying. I can't believe no one discovered that the real Pepa Tiamie Junenten Harris was in a mental institution in Arizona. I was also grateful that they had not discovered that all-points bulletin that was out for me. Another blessing.

I would continue my talking to God and thanking him for all the protection he was giving me through his angels. There would be many times I would go into deep discussions with anyone seeking as I was. The supernatural things were always something I could not get enough of. I knew I was alive only by his grace and love. The incident I am about to lay out here is one time in my life I do regret. I only tell it to let anyone else who had gone through the same degrading thing to know they are not alone in this appalling action done to them.

I had been working far out on Long Island and needed to take the train back as usual, only this was during the time when I was trying to save money. When the conductor came around and saw me, he gave me the option of sitting in the last seat in the last car and he would not charge me train fare. I thought that would be nice, so I did just that. When he came back after doing his rounds and sitting in the seat opposite me, he went on to request that I open my blouse. At first, I thought he was joking, and I laughed, but he went on to say then I could just pay for my ticket instead, but by that point, I knew just paying for my ticket would not be enough; his demeanor told me that. So being underage, I did not want to get this adult angry with me. I remember that I did slowly unbutton my blouse and had to sit there while this pig gawked at my chest. I can't recall how many times he came back after his rounds to repeat this action. I could not get home fast enough. Back at the Chelsea, I resumed life in the city. The Allman Brothers were back in town for a week or so. Duane would come and stay in my room some of the times. It was when he would take off to join up with someone from another band he wanted to jam with, not to mention the high he would get in more ways than one. Then he would come back to my room. It was also during that time he gave me crabs. I was horrified. He went to the drugstore and bought a couple of boxes of the product that eliminates them. I not only used the stuff, but I shaved my complete lower half! I was so mad at him for doing that to me. Oh well, that would not be the last time I contracted them. You can catch crabs just by sitting on a bed where someone previously had been with them. Horrible feeling. One of the times, he had come to me to say, "I just kicked the ol' lady and the kid out." I was feeling odd about the cold way he had said that to me. Alas, I did not know anything other than that she had approached him, and I asked if he wanted to "ball," and that is when she got pregnant. I did not know her side of the story, but I believed him. I did not expect that to change how we were together. I was happy to be with him. I would be so jealous of his always leaving to go off without me that I took a lot of downers and threatened to jump out the window. Red Dog had come to my room to read me the riot act and to grow up. When he left, it was with kind words—harsh, but for my own growth, as I fought my emotions. Rooming with Jojo would not guarantee total security from ugly things happening to me. I will never forget the time she showed up with two guys. From where? I did not know. She was having fun with one of them, and the other thought I was there for him. This gent was about seven feet tall (I am not kidding), and when he started to put the moves on me and taking my disinterest as a challenge, I guess, because he became forceful. I was in no position to scream, and Jojo was not even paying attention to me. This giant began yanking my jeans down and sticking me with his log only to realize there would be no entry. He was huge. So he flipped me over and tried the back-door angle. Now I was really fighting back, but it was like I was just a rag doll to him. Without mercy for my little self, he tried and tried to force his way in. Finally, he gave up. He left. I cried. I was a mess. Till this day, I have serious issues.

One day, I was to be booked in club that was in an undesirable part of Brooklyn, although the owner and patrons were very nice and respectful. A little while into my second set, two hell's angels sauntered in, looking arrogant. One of the patrons mumbled something like, "Hell's angels, harumph!" It was just loud enough for one of them to hear. That was enough to send them both into a raging frenzy where they proceeded to punch this poor fool in the face, breaking bones, and while he was on the floor, they continued to kick him repeatedly with hobnail boots. Mind you, I was onstage with a clear view of this horrific scene. Moaning and in the fetal position, those maniacs were not quite finished yet. Between kicks to the head and back, they would repeat, "So waddya think of the hell's angels now, huh?"

Still not happy with the beating, they now pulled thick chains off their shoulders and swung them with as much force as they could and continued to bash this poor guy all over his body. No one could help him for fear of being the next victim. When they had satisfied their blood lust, they proceeded going up to everyone's face asking, "So waddya think of hell's angels?" Naturally, everyone gave satisfactory answers and was left alone. Now it was my turn. I was practically stiff frozen. As I was the only girl in the establishment, I was again saying those silent prayers. "So waddya think of the hell's angels?" All I could muster was "I don't…" The creep stared at me for the longest second in history, then he slowly turned away, and the two of them walked out the door.

An audible sigh of relief swept through the room as people rushed to help that poor man on the floor. At that point, I asked if I could leave. How could I dance while a man lay half beaten to death on the floor? I don't know if they called an ambulance or what. The one thing club owners don't like to do is call the police in for any reason other than a death.

I waited in the back room for a while just in case those two characters were hanging around. After enough time elapsed, I called a cab to the subway station, which was only a couple blocks away. But why tempt fate even further?

During that time, brother Dave and Darcy were staying with me, and I was working. Duane showed up out of the blue at my room with another woman in tow. He asked where I was and proceeded to help himself to the greenies in my little fridge, after which he and the girl drew out lines of cocaine and then started making out right there in front of them as if they were not there! After a while of that craziness, they both left. My brother was stunned, and when I got home a couple hours later, he immediately told me what had gone down. I knew the young woman he was with. She was a white girl raised in Jamaica.

Incidentally, it was the aforementioned girl whose peace symbol tattoo I had copied, only hers was well done and really small. So I had her friend, also from Jamaica, using a needle and Indian ink, tattoo one for me on the back of my hand, only the job he did on me was terrible. Even so, I thought it was so cool. Regardless of the fact that it looked like an old truck's steering wheel, I was so proud of it.

Anyhow, that girl was my friend, and I don't think her intentions were bad, but simply drug-induced. I was learning quickly; it didn't sting as much anymore, Duane acting that way. I just didn't have to like it.

About a week later, as I was sitting with Dave and Darcy in my room late one night, we heard the screeching of tires just below the window, followed by a crashing sound. Looking down, we saw a long large car that had forced its way between two other cars parked where it now was! We started laughing at such an incredible action that person had done and wondered if anyone else had seen or heard it too. It was only about four minutes later when Duane was banging on my door. As I let him in, the first thing out of his mouth was, "I just smashed somebody's car, I don't know if anyone saw me." We all looked at him and said, "That was *you*?" His reply was that he had borrowed someone's car after he got finished playing with Bonnie and Delaney. He had obviously gotten very high before taking the car and racing along the Long Island Expressway into Manhattan to see me.

After getting a greenie (Heineken) for him (of course the stash of beer was for whenever he came over), we walked over to the chair, the one by the window, and I sat on his lap. He kissed me, and then we worked our way to my bed, which was next to my brother and Darcy's. They too had retired, only to keep giggling at us as Duane was getting quite active and saying to me, "I never seem to be able to satisfy you. What do you want me to do?" Oh man, I was mortified as I knew those guys were intently listening, and Duane didn't seem to care one iota. Ah, the giggling and whispering continued, causing me more and more anxiety. I could never relax in such an environment. I was overwhelming happy when Duane said, "Come on, let's get outta here," at which point we went down to the lobby to get our own room. It just happened to be one of the first rooms I rented on my own months earlier.

While we were on our way back up the elevator, we ran into a friend of his whom he had jammed with on occasion. I can never recall his name, but the word Blue was part of the name of the band he was with. He walked with us to the room and hung with us for only a few moments, but in that time, Duane put his arm around me and, looking at me, said, "I will love her till the day I die, and she'll love me till the day she dies." That guy soon went on his way. Duane and I were finally alone for the next twelve hours.

Upon waking up the next morning, Duane went out for a little while, coming back with some packets of methadone. He wanted to share it with me and proceeded to chop it up and make lines to snort. This drug was not meant for that, and so it was very chunky and harsh, but against my better judgment, in wanting to do just once what he was doing, I went ahead and did the best I could to snort this abrasive chunky powder up my poor nose. To be honest, I didn't feel anything. I knew it was the drug used to treat heroin users who were trying to quit. It broke my heart to think Duane had possibly become a junkie. I didn't always know what he was on; all I knew was that it was the heroin and cocaine that were the worst evil.

Years later, I would first-hand find out just how evil cocaine was and still is. That is a story for later. After we had enjoyed our time together, he had to get back to Long Island.

It would be a few weeks from that time when Duane would come back and spend time with me. And then he'd be off again.

Not long after, my brother Dave and his girlfriend moved in with Val, Paul, and little five-year-old Camille. Once again, I was booked for a couple of weeks out of town, and upon returning, not only did I find a padlock on my door, but my things had been put in the storage basement until I had paid for those weeks I was gone. Plus, I was told that Dave and Darcy had left for Danbury, Connecticut. Feeling discouraged, lonely, and hurt, I went to pay to get my things back only to find not everything could be accounted for, like some of the T-shirts Duane had given to me. With what was left of my things, I got into the elevator to where I did not see a floor for me, and realizing just how alone and lost I was caused me to have my first real anxiety attack, which caused me to hyperventilate and collapse on the elevator floor. Val and Paul happened to be waiting to get on, and as the doors opened, they saw me lying there, shaking violently. Immediately, they picked me up and took me to their suite, where they put me to bed and said I was going to be all right. It was during the time I was staying with them that I began to believe in ghosts. In the middle of the night, when everyone was fast asleep, something would fall off the counter for no reason, and when I would go to investigate, I would see things on the floor that I had heard crash down. I never even gave one thought to the possibility of a rat! I was convinced there was a ghost or two haunting the place. After all, the Chelsea had a long history.

In a few days, I began to feel stronger again, therefore able to go back to dancing. Some weeks later, they decided to move to another hotel with more room and less money. We had been paying the big bucks for the location and the name. Into the hotel in the East Village, we moved. It was not far from NYU, so the area was not too skuzzy. We had two large rooms and a big bathroom. Camille and I had one room while Val and Paul had the other. It was at this time that Val got pregnant and was getting welfare. That was all well and good for her, but I was brought up to never ask for handouts. My mother raised all of us kids on her own money as my father only gave her $10 per child a month, which even back then was almost nothing. Yet my mother never took welfare. She worked a full-time job as a nurse while trying to raise us to be self-reliant. Still, Val tried to convince me the government owed me. Whatever it was she managed to not only haul my young little white butt down to the welfare office, but she somehow got me to actually give them a sample of *her* urine (saying it was mine) so that I would get a bigger welfare check. What brass ones she had! To add insult to injury, I looked like I was pregnant, being drained and pale as I was.

It took a few weeks to begin receiving my checks. When the first one arrived, Val was so excited, but I was having terrible gut feelings of wrongness. I had the brief sensibility to know there would be serious repercussions when they discovered the truth. Val didn't seem to care as she tried to get me to give her the check to cash if I didn't want it. My instincts had become so overwhelmingly strong that I made up my mind in an instant and immediately tore up that easy money. I don't think I ever went back, although I had to have called them to cancel any other checks that were to come.

I have to tell this one story about Camille and me. Strange as it seemed, this little black child looked just like me, only darker. One day as we were sitting on my little bed, she was sitting with her head (which sported the cutest Afro) leaning on my shoulder. A friend had taken a picture of us. I must say, although I looked pale, pitiful, and waiflike, it was an awesome photo. We were both in our PJs. It was later told to us by some lady that upon showing it to an artist friend, she was immediately asked if he could make a painting of it. He then sold it for big money in Mexico. Impressive, I thought. I wish I could have seen it. I did manage to get a copy of the photo, which I kept for years as a precious memento of me and my little friend. I actually kept wearing those PJs for many more years. I have another story of mine (which I will get to later) again wearing those same pajamas.

CHAPTER 10

I continued to dance, and my life seemed to be more organized now that I was paying a lot less rent and had a family to love me and me them. Camille and I did a lot of fun things, and I was amazed at how many people really thought she was my daughter! As I mentioned earlier, she and I had similar features. We, Camille and I, got such a kick out of those remarks. And on we went over the next few months.

By then, I had become a regular at the Fillmore East backstage group. Thinking back on those days, even though I would be with one of the most popular groupies, I was not considered as one. The backstage crew and I became good friends, and they would protect me from any danger, and there was plenty of that!

While Beth was off doing her thing, I would be helping the stage manager, Michael Ahern, by delivering messages or getting something or someone for him, or I would be just hanging out (as we called it in the late '60s), rapping with a band or crew member that was booked to play that weekend. There was never a dull moment. The only person I would have ever been seen going off with would be Duane when the Brothers would be there.

Paul had been looking to get a job as a teacher but was having a tough time finding one. Hmmmm, could it be because he and his wife were part of the Black Panther Party? Oh yes, they had me practically convinced of the cause so much so that I even went on the march and stood outside the prison doors, awaiting the transfer of activist Angela Davis. There were a few white faces dotting the sea of black ones, with all of us chanting at the top of our lungs over and over for hours (so it seemed): "Free Angela Davis! Death to the fascist pigs! Right on!" After which, we just went on with our days.

One day, Val and Paul told me that it looked like Paul might have found a teaching job but would have to do an interview with some agent from the FBI. When that day did arrive, they told me to hide out in the closet, which had louver slats. Why? I guess it might have to do with my age or skin color. They did say, "We can't let them find a white chick with us." That made no sense to me, but I did as they requested when the agent made his way up to the room. I had never seen an FBI agent in person, so it was exciting and scary all at once as I looked through the slats of the door. Just what would happen if he did a search of the room (today they would have), but phew, he did not. I got to watch and listen as the man asked Paul what seemed like normal questions one would ask of anyone looking to work in the education system. And yet I suppose it was because Paul was on the grid as a somewhat undesirable being involved with the Black Panthers, no matter what the degree.

With that done and the agent gone on his way, I was allowed out of the closet. Oh god, I couldn't wait for my eighteenth birthday when I could truly be the boss of my own life! Thankfully, that was only a couple of months away. My only fear of discovery was that damn reform school that hung over my head like the proverbial Damocles' sword. Oh, and the fear of those guys in Buffalo finding me as well.

Life with that family was beginning to get a little odd. They decided they wanted to dabble in the occult. Day by day, they would come home with books and other material on witchcraft and other occult paraphernalia such as talismans and ingredients for spells. I tried to ignore their actions. I went about my life of dancing during the week as well as some weekends, unless there was a band I wanted to see at the Fillmore. Sometimes someone would contact me to come in to dance in the light shows. One of the groups was Savoy Brown. They had a perfect song for my dancing too. I think it was called "Dancing in the Streets." While at the concert, one of the roadies and I became friends, and for the time the band was in town, he and I hung out. They were staying of course at the Chelsea. It was weird to be entering that establishment again. He was so fun and cute that it didn't take long for us to—well, you know, somehow we ended up in his bed. Laughing and tumbling around, we finally got to the serious part when he was about to climax, at which point he did the funniest thing—he pulled free and let it rip! That was so weird. I had never experienced that. Then again, I had only been with someone when I was sixteen and Duane. Neither of them ever did that! So now I ask him, "Where did it go, the stuff?" In his cute British accent, he answered, saying, "I've not a clue, let's look for it." Now here we both were hunting all over the bed, walls, floor, even the ceiling! Ha! It was a learning curve for me, I must say. Did we ever locate the missing goo? I can't remember if we did, but I do remember laughing so hard at the craziness of it all.

Something strange was happening to me at night while I slept. First of all, let me say that I would hide my money that came from all the dancing jobs I had done under my mattress. During the nights, I began having terrible nightmares, and sometimes I would wake up still in what felt like a drugged groggy state of mind (normally I would wake up immediately) while Paul would be whispering to me and tucking my covers in for me. Upon waking up and getting ready for the day, Paul and Val would remind me of my nightmare and having to calm me down. Okay, that made sense.

A funny thing while living there was how they thought it was interesting that I never called them the N-word. They used the word, but I just could not! Day after day, they would tease me, trying to make me say it. Not in anger but the way blacks would do themselves. Finally came the morning while I was taking a nice warm shower when Paul snuck in and threw cold water over the shower curtain, hitting me with the shock of cold, scaring me, and in that moment of sheer shock, I used it! I called him a N***r, sending them into gales of hilarity, congratulating themselves at getting me to break down! That was the only time I was to give them that satisfaction. All seemed fine until when I went to get my money from under my mattress only to find there was a lot of it missing! Those two kept insisting that it had to be the maid. I was so angry as I had stashed quite a bit.

CHAPTER 11

Finally, it was the eve of my eighteenth birthday. The first bit of action was to call my mom. I was now safe of her well intentions. That night, I sat down and dialed her number (my former stepfather has that number to this day). As soon as I heard her voice, I began to sob; I had missed my mother so very much. The first word she said after hello was, "Peggie?" That sound tossed me over the edge of my emotions. I proceeded to tell her how I wanted to call on so many occasions but was too scared of *the reform school*! Whatever her reply to that was, I cannot remember at all. She was so happy to hear my voice too that she cried. Above anything else, I knew my mom loved me. At least now she could let the control issue go for good. Now the only hiding I had to get through was the Buffalo thing.

One other important move I wanted to accomplish was to get that talent agent for dancers who handled all the swankiest lounges and the best and prettiest ladies. His gigs paid better, and I would get more steady work right in the city.

Okay, so now finally, it is September 23, 1970, and I am eighteen years old officially! That night, I was to dance in a light show. When the gig was over and the bands and crowd left, I walked from the stage area, and stepping through the curtains to the lobby, everyone from the stage crew and Beth started singing "Happy Birthday," and they actually had a cake for me! I almost cried. So I guess I did get a real surprise birthday party in my life, for the most awaited one as well. What a wonderful thing to have in my bank of memoirs. Until now, I had forgotten about that, and years later, I would be heard complaining how no one had ever thrown such a thing for me. It is only now as my memory comes flowing back that I begin to recall those happy times. I wish I could thank them all for being my friends during such a rough time in my life. They had remained my friends until all of us eventually drifted off onto different paths. I have always wished them well, and still do.

I was now perfectly safe to go visit my family, so I boarded a Trailways bus out of Penn station to Worcester, Massachusetts. My mom was there to pick me up. It was a bittersweet moment. As we drove back to Webster, where I once briefly lived with her and all my other siblings, I was noticing how odd it felt to be back in a small town again. I had gotten quite used to city life and all the close-at-hand conveniences. Nonetheless, I was so happy now that I was able to hold my little Lorne pie again! He was almost four years old. He was my sweetheart boy. He and I had been nearly inseparable for the first two and three quarter years of his life. I had missed him so very, very much. I believe it was at that time I brought him a Dr. Dolittle "push me, pull you" llama stuffed toy from FAO Schwarz. He still remembers it to this day.

While back in New England, of course I had to go see my friends in Oxford. They were all somehow connected with my brother Donni in the popular local band Section 5. It was so good to see them all. As I waited for my brother to come pick me up at the Newsroom on the corner of Main Street and Sutton Road, I heard a distinctly familiar voice say, "Hey, Tayer [he couldn't pronounce the *th* in my last name]. I tot you was dead!" I laughed as I turned around, knowing exactly who I was to see—Greg Spadea, with the look as if he had seen a ghost. Greg went on to say, "Yeah, your brudah didn't know where you was. You never called him, so he was afraid you was dead!" It felt good to belly-laugh again. There was a calm that quieted the raging storm in my soul for so many months, which felt like years. Yes, indeed, it was wonderful to feel the ripples of sheer hilarious joy exploding out!

My brother showed up to get me, and we went back to Paul Tringuk's house, where he grew up with his mother, Meg, and his stepfather, Dick Gould (a.k.a. the Mgr, pronounced Mahger) as he was the band's manager. Also, the band practiced in the basement of that house. A lot of memories down on Marshall Street there. Besides

Chris Boutillette's house or the Paradise, Paul's was the place to be in town. The band was the pride of Oxford, not Webster!

The fact that I had been in close contact with a lot of well-known bands did not one iota cause me to think less of this band. If anything, I was hoping to use some of my contacts to help them climb that impossibly-wide-apart-rung ladder. They were that good; I had such faith in them as musicians. I spent that week in Massachusetts before heading back to New York City. Feeling recharged and ready for the next phase of my life, I boarded the Trailways bus for my return to my now beloved concrete jungle, better now knowing I can return to my family whenever I wanted.

Now that I was eighteen, I could go see the elegant agent Mambo Hye, hoping to get work through him. After having me do a slow turn in front of him as he sat behind his big desk, there I was, looking at this tiny Jewish man with a head of curly dark hair (I think it was a wig) looking back at me with a grin on his face. He said, yes, he would be my agent. Mambo was very protective and kind to all of us girls. We were known to have more than some of the other agents in town. Our costume maker worked on the premises and made our outfits to measure. She was a master at working with beads, crystals, rhinestones, and sequins. They were exquisite pieces. They were expensive, but well worth it. He also had a standing rule that we had to wear two pair of hose, and we had to wear silver or gold high heels.

Mambo booked me in a really nice club in New Jersey for a start. In New Jersey, we had to wear full bra type or bathing suit type costumes. I had one of the prettiest beaded tops that sparkled like a rainbow to match the bottoms. Because we were not wearing the small pasties that we did in New York, we got paid less. That was okay with me. Those were usually short easy gigs, and we were not allowed to fraternize with the customers. Again, that was really fine by me. What I would end up doing was to sit in the back of the lounge with a "friend" of the club owner. Okay, this guy had one arm and talked like "dis." I was being told to go sit with him as he sat in a darkish corner, making me nervous. Truly, he looked like a hit man! Then I was told in confidence that indeed he was and to not mention anything like that to him. Whoa, check, no problem in that department for sure! It was also added that he had gotten his arm chopped off while doing a job. Phoo, now I was really feeling the love—not. Very unaggressively, I slowly approached this giant one-armed Italian as he watched me closing in on his space. When I had closed enough distance, he looked at me with those eyes that had seen death on a regular basis and proceeded to tell me, "Hey, kid. Go get me a cup of coffee. Get yourself one too. Don't be scared. Wattya afraid, I gonna bite you?" He followed with one of the gruffest guffaws I had heard to date (I would meet a woman in later years that came a close second).

After a while of my being a steady at the Fillmore, Michael Ahern started having me dance in the Grateful Dead's Pig Light Show. It was a psychedelic show of dripping and blending, swirling, waving peaks and valleys of kaleidoscopic brilliant colors. Thank the Lord, I no longer did drugs. I would be wearing micromini skirts or a pink hot-pant jumpsuit. The light would project a superimposed image of me over the trippy colors all throughout whatever song I was to dancing to. I think I must have looked about ten feet tall! That was a huge hit with everyone, and Michael began putting me in other songs (band's permission or request naturally). That became the norm for the rest of the Fillmore's run. We had so much fun. We would always go to the backstage door and pound three times, then one of the stage hands would open the door for us but would then have to quickly slam it shut before anyone else could try slithering their way in. There would sometimes be nobody there, depending on what band was playing.

The Allman Brothers came back to play and, soon thereafter, became what was considered a huge coup in the industry to being a house band in that they would be booked to play there whenever Bill Gram wanted. The Grateful Dead were the only one till the Brothers came along. What an honor! I remember when we first got to the city and how excited the guys were at seeing their name, the Allman Brothers Band, up on the marque. How remarkable. I knew they would be, and here was proof! Bravo!

Peter Green, lead guitarist for Fleetwood Mac, had come back, and they were booked to play the Fillmore at that time. It was then that Peter told me about Jeremy Spencer disappearing off the planet in LA. After having no luck in finding him, they asked Peter if he would come back to play. Apparently, Jeremy was seen to be talking with some religious cult from Europe who had convinced him to just up and leave with them. I was shocked as I knew his wife, Fiona, and his little son, Dickon. They were such a beautiful family. Fiona was absolutely gorgeous and gentle and was such a soft-spoken lady! How could this happen? My heart broke for her, but I was disappointed for the band as well.

It was so odd to see the band without Jeremy. Danny Kirwin looked sad, I thought. Perhaps angry? Oh well.

While everyone was arriving and the concert hall filling up, everyone in the house would be visiting or jamming during the wait. At some point when Peter and Duane were alone having a conversation, Duane related to me how Peter had told him to take care of me. I never did question further just what Peter meant. I was amazed at how much he cared. I know I cannot see Duane again, but maybe someday, somewhere, I will get to visit with Peter again. During one of those evenings at the Fillmore, I was to meet and become good friends with Mickey, a gentle and kind, not to mention patient, young man who would be my champion in a situation. I could have not handled nor understood without him. As our friendship grew, of course, I would mention the odd behavior of my adopted family. I would explain to Mickey how being around them was becoming more and more weird and uncomfortable. Therefore, returning to the hotel, which was once my sanctuary, no longer held that comforting feeling. Showing concern, Mickey asked to accompany me up to the rooms so he could see what they were involved in and how deep. Upon reaching my floor and as I put my keys in the lock, Val yelled at me to go away for a while as they were busy. At that, my entire body began to violently shake enough to spill the cup of coffee I was holding. It was not shaking from anger; it was from fear of them. At that point, Mickey had me sit on the steps leading to the next floor up, and in a calming soothing voice, he explained to me that no matter what they do, they cannot touch me and they cannot affect me at all. I am protected, and he quoted a Joni Mitchell lyric

"Only with your laughter can you win." Right then in an instant, I found strength I never realized I had. Immediately I got up and proceeded to put the key in the lock and open the door with confidence even though I could smell goat and something burning. We walked into a scenario that will stick in my brain forever. There was a brass cauldron with something in it that had been burned. Somehow, the sight made me laugh with conviction, enabling me to carry on with collecting as much of my things as I could. All the while Val had had her baby by then, and she was born with teeth already, so they named her Aphrodite. I have never, since then, seen a baby with a full set of teeth! It was the freakiest thing I've seen to date! A newborn with teeth!

Now I am out of that den of nuts. It would be later that I would realize that these two were somehow drugging me enough to enable them to rummage through my things, looking for where I had hidden my money. Actually, I had been booked as a regular dancer at the Metropole, and unbeknownst to these characters, I had been leaving my money with the manager who doubled as a mom-like confidante. Gerry Siner would keep my money in the club safe.

I started to do that after realizing that I had put a one-hundred-dollar bill in the back pocket of my jeans and forgot about it until one day I found where I had stuffed them in the back of a drawer. Upon finding it, I squealed with delight at finding that treasure. Val was standing there and witnessed my find, at which point her jaw dropped and her eyes said it all, "I missed that?" I just knew then and there. It was this revelation that gave me the creeps. I thought I could trust them, but alas, it was not so. When Mickey and I were grabbing my things, I kept thinking about all the things that were done to use me all that time. Oh well.

Thanks to my armor of God and my angel, Mickey, coming to help me; they could not harm me in any way. Mickey took me to Neith's apartment, where she immediately took me in. I will forever be grateful to her for that.

When I did not see Mickey after all that, I went by where his apartment was, and I was told that no one of that description lived there. I was shocked and could not figure out who, how, and where he even came from. He was there at the dire straits of my life and gone when I was safe. I have my beliefs, my faith. I will forever believe Mickey was the angel outside my window when I was five years old. I guess it was me he was interested in.

Onward to the next phase of my life of living with a new friend. Neith was like the older sister I never had. She taught me many things about street life in general. She tried to teach me how to spot trouble and stay clear, but also how to be more refined. We would shop, go to Nobody's, or just hang out at her apartment. Sometimes we would travel to England together.

I would, of course, return to Massachusetts on a regular basis. I will always remember, upon learning that the rhythm guitarist for Section 5 (the band my brother Donni played in) had quit for some reason, I was really disappointed in the change that was to come in the band, with having to get used to someone new after all the years of Mike "Head Bone" Goff being part of a family I was familiar with.

One afternoon when the guys were getting on the bus to go play out, I arrived just in time to get on it and find that there was the new guitarist who was replacing Head Bone. I knew who he was. He had driven me home from a gig at a local school in Oxford only a couple of years earlier. So Chris Boutillette was the new guy. I had grown up quite a bit since that last time we met, and I had the instant desire to sit next to him while on the way to where they were playing. Chris would be with them for the rest of the band's existence.

A funny thing happened one day while my brother and Diane (Spooky) and I were at a carnival and Spooky and I went into the ladies' room. As we were stepping into our chosen stall, she then asked me if I had a boob job. Naturally, I said, "No, but why do you ask?" Her reply was, "Well, when you left last year, you did not have them and now you are a lot bigger, so I was wondering if you had something done. I know they do it there, so I thought that is how you got that big so fast." I told her that I had done some pectoral weight workout before I even left home, but nothing happened. I guess when I actually did begin to develop, it just added on to the little bit I managed to acquire from those exercises.

My size and bone structure was petite. I was 5'1" and weighed about one hundred pounds, so having any boobs would make me look bigger than I actually was. Optical illusion became my best asset. My measurements were, at that time and for quite some time after, 36–23–34. I would like to wear clothes that were fitted, as anything else would make me look like a box. The only problem with wearing things that were curve-revealing was that I got more attention for the wrong reason. I have such revulsion for being short that wearing anything baggy would not only make me look like a box but a fat one. It was having a nice physique that allowed me to work in the best clubs that my agent handled.

I had now worked as a regular at the Metropole, long enough to have saved up for the next available apartment in Neith's building. One did on the second floor. It was a wonderful feeling when those keys were handed to me and now to feel truly independent.

The first order of the day was to call ConEd (electric) and the phone company, as well as getting wall-to-wall carpeting and matching ceiling-to-floor curtains. This took about all the money I had saved up, and I spent it with a huge smile on my face. Neith gave me a silver crushed velvet love seat that she was done with. I then put two twin mattresses on top of each other and would unfold them to create a king-sized bed.

My little studio apartment was my new sanctuary. There were times when I would just close myself in for a week at a time, not seeing or speaking to anyone.

There was one breakdown I had that had me shut in for two weeks, and it was not until Chris Boutillette came down from Massachusetts to get me to come out. He was the only one who could make me come back to reality and stability and make me feel better about myself.

While I was onstage at the Metropole, I looked out the door, as I often did, when I saw a sudden flash of red hair, and I just knew it was the Oggie Doggie Red Dog. It took a couple of seconds when he backed up and looked in, and when he saw me, he came in. He bought a beer, and we chatted while I finished my set. When I was done and had an hour break, I met up with him around the comer as we were not allowed to meet customers anywhere as long as we worked at the Metropole. They were very strict, and that worked fine with me, but knowing my ties to this person, Gerry gave me the green light to meet up with him instead of taking two cabs to the hotel where the guys were staying. Throwing a light coat over my costume, I joined Red Dog. It was a really nice hotel they were staying in these days, and it just felt weird for some reason. For so long, it was funky rooms with a lot of character. Anyway, I saw Dickey and Butch along with some of the other guys. I guess I must have looked a sight with all the stage makeup and high-heeled gold shoes and fishnet stockings on. When the time came for me to get back to work, I was told to make sure I came to the concert, which was at the theatre out in Westchester. I promised I'd be there. That evening, I caught the train out to the place and proceeded to find the guys.

Dickey and I hung out for a few minutes, and then as I was walking past Duane, he reached out to me and kept his arms around me. He told me how he found out I was living in a bad situation, and he wanted to come and get me out of it himself but had gotten sidetracked. I wonder what that could have been. He even showed me my name and address written on the inside of his leather jacket. I think it was a white leather jacket, because somehow I seem to remember thinking of how that was ruining it yet, on the other hand, knowing that he did not care about that. I was so flattered. I wonder who's got it now.

When the gig was over, he asked if I would come back to the hotel with him. I had to refuse as I did not want him to think all he had to do was snap his fingers and I'd follow. I wanted him to come get me himself, go out of his way to be with me. Plus, I knew if I did stay with him, I'd never make it back for work the next day. It took all my resolve to walk away. I knew the Allman Brothers were to play at the Boston Tea Party again, so I made sure I went. I took the bus as usual to Massachusetts to my Mom's house for the weekend. I called some people and asked if they wanted to go.

When we got there, I had a pass waiting for me. While backstage, before they went on, Duane (with his arms around me and in one of the most excited moods I had ever seen him in) replayed the scenario of when he first saw Eric Clapton in the audience while the Brothers were playing. Duane demonstrated the face he made upon noticing him there watching him play, then how he and Eric became friends, and the recording session of Layla. I was happy for him as it meant so much. I wish I could take back my attitude when I tried being fresh by huffing on my bent fingers as if to say "Big deal." I feel so awful about that even to this day. I don't think he even noticed though. I am glad that I had said "That's great" at least. Duane was floating on cloud nine all evening long. The last time they played there, they were the opening band; now they had top billing. They were the stars.

There was this club I would dance in a cage at in the Village, and I always had fun there, especially this one particular evening. Sitting at the bar among others was this man wearing a hat similar to the one a southern man would sport, not exactly a cowboy hat, yet nothing an East Coast gent would wear. I always scanned the crowd, and upon seeing this character, I just had to accept his invitation to have a drink with him. My drinks were always specially made with only a dribble of alcohol across the top. Once settled in my seat next to him, he went on to tell me his name. I almost gagged on my drink when he said, "Butch Trucks, you know the drummer with the Allman Brothers Band." I would laugh and say "Okay, what's the punch line?" With a touch of irritation, he went on to say "I am Butch Trucks, and I have a Cadillac outside and fifty dollars in my wallet that says, 'I'm Butch Trucks!'" I could not help laughing so hard I almost fell off the barstool. I asked him if he knew who I was or had he seen me with the guys. Not even acknowledging what I was saying to him, he adamantly insisted he was Butch. When I realized he was truly trying to trick me, I had to at that point tell him that Butch and I were good friends and "You ain't him!" I tried one more time to get him to own up to his ulterior motive. I said "Okay, if you are Butch Trucks, then you know what your real first name is." Ignoring me, he continued with his litany. I gave up, realizing this person was a nut job and getting scary. I moved on to another set, allowing me to get away from this delusional character. I could not wait to tell this story to Butch. When they did finally get back to the city, I got to relate the incident to my friend. He just laughed and told me I should have asked to see the mushroom tattoo on his knee. I had totally forgotten about that. Oh well, not that it would have changed his mind.

It had been a little while since seeing the Brothers back in Boston, and now here they were coming back to play the Fillmore East and were to record an LP at the same time, later to be titled *Live at the Fillmore*. It will always bring back bittersweet memories as I stood next to the photographer as he and the guys got situated—lots of laughs, some impatience (nothing new in the family portrait scenario), then the moment that will forever be frozen in time in my mind as well as in print. Someone or something happened to make us all bust up laughing, and the shot of them will forever live frozen in time on that album cover.

That was the concert I sat on the dolly of Greg's Hammond organ and watched them play. There was one moment when Duane was introducing an Elmore James song "Done Somebody Wrong," and if you listen carefully, you can hear him say after that "I wonder who" and then looked over at me sitting on the dolly. Later, I think I know what he was talking about. There were a number of occasions when Duane would try to walk up to me but to quickly turn the other way. One of them was when I was sitting stage left with my back to the curtain. Duane saw me and I him, so he began to walk up to me only to suddenly turn around. I looked up to see what he was looking at. It was the lady he brought with him. If looks could kill, one of us would be dead on the spot.

They played every night all night right into the dawn. On the last night, they had really played long and hard, so when they had headed back to the hotel where they were staying in the Village this time, I of course went with them.

Duane was sitting alone on one of the beds, and we had a nice conversation. When he got up to leave, he tousled my head and said, "If y'all come on down to Georgia, I'll give you a ride on my motorcycle" (he pronounced it to rhyme with *pickle*). I said I'd like that a lot.

I knew he would be involved with women, and I wanted him to get all that out of his system, and if I did not meet anyone before he came to realize that, then so be it. I also knew he was into serious drugs. I was also told (I won't say by who) that the woman he was with was also his dealer, and one rumor was that she even sold some of her furniture (couch) to buy more drugs for him. I knew that I had a long wait. I would enjoy just being with the guys as they were family to me. I would have to enjoy watching him and feeling him through his music.

One night, Michael Ahern was excited about an idea he had. He thought it would be very cool to have me attached to a line and low-ered down to the microphone to introduce a new band. I was to be dressed in a black flowing gown, sort of like a little fairy witch. Once being lowered down, I was to introduce the band Black Sabbath. As soon as Bill Graham got wind of that idea, he immediately said no as he wanted to introduce the band himself. Oh, if he only had more imagination than pride. I was so looking forward to flying around on the drop line zip line or whatever it is called; I wanted to do that so much. I ended up just going up to the sound balcony and sat up there with the soundman. Bill Graham came out and so very boring introduced the band. I really liked them and was bummed out that I did not get to make their Fillmore debut a more memorable one.

It was Bill's way to be gruff, but he was a good guy to me. He never said anything mean to me.

One evening, my roommate Pam and I went to our hangout Nobody's on Bleecker Street in the Village. I always would stay till closing at 2 a.m., but this day, I developed a sudden headache so left early.

I had hailed a cab, and after I gave him my address and pro-ceeded to relax, trying to get rid of a headache I felt coming on, when all of a sudden the cabbie, all excited, asked me if I had heard about what had happened to Duane Allman from the Allman Brothers Band, at which point I asked him if he knew me. I thought it was odd that a random stranger should mention him at all to me. I had not fully realized that he now was famous. I thought I would play along and see where this was going, so I asked the cabbie what he was talking about, and he went on to tell me that Duane had been killed in a motorcycle accident that afternoon. I could not believe what this man was saying to me. I kept asking him if he knew who I was. Each time, he said, no, he had never seen me before, but because I came out of a musician's hangout, he assumed I knew already. As far as I was concerned, I was convinced that this joker did indeed know me and was playing a very sick joke on me. After dropping me off at my apartment building and as soon as I got in my door, I immediately called Nobody's and asked to them if they had heard anything about it. To my relief, no one had. I then let out my breath. I told myself it was not true at all, and I just had my chain pulled.

I had already planned on going back to Massachusetts to hang out with my brother and the band. They were going to play at the High Street Conspiracy in Gardner, Massachusetts. Upon arriving at Paul's house, to begin loading up the bus, of course, I sat with Chris. Diane Paradise (Spooky) was with my brother Donni, and I have no idea who else was on the bus that day as I had been given a shock the moment I stepped into the house when someone handed me a newspaper, at the same time saying, "Hey, did you hear about Duane Allman getting killed in a motorcycle crash?" My face in that moment must have drained of all its color, and my eyes round as plates as in that instant I knew now for sure that stranger had been right. I think I was still in shock for real this time as I read the paper. I could not talk. All I was capable of was looking out the bus window. By the time we arrived at the High Street Conspiracy, which was about an hour's drive, I had not gotten my mind and heart to accept what was obviously true.

The roadies and band members went in to the club to prep for the first set. Spooky was staying by my side as she understood exactly the state of my being at that time. Her dad was a funeral parlor director, Jules Paradise. The entire family worked together for many years and many more to come. Diane was so knowledgeable in recognizing grief and its effects. She knew I was going to break at any time. Indeed, it happened when all of a sudden the band broke into "Trouble No More," the Allman Brothers' version of the song no less. They sounded so much like them that I could not keep from shattering and imploding, screaming, and just running to the door. I had to get away, run in circles or in front of a car, anything to stop the annihilating pain that took the place of every fiber of what was me. We were supposed to go riding his Harley when I finally made it down to Macon. Diane just ran right along with me. She grabbed me and crumbled with me as I threw my head back and wailed like a banshee. Diane stayed with me then until the end of the night. The rest of that weekend is still a blur to me. I don't even remember how I got back to the city, because my first memory I have after that was being back dancing at the Metropole. I was struggling to control my sorrow. Gerry Siner was so gentle and kind. I can still see that tiny woman of about sixty years old or so with her pale skin, thinning red hair, and Coke bottle thick glasses (making her own eyes look hugely magnified) as she looked up at me weeping. She suggested I go to the funeral in Macon, Georgia, but both Neith and Engie thought I would not be able to handle it and, therefore, advised me to not go. I did not go. I did not want to see the woman he had been with. I couldn't bear the thought of not being able to see him alive. So no, I didn't go.

I continued to work and hang at the Fillmore on most occasions, unless I was out of town. Sometimes Mambo would switch up the rotation of us dancers so there was some variety. We were still the main dancers; we just got a break now and then.

The Brothers were to play in Carnegie Hall only about two months after Duane died. There were a lot of critics out there, and licensed or not, they had to put their two cents' worth of criticism over the media as to whether it was right or wrong to go on with the gig. Duane was so ecstatic over the booking of such a prestigious, if not the ultimate, top gig to have. Like the song says, "If you can make it there, you can make it anywhere, New York, New York!" This was proof.

CHAPTER 12

As time went on, I was to be booked for a month at a time in places like the Flamboyan Resort Hotel in San Juan, Puerto Rico. It was beautiful beyond my wildest dreams. I could not believe the lobby had no walls or doors. You just walk up the wide steps into the lobby where the reception desk was. The entire place was filled with lush greenery, colorful flowers, and palm trees. I had a whole month to enjoy this place. Wow, was I ever going to have fun. The room I got was gorgeous and large, and I could see the ocean from the huge windows. Oh yes, I was already tasting heaven. Ahhhh, and the beaches!

Upon returning to the city, I would continue to get more gigs out on Long Island as well as in the city. Come New Year's Eve, all of us that worked during the day at the Metropole would either leave town or head out of the city. I would usually get a gig in the Village (Greenwich).

Going more frequently to England, I would have so many adventures I can't possibly mention them all, but there is one I need to tell. I would run into Mick Avory, who was the drummer for the Kinks. I had met him back in USA through another friend Ron Shelly. We ended up going to his flat for the evening. At some point during the night, we needed to go out to buy cigarettes from one of the many street vending machines. One interesting thing I noticed is that not only were there cigarette machines but unrefrigerated milk that came in triangular pint packets. I wondered why we did not have that in the States.

While I was in England, my friend Barbara Goodman stayed in my apartment. Upon my return to the States and trudging into my place with all my suitcases, I was to walk into a spaghetti party with the guests being the band for Cat Stevens, only the man himself was not present. Upon seeing this gathering of not only the guys but a few ladies I did not recognize as well, one of them turned to me saying, "Who are you?" as if I was a party crasher. I came back with the answer, "This is my place." At that, she humbled herself. Even though I was exhausted, I did enjoy what was to be a pleasant evening with some really nice people.

I would again get booked at the Flamboyan Hotel in Puerto Rico for another month. I took my Siamese cat Crumb with me that time. I lived in a studio apartment at the time. Living in that big room was not different, so the cat was fine.

There were two clubs. One was the smaller one, where I was working, and next to it was the big room, where the famous people worked. One of them was the comedian Professor Irwin Corey. This tiny little man was so funny I could not hold back my insane loud laughing. I was to be the brunt of some of his joking statements of which I was not insulted but laughed even harder. I was making myself choke while tears streamed down my face. I had to go see him again the next evening. Sitting in the back, I was not noticed. When he came to the statement that "there are two great life urges—sex…" (He was pondering a few seconds.) "I forget the other one!" Of course, the audience laughed, but I yelled out, "Going to the bathroom," which sent another gale of laughter. After the show, the professor came up to me and asked if I would do that again the next night and then on his last show. Of course would. I still maintain that going to the bathroom is a greater urge (at least for me) than sex.

Over the month, I would become friends with the wife of a famous baseball player. I can't remember his name, but I had heard it many times when my brothers would talk baseball. The reason I mention this is because upon meeting this person's wife and five-year-old daughter, I would become close friends with them and would babysit the little girl while the Mom went out shopping and such. I would take her to the beach, and we would enjoy the beautiful weather. Sharon had told me that she and her famous husband were getting a divorce, or they were separated and constantly on the phone, arguing. One day, the five-year-old child while preoccupied with a project so not even looking at me said, "You like my dad? You want him? You can have him." She said it as calmly and matter-of-factly. I looked at her and had to laugh. It really was not sad. She did not seem to care one bit at all. I thought that was odd. Oh well. Live and learn from a child.

By the end of the month, I had to get back to the gray jungle. It was home, and I did not mind the hustle and bustle. I thrived on it.

I was now a student at HB Studios on Bank Street downtown. Herbert Bergdorf began the school for acting in 1945 and is still there now. I had some really fabulous teachers there. I had wanted to study with Uta Hagen and knew I needed to audition to get into her classes, but life took so many wild turns that I ended up leaving the city before I could accomplish that. I sometimes see a film where someone who was one of my teachers appears. I loved seeing some of my fellow students that have made it to the big screen or stage.

Almost exactly one year later, I would hear of Berry Oakley's death. It was a block from where Duane had his accident. From the way I heard it, Berry thought he was all right and refused to be taken to the hospital. Later that night, he got a massive headache and died.

That was just too much for me. If I believed in curses, I would say the Allman Brothers had a huge one hanging over them. I could not stand hearing all the terrible things happening to them.

Whenever I read or heard that the Brothers were going to be appearing somewhere close enough to go, I just could not. I could not bear to look at them with new members. God bless them for carrying on; after all, the music really doesn't die. I just could not handle not seeing Duane anymore or Berry, my sweet friend.

It must have been about a year or so before I would accidentally run into some of the guys in a new hangout for everyone. Upon asking how the gang was holding up, they suddenly went quiet, wondering, what in the ——— happened now? I asked how Greg was holding up, and that was when they told me about how he turned to his friends. I'll say no more as I'm sure it is in his memoirs, and if he wants the world to know his past sorrows, then it is his to tell. I felt so sad for him. The sorrows he had inside. The demon's claw.

To this day, I can't play their songs, but if one is already playing within earshot, I will listen and remember. No, the music does not die, only the musicians. I was going through life, working, dating, traveling back and forth to Massachusetts, and so on. Neith and I would hang out less and less as she and Gerry became more involved with each other. That was fine with me. Sometimes we would fly to London together and go our separate ways. Joyce, the secretary of Electric Lady Studios, and another friend I met through Gerry would meet up with me in London a day or so later, and we would share a room in a tiny hotel. It was at this time Gerry introduced me to his good friend Tappy. I was to help him set up the Jimi Hendrix concert film to be shown in a local theatre. Gerry and Neith were on to something else.

For the next few days, I was to help and learn a great deal from Tappy. I would be shown how to get the job setup organized and all the extra things one would not think of to do. I had to keep checking on the box office for how many people were showing up and making sure the money matched the headcount. I also had to organize the time to start as we were having brownouts daily. Brownouts were when lights had to go out for a little while every day at intervals. Blackouts would be when all lights went out. I did not have to worry about that though. I had to figure in the intermission to coordinate with those. My plan was to be the road manager for a European tour with my brother and Paul Tringuk's band, Hard Road. A new record company, Virgin Records, was going to back the tour but not record unless they became a hit with the live audiences throughout Europe.

Upon my return to the States, I was so excited to tell the guys about the tour, but alas, the band had just broken up. Like a balloon that got stuck with a pin, I fizzled my way back to the city. That dream fell flat for all of us.

One day, I was walking into the Electric Lady to see Gerry when I ran into Robert Plant. Before getting past him, he reached out taking my arm and, with a lewd attitude, asked who I was. After telling him, he went on to say, "Oh, are you Peggie the Plaiter?" Knowing full well what that meant, I told him no and that he was disgusting, continuing on my way to my original destination. Forget about that pig. Such is my recall of him.

Going on from there, I kept dancing and traveling back and forth from here to there, yet I felt like a gypsy wagon without wheels. I was traveling all over the East Coast and Puerto Rico, yet I was going nowhere. I was in the beginnings of another of my depressions.

It was when Neith and Gerry wanted me to meet some nice man—some nice Englishman, preferably. I flipped out, saying I did not want to meet anyone English—American or otherwise. I wanted to be free.

As time went on—and I did live each day to the fullest—I would meet many famous people while hanging out at the Fillmore East. It was there I had been abducted by the Steppenwolf band's keyboardist as they were driving away in a limo. I was just leaving the backstage door to catch a cab for my apartment when all of a sudden the big bushy-haired keyboardist from the band jumped out, grabbed, and pulled me into the limo with him, trying to orientate myself to my situation as I was dumbfounded for a few moments. My first thought was why, how, and who I was with. I was not fearful of being in danger as they were famous and if he did anything to me it would be bad for the band. So I thought perhaps this guy who told me his name was Goldy would be fun to hang out with. When we pulled up to the fancy hotel they were staying at, I was sure nothing disagreeable could happen, so up to a suite of rooms he led me. We were alone. *Okay, so what are we doing?* I wondered as he sat down across from me and said, "Take off your shoes." I was thinking he thought I was uncomfortable or something, so I told him I did not want to. He came over and began to unlace my granny boots, and then it all began to get fuzzy as his hair was when I was not letting him do what he wanted. As he was getting upset, I was preparing myself to run out the door. He then said to me to "take off your fucking boots or I'll throw you out the window!"

I told him "No! And I will jump out the fucking window before you can touch me!" With that he said, "Come, I want to show you something." Leading me to the door to one of the other rooms in the suite, upon opening it, I saw something that looked like a scene out of Dante's *Inferno*! There were about five or six bodies writhing and crawling all over one another in an orgy of sex. I almost threw up. At this point, he went on to say, "You recognize your friend there?" He made me look till I saw her in that pile of perverts. I was so disgusted I turned to leave, but he was having other ideas. Before he could make a move, I made a mad dash for the front door. I got out and ran to the elevator. When it arrived, I stepped in to find John Kay in the comer, heading to his room. I told him I was not into what his friend wanted so I was leaving. John invited me to come hang with him for a while. In his quiet room, we talked about his traveling and missing his ol' lady. He told me he was diagnosed as being legally blind and did not get to see the details of things. He showed me what he had gotten for her while in the city and asked me if I thought they were nice and if I thought she would like them. I certainly did, so I knew she would as well. While rapping for a couple of hours, I mentioned how I wanted to move to a cheaper apartment. He said he thought a friend of his had one available on Avenue B downtown. John gave me a number to call. After a while, we fell asleep. He was so nice and such a gentleman, I regained respect for men. Not all of them are pigs. Now to deal with Beth. She had become disgusting to me. That was so disgraceful and degrading. She too felt bad about allowing herself to get into such a thing. I was happy to hear that, as I did not want to have to stay clear of her. We had gotten really close as friends.

Before calling the number John had given me, I thought I should check out the area and see for myself if it was as bad as I thought. Oh, hell yeah, it was! As I was getting ready to cross the street, I saw two guys arguing when all of a sudden one of them pulls out a gun, and thank God, he did not shoot the other guy, instead wildly pistol-whipping him. I turned and quickly got out of the area as quickly as I could.

I would try finding another solution for a less expensive place. Wanting to do summer stock theatre meant I would have to go out of town for a couple of months, and I would not make any money doing that. I had a lot of figuring to do.

Joe Cocker with the *Mad Dogs & Englishmen* was scheduled to play in the city, and meeting the road manager in Nobody's, I would be invited back to where he was staying so he could explain and describe what the job he offered me would entail. I was to be a dancer who would come out onstage to dance around. He showed me the airline ticket for whoever got the job. He said I was perfect for it. Of course, I let him seduce me. I didn't think it would matter. The next morning before we parted ways, he told me where they were playing next and to meet them there and he would give me the ticket to fly to the next gig with them. I bought that hook, line, and sinker. I went home to immediately begin getting in touch with friends I knew would live in my apartment for a few weeks while I did this gig. I then packed up a bunch of clothes and anything I would need for being on the road. My gypsy dream was getting momentum.

That weekend, I boarded a train for the long ride out to New Jersey, where Nigel told me to meet up with him. From there, he would get me hooked up to do the gig he promised, and I would get my plane ticket to travel with them.

Upon arriving then catching a cab to the location, sure enough, the band was indeed booked there, and I felt excited to get to the place and pick up my backstage pass at the "will call" window. I can't describe how shocked I was to find none there. I tried to get someone to find Nigel and tell him I was there; well, I waited and waited. Nothing. I learned another life lesson right then and there. It was to never trust a promise from a man I had just met and the tricks and depths of deception they will go to for seduction purposes. I felt foolish, gullible, cheap, and dirty. Catching the next train back to the city and upon reaching my apartment, I was mortified to tell the truth to my friend who was staying there. I could not stop crying. Why? There was not an answer or a pill to cure stupidity. Live and learn is always the way it is and always will be.

Chris Boutillette sometimes would come to NYC to just hang out with me. One particular occasion, he was visiting another friend showed up at my door. It was Randy Hobbs, and Chris immediately recognized him as he was the bass player for the Johnny Winter and Edgar Winter bands, as well as Rick Derringer among others. He had also played bass with Jimi Hendrix on occasion. Those guys ended up hanging out for the rest of the afternoon, drinking tequila until it was gone. It was at that point Randy told Chris, "Well, I guess she ain't coming back. Tell her I was here." And then he left. Chris was so amazed at how much Randy drank and still was able to walk out with only what appeared as a slight buzz. Actually, Chris said when Randy would pass the bottle to him, he would only take a sip. By the time they got to the worm, Chris had only really drunk about one-fourth to Randy's three-fourths.

I have to add one little piece here of when I was in England and was told what Randy meant over there; I thought it funny and said, "Oh, I have a friend whose name is Randy." The reply to that was, "Then I shall call him Randell." Randy is the slang word for *horny.*

There is another time when Chris came to the city while I was working at the Peppermint Lounge. Bringing along his friend the Goon (Mike Dushane), they came to town for some music business. I had been bringing my flute along to practice while on breaks. Incidentally, Chris bought me that flute when I was nineteen. Okay, so while I was dancing my set and my friends were sitting at the bar, who should walk in and plant himself right next to Chris and the Goon but David Cassidy, who was a huge TV star on the show *The Partridge Family.* Chris reminded me how David was sort of a jerk. All I remember is that I thought this character only looked like him and was going to try convincing me that he was. Before my set was done, this David lookalike with someone who was acting as his bodyguard left, and I finished up my set. As I sat in the break room, practicing my flute, the boss walks in all excited that David Cassidy came back, asking for me and if I could sit with him (and his bodyguard). The boss told me to order champagne, and I quote, "The kid's rollin' in dough," but I did not want to do that for more than one reason. I whispered to David that I had to. No problem there. Champagne was ordered. It was not the fact this young man was very wealthy; it was the idea of taking advantage of someone. I was not the material for that kind of work. Extending my good-byes and thanks for the drink, I had to head back to the stage, at which point they left as well only to return half hour later to ask me to breakfast. I thought that would be nice as his choice was the Brasserie, a fine French dining restaurant. I would never spend so high a price to eat as that place was very expensive, so this would be a rare treat indeed.

As we hopped into (of course) his limo, we were driven up to the door of the establishment. Walking in with all heads turning our way, I proceeded to keep my face turned sideways and downward. It was unnerving. I kept my eyes on my date and ignored the rest of the place. Ordering eggs Benedict and coffee, I would quite enjoy his company. When we had finished eating, we headed back (in the limo) to the Plaza Hotel next to the Central Park. Upon entering his gigantic suite, we sat around the living room, chatting. I do remember David being fascinated with my flute. After an hour or so, I had to lead him to his bed as he was literally falling asleep to the point of passing out. He looked so lonely and sad in this vulnerable state I had to lay down next to him, and I fell asleep as well.

Waking up at the crack of dawn, we sat on the huge bed, talking about his place in California. He mentioned how he went to great lengths to not ride on his father's (Jack Cassidy) coattail to achieve his success. He even changed his last name for a while so the playing field was even. I think he wanted to make sure he had what it took to be successful on his own in the industry.

At one point, David asked if I would come out to Los Angeles. I could stay with him, and how I would love his dog and his mother— funny way to invite someone to stay with you. He went on to tell me that he could set me up with agents and get me into the chorus line of some play. I did not want to look like an opportunist appearing as if I was only using him to further my own career. *Naive* is too small a word to use here. *Idiot* is more apt. Actually, it just did not feel right. I had commitments, family, friends, and there were so many cons to one pro. Giving me the phone number for his dressing room at the studio in Burbank, California, he asked me to call him in a couple of days when he would be back there. I thought that a better idea.

A few days later, I did call him, and we chatted for a while, during which he asked if there was a phone number where I could be reached. I had to give him Neith's as I no longer had a phone. The first few times he called Neith would have to get into the elevator from the seventh floor down to the second to get me, then go back up with her. Suddenly, he stopped calling me. I thought he was tired of just talking to me. When about a month went by, I thought I'd try to give him a call at the studio. In those days, you had to have the operator make a long-distance call when the charges were reversed. (He had told me to do that the first times I called him.) David answered the phone, and as we talked, the operator stayed on the line, listening to our conversation. I finally said something at which point David began telling her off. The woman kept insisting that she only wanted to make sure the call had been completed and kept arguing with him! I was so amazed at the audacity she had. Yes, she knew who I was speaking to because that information had to be given for reversed charges. Finally, she hung up, and we continued to visit. He then told me about the last time he called but my friend said I was not at home. He tried a couple more times only to get the same response. I was stumped as to why Neith would do that. I definitely planned on questioning her. The last time he tried calling, he wanted to ask if I would join him on a short European concert tour. He was planning on stopping in New York and would have picked me up. I was speechless for more than one reason to say the least. I would have gone. At least he knew, and I knew that neither one of us was trying to avoid the other. Anyway, that is my story about David Cassidy.

Upon questioning Neith about the calls and as to why she did not even tell me about them so I could call him back, her reasoning was that she did not feel like riding up and down the elevator to fetch me whenever he called. When I had asked why she did not tell me, at least she went on to say, "I'm not your personal secretary." I did not have much luck in retaining a close friend.

CHAPTER 13

I would get booked again at the club in Norfolk, Virginia, for about two weeks, maybe longer. Some club owners would like a particular dancer and request the agent to extend the gig. I would have that happen a few times. This was one of them.

One of the waitresses there, Peggy, who claimed to be one of the first Formula 4 race car drivers (I think she meant in that town), and I hung out together, and one evening, we had been cruising around after work when the car ran out of gas! My first thought was, *For a race car driver, you'd think she would have noticed that her gas level was low.* Peggy told me the gas gauge was broken. Still, person claiming to know cars well enough to qualify to be licensed in a Formula 4 category should know enough to check for the gas level in the tank. Now here we are, and it is after midnight, and we are two women alone on a dark road, trying to hitch a ride. We had no other choice. It did not take long when a sports sedan pulled over, and upon seeing a pair of baby shoes dangling from the mirror and a preteen boy in the passenger seat, I thought we would be fine. We were for the first part of the trip to the gas station, where the man driving us took the can and had it filled up for us.

Putting it in the trunk of the car, we proceeded to head back to where the car was stranded, but as we approached the entrance to the park, instead of going straight back the way we came, our gentleman driver suggested we take a ride through the park. Suddenly, not feeling right about doing that, Peggy and I both looked at each other and said no, and we asked to be taken back to the car. He did not listen, but instead, he took us into the deserted park, all the while ignoring our pleas to just take us back to the car like he promised, but to no avail. When he had driven deep enough into the park, he decided to stop the car. I have to say that it is absolutely amazing how quick the brain thinks in such moments. I was able to evaluate the fact that this vehicle had bucket seats and the back of the seats could go forward to allow for climbing in the back. Then I noticed the door handles were flat and had to be lifted up to open the door. I also calculated the time he would manage to get in the back seat by leaning over, causing his seat back to lean toward me while he started to grope Peggy's leg, ignoring her protests, not to mention the boy in the passenger seat pleading with that man to let us go. I knew if I could get out of the car and run down the street far enough, it would give me a chance to stay in view of Peggy and yet far enough to get away.

The fact they were black and it was early '70s in the south was threat enough. They would get caught and severely punished for attacking two white women. I would be able to get away and describe them and their car exactly not to mention the gas station attendant having seen us with him. All this ran through my mind in a nanosecond, and that was exactly the way that it played out. I got far enough down the road and all the while screaming at the top of my lungs (vocal breathing lessons came in handy). When I had gotten far enough for safety, I began screaming and screaming for help. Suddenly, Peggy jumped out of the car, and the man gave her the gas can from the trunk, at which point, Peggy came as fast as she could, considering the can was heavy. As soon as he got back in his car, he tried to run us over, but because we were surrounded by trees we were able to dodge him. It must have dawned on him that if he got one of us, there was always the other person to have to deal with and that the chances of succeeding were slim, so he had to leave and hope we would not go to the police. After we felt sure enough they were truly gone, we attempted to make our way to where her car was. It was not long when an elderly couple driving through the park stopped and offered us a ride. For a split second I was thinking maybe they were nuts as well, but that did not last long, and we got a nice safe ride back to her car.

When we got back to the apartment, we called the police and explained everything. The next day, an officer came to see Peggy and me to inform us that the two we had described had been found and brought in. The officer also asked if we really wanted to make charges against them, and when we said "Oh yes," he went on to say that this man had no priors and was not a bad man, he just made a wrong decision, and maybe we could drop any charges as he was remorseful and scared enough. Peggy and I were still shaken up and angry, so we did not care about how he felt now that he was caught, and since he tried to kill us by running us over, oh no, we wanted to make him pay. At that point, the officer went on to tell us a little more information about how seeing that they were black folk they would get the book thrown at them, and more than likely, they might never even see a trial because white folk down in the south would very likely grab them both and hang them from a tree or lamppost. Could we live with that? Had the crime fit the punishment they would receive? After hearing that, I was so shocked that that could still happen now! The cop assured us it was so. Peggy and I figured okay that had to be scaring the crap out of them right now and that poor innocent boy would pay as well for something he did try to stop, so we dropped the charges. I never regretted it either.

As I got close to my appointment with Edgar Cayce (the sleeping prophet) I got a call from his secretary to tell me that he would not be able to see me but that his son would. I wanted to see Edgar, so I declined. I thought it also odd because this would be the third time I had tried to have a physic reading and they too had been unfulfilled. Being that I was to leave the next day, I was unable to reschedule. As time went on, there were many other times I had attempted to have a reading of tarot cards, my palms, or even tea leaves, but one after the other would be squashed. Years later, I would realize why.

CHAPTER 14

After I had been working in Norfolk, Virginia, for a couple of weeks, I had become friends with some navy folk, and at one point, I was taken on board a submarine and was quite impressed with how close quarters those men had to live for weeks at a time. Funny because in twenty years or so, I would have a niece that would be stationed on one of these tin cans. She had not been born yet. Just the thought of being under so much water in only a metal case was overwhelming to me.

One night, while at the Fillmore, I met Mel Collins from King Crimson. He was the saxophone player, and he also played the Moog synthesizer, which he would later tell me how he hated that thing. Mel played piano and thought the synthesizer was so fake, but he needed to make the sounds that machine could create. Mel and I started to see each other while he was in New York, and before he left, he asked if I would come to stay with him in England. I really liked him and thought that would be great.

A couple of weeks later, I would fly over to London for a month. Mel picked me up from Heathrow, and we headed on to his home, where he lived with his parents and sister in Banstead, Surrey. It was only about twenty minutes out of London. I will always remember how English quaint the house and gardens were. Mel's mom and dad were wonderful people, and I fell in love with them all immediately. His dad, Derek, worked for the BBC in the orchestra. He too played saxophone while his mother was a retired vocalist, and his sister Cherry was a vocalist as well. Cherry would take me to some of her gigs when Mel was working in the studio in London. She would get booked to sing in nightclubs or dinner clubs, bringing her arrangements for the house bands to follow. I thought Cherry was an amazing lady. I would go back and forth between NYC and England quite frequently and so becoming more and more a part of the Collins family.

Sometimes I would go to the studio with Mel, and there I would sit in the mixing room and listen for hours to take after take.

One of the sessions had Greg Lake of ELP (Emerson Lake and Palmer) sitting in on some tracks, or maybe it was his LP that Mel was working on. There were so many recording sessions and musicians coming and going either to add their talent to the mix or just to hang out. All in all, they were good times. I'd get pretty tired and get anxious to get done with the studio at times when we had been there for almost eighteen hours!

It was interesting to hear the separate recordings of the vocals. Once in a while, I would feel sad when they would take a beautiful instrumental and then add the voices. Oh well.

I would again head back to the States. My mother was remarried and was trying to get pregnant one more time. She wanted to try for a girl, seeing, as the order of gender all us kids came in stood in her favor, that she would indeed get her wish.

My sister Heather was born on June 30, 1972. We were all so happy to have this adorable and intelligent little person added to our family. We would be two months shy of being twenty years apart. Funny as it seemed no one ever asked if she was my child. I have a picture of myself holding her as a newborn up in the air (yup, she drooled in my mouth) while Chris took a picture, freezing that moment in time.

One of the times I was in England, naturally I had told Bebe (Mel's mom) that my mom was about to have the baby. The next time I was visiting Mel and his family, Bebe gave me a precious hand-crocheted yellow dress that she had made a few years earlier herself when she was expecting her third child only to miscarry. It was devastating for her, and she held on to that little dress for long enough. With a very heartfelt explanation, she gave it to me for my new baby sister. I gave that dress to my mom and told her the story behind it. My mom was so touched she immediately sat down and wrote a wonderful thank-you letter to Bebe. Heather would only get to wear that little outfit a few times before the cat, Crumb, would eat a huge hole in it. This would not be the first thing she had eaten. For some reason, she had a thing for wool. Not just any wool, but it had to be the expensive kind. When I had her in my apartment, she would eat my things, and when anyone slept over, they had to be careful to hide anything made of the delectable material; otherwise, that said item would end up with great gaping holes in them, rendering them unsalvageable. I will never forget the morning my friend Beth went to put her socks on only to find that the entire heel on both socks were gone. She was so funny when she put them on and half her foot hung out the back. I still laugh hard when I get into the story. Beth went on to tell me that those were her late grandfather's. Beth loved them dearly. Who knew the cat would eat them! Eventually, I would take her to my mother's house so I could sublet my apartment and be free of the rent for a while, as I had hoped to work in a summer stock theatre over the summer months. That would not happen for a while yet.

Yet again, I would find myself on my way to England, only this time Mel had shown some unfavorable traits that I knew would not fly in my life.

One evening, when we were leaving the nightclub (the British equivalent to Nobody's), another friend of mine, Victor, said, "See ya later." Victor worked as a roadie for one of the British bands that had come to America. Victor and I were good friends and nothing more. So it came as a natural response to a good-bye to say "See you later." No sooner were we in the car when Mel asked me in a very serious voice, "What did he mean 'See you later'?" I was so surprised that he would have misconstrued the meaning of such a simple statement. I had to convince him that it meant absolutely nothing. That was the first serious flag to go up in our relationship.

One day as we were driving past Old Bailey, he made a comment that we could just walk in there and get married. When I asked if he was serious, he answered me, saying he was. I had to quickly get his mind off that train of thought.

It was on one of those trips to England that I was to attend the wedding of Mel's sister Cherry and her fiancé Bernard. It was a beautiful day for the wedding they had. The wedding ceremony was exactly the same as I always knew them to be in New England. Guess some traditions never change.

After the reception, some of the guests were invited back to the house for more festivities.

I would continue to dance with Lou Christie, a singer from the mid '60s who was touring England and had hired Cherry for backup vocals. Cherry had naturally invited him and the other members of the band to her wedding. He and I were the only Yanks present, and I think he just wanted to hear the accent to feel a little bit of home. One thing about Lou was that he was very gay. Everyone knew that, and so I did not feel like I was dishonoring Mel. Mel did not want to dance at all, and I liked to, so therefore, I had chosen to dance with Lou. No threat there; I was positive of it. But no, Mel pouted. I kept dancing and enjoying everyone's company, including Cherry and Bernard, not to mention Bebe and Derek as well. After about an hour of this, I noticed Mel had disappeared. I knew just where he had gone, so I went looking for him, and finding the door to his bedroom locked, I knocked. Mel was not pleased and thought I should come up to the room to stay with him. That was not going to be fun at all. I chose to remain with the party of happy people. That night, when we all retired, Mel was not speaking to me. I was baffled at how immature he was acting. There was something about him I did not understand. I had learned he could be very moody often, and he was always questioning me about this or that guy I might say hello to or even look at. I don't know. Maybe I imagined the whole thing.

Normalcy resumed for us, and we enjoyed being together. One evening, he told me he was going to have a blow (jam) with some other musicians out at one of the guys' home. Ian Anderson and Alvin Lee were among some of the lads playing together that night.

Mel brought home the tape of that session. I listened and was surprised to hear a sweet blues sound coming from Alvin. He really could play tasteful guitar. Not that I did not like his other way of playing. One day, while I was playing a Ten Years After's LP for Duane, I asked how he liked Alvin's guitar playing. His answer was, "Hell, he's just a fast guitar picker." I took that as meaning he was not really a good musician. The moment I heard the blues so wonderfully played by Alvin, I wished Duane could have heard it.

I returned to the States and knew I had better make sure I could handle moving to England.

I would fly back in December for Christmas. Mel and I were going to stay at his parents' villa in Majorca, Spain, then later go on to France and Scotland. When we tried to catch a plane over, something was not making it possible. I think our flight had been cancelled and there were no others to be had. We spent Christmas just the two of us at his house. No one else was there for the entire holiday. I was so depressed. I wanted to be with my family back in the States, celebrating Christmas as I knew it and with the little kids as I would watch them open their gifts. I had dreary drab holiday. Could I do this year after year if we got married? I had serious doubts. Mel spent the entire time working on arrangements of music and writing pieces for another band. He was a genius at it. Maybe that is why he was the way he was—moody, glum, and worked constantly.

When I had arrived just before Christmas Eve, Mel took me to the house he had purchased. He was so excited to have been able to do so. It was a fixer upper and did not look at all appealing to me in the least. I had a vision of me always being chilled to the bone and scrubbing walls and floors. I could not even imagine what all a fixer upper would entail. I just knew it did not make me feel one bit domestic. I knew then I had better make up my mind fast.

New Year's Eve was spent at a friend's flat in London. I was told the belief that how you spend New Year's Eve would be how the rest of the year would go. I had a great time at that party and couldn't wait to see if the saying was true or even close.

I would head back State side a few days later. The phone calls between Mel and I became less and less. Then I found out he had met a lady named Maggie and had become serious with her. I was only a smidgen jealous and slightly wondered if I had made the right decision in not wanting to marry Mel. It was only moments later when I felt a relief and was happy for him. Onward with my single life. I was quite happy with it.

CHAPTER 15

I had been a student at HB (Herbert Bergdorf) Studios on 120 Bank Street. I took Method Acting Tech 1, 2, and 3, modern dance, and speech.

I would audition for Broadway plays and some off Broadway. I will never forget auditioning for Rosemary Rosenblum on the *Jesus Christ Superstar* stage. It was slanted, so when I went to walk down to hand my sheet music to the pianist, I actually tripped over my own feet and did a little roll down the stage before catching myself and gathering up my music and handing it over to the accompanist, only to find I was so mortified that I could not sing very well. As the director sat (not the first row), he never even cracked an expression once. I knew I would not be getting a call back. I would be constantly hauling props for my acting class scenes, and taking the subway proved to be so cumbersome that I decided to go for the cab instead on those days.

Ed Moorehouse was my teacher, and he was fantastic. I learned a lot from him. Once in a while, Bill Hickey would substitute for Ed when he was out.

We had so many talented people in our class. Actually, all the students at HB were wonderful. We were not pampered. Many famous actors came out of that place. At first, I wanted to study with Stella Adler or Stanislavski, the other highly respected teacher. I had also wanted to study with Uta Hagen who taught at HB. I was to leave town before that could happen.

Now came the time when I really wanted to get some full submersion in acting, so decided I would go try for some summer stock. Before I would find anything out on how to go about auditioning and other prerequisites, I had asked a couple I knew who was looking to sublet and apartment for a few months. I gave them that opportunity; I then went in search for a company that was preparing for the summer stock only to find out that had already been done. I was too late. My fault. Another of life's lessons to be learned.

I now find myself without a place to live, but fortunately, I met a young lady, Sharon, who was staying with her dad in a hotel on 57th Street. Her dad, Bob De Orleans, was an engineer for Mountain, a rock group in the '60s and '70s.

Bob engineered another LP for Maggie Bell from Stone the Crows, a rock group out of Scotland. I listened to the master tape and wished I could have had a copy of it. Maggie sang a few of her tunes in old Scottish Gaelic, which was almost obsolete in the twentieth century. I thought it was one of the most beautiful pieces of music I had ever heard. I never did get a copy of the master tape as I was promised. Ah, well.

Maggie Bell had a tragic story to tell. While she and her husband and the rest of the band were onstage doing a sound check (I believe or perhaps they were actually doing a performance in Scotland), her husband went up to the microphone to begin singing when he got electrocuted (the mike was in a puddle of water as there had been a rainstorm earlier) and got shot across the stage, where he died immediately. I was never able to find anything from Maggie Bell since then—sad because she was good.

Bob would take a shine to me enough to ask me to come to Bermuda with him where I got to watch a full-blown hurricane from the hotel room. I watched the huge beautiful palm trees getting ripped out of the ground roots and all and flying right past me as I sat in the hotel window. What did I know of safety in those young days? The image will remain on the screen of my mind forever. Bermuda was so beautiful. I had thought it was such a paradise. I thought the police in their cute Bermuda shorts and high white socks with the high hat were intriguing. Almost everyone rode around on Vespas. The streets were small and quaint. So many flowers and sweet smells. The ocean was wonderful and not too cold. I could stay in that water for hours.

One day, Bob rented a couple of those little motorbikes for us to do some sightseeing. Being in Bermuda meant that driving was as it is in England. Driving was on the opposite side than it is in America, so as we were tooling around and having a great time at one point, I noticed that Bob was not with me. I turned around to see where he was, and I saw him lying in the road. He was on the wrong side. I don't remember if he was or the automobile was on the wrong side. Any way, he was all right—bruised and achy, but all right. I could not stop laughing. He looked so funny in the road with his bike on its side. I don't know why I thought it was humorous; perhaps he too was laughing.

The next day, he had to go take care of some business he came down there for, and I hung out with one of the waiters, Tony. Of course he was from Italy and so good-looking. Tony first took me to his little apartment, and then we went to the beach. What a fun time we were having, jumping and playing in the surf. At one point, Tony was looking at me, and all in a fluster, he kept waving his arms in all sorts of gestures, and his English was compromised, so I could not understand what in the world he was trying to say. Finally, he was able to get it out enough to say, "Your things, your things are out! Your things are out!" All the while, he was pointing and looking at my chest. I looked down to see my bathing suit top had ridden way up over my boobs, and I was just going on about my playing, never feeling the change in the position of the top. Naturally, I yanked it back into place. I was a bit embarrassed but not too much to spoil my fun. Tony and I would finish up our outing at the beach and head back to his place, where we had some more activities to see to. I finally went back to the hotel, and Bob had gotten back and was taking a nap. He never once asked any questions. I somehow didn't think he would.

Back to NYC we went, and I took some pretty awesome memories with me. I'd like to go back someday. Sharon and Bob would soon be moving out of the hotel. I did not want to follow them, and so I went to stay with Dennis Marino, a friend of Sharon's. Dennis told me I could stay at his place that he shared with a young woman, Symie. Symie was about twenty-two and being supported by Ace, an older man in his sixties. Ace owned a very successful construction company, therefore quite wealthy. Dennis, if I remember correctly, fixed them up in the first place and so was allowed to share the apartment on the fourth floor in an exclusive building on Madison Avenue. The furniture was sparse, and I did not care as long as I had a roof over my head. Dennis and I would have a brief entanglement. I was not looking for anything anyway in the line of boyfriends, so not sharing his round bed with him was not an issue. I slept on a bunch of pillows, and that was fine with me.

Symie, I thought, was a kick, and I liked her. I admired the way she did not care that the man she would go out with and go on cruises with was old, gray, and not handsome at all. His body was not anything to desire, but she did not give a hoot. She told me she had gone on a cruise with him, and she took along a girlfriend, and he paid all expenses for her as well. Symie did not have to tell me anymore for I already figured it out what that deal was all about. I was getting an education as I went through my years in the city.

On one of the occasions, Ace was taking us all out for lunch. He proposed that he would set me up in an apartment right down the street from the HB Studios and he would pay for everything, even my classes. He would take me on trips with him, and he would provide me with a driver whenever I needed to go somewhere. I must say it made me think a little. By then, I knew I was not a bar of soap and would not wear out. I did toy with the prospect of having all that was offered. It was the cost of all this that I could not bring myself to pay. Just the thought of it made me ill. How did Symie do it? How did all those other beautiful women do it? I knew it was for the money only. That was not my agenda. I politely refused a few days later over another lunch. Ace understood. Besides, he was a married man.

Hanging out at the club Nobody's on Bleecker Street in the Village, I would hook up with friends and just drink and be merry. A lot of the time, I would hook up with Gerry Stickells there. He and I were sort of in a relationship, nothing serious, but I knew he would really like to meet someone to have a real relationship with. That person I knew was my friend Neith. It would take a bit of patience to get her to come around and realize that Gerry would be the perfect man for her. Eventually, that did come to pass.

After moving in together, life was looking up, until one day out of the blue when Neith wanted nothing more to do with me—even to the point of not inviting me to their wedding. I was so hurt. I had no idea what I could have done to upset her, and it was the worst part.

Eventually, after I had moved out of the building we lived in (when I got sub letters) and I was now staying with Dennis and Symie on Madison Avenue, I got a phone call from out of the blue, and it was Neith. We talked for a while, and part of the conversation was to tell me it would help Gerry out if I were to join them both on a business dinner date with one of the guys from Three Dog Night. They thought we were a smart match. I agreed. I really was hoping to get back in good graces with this lady who meant so much to me. Alas, when the date came—and went—I had not shown up. When Neith called to give me a piece of her mind, I was at a loss as to what her problem was! I had written down the wrong date. She did not believe me, and after her tirade, she hung up. Every time I went to call her back, she would pick up the phone and hang it up. That was truly the end of what was once a wonderful relationship—not to mention losing another friend, that being Gerry. I had to move on.

I knew Neith would have a full and exciting life with Gerry, seeing as he was the road manager for bands such as Fleetwood Mac, Three Dog Night, Elton John, and Queen among others, but it would be about a year later before I would see my friend again.

Neith and Gerry had moved out to Burbank in Southern California, so I really did not expect to see her ever again, yet one evening, who should stroll into the Ropewalk where I was bartending but my old friend—only this time her mouth was wired shut! I was shocked to say the least. She went on to tell me that she had a near-death experience, which caused a change in attitude. Apology was her mission. I forgave her, and she invited me out to Burbank. I did not think I would be doing that in the near future at least, but it was wonderful to have her friendship back. Incidentally, the reason why her jaw was broken was that she had been crossing the street with her horse when a car hit them, sending her flying and breaking her horse's leg. Airborne stood over where Neith lay all broken up in the bushes where the police found her. If it were not for her devoted horse, they would not have found her in time. That was Airborne's final act before he had to be put down because horses don't recover from a break to their legs. Very, very sad time.

CHAPTER 16

I have to tell the story about Peter Max, the artist that was famous in the '60s and '70s. I met him through Dennis at a party at Peter's Brownstone on the Upper East Side. I thought he was very cool, and I think he felt the same about me as I ended up spending the night with him. The next day, I would find out he and his wife were divorced but still very good friends and remained close. Peter had a hole cut through the floor of his apartment and had a spiral staircase put in so they could remain in the same home for their two children, Adam and Libra. I liked to call her little Libra Sagittarius. Those kids were so adorable and smart. Libra had a habit of hitting her dad on the face, and he would not scold her. He would just let her wail away. When she tried that on me, I did not allow it. Oh, hell no. She liked me anyway. Peter had hired me to take care of them whenever he and his wife were out of town.

We would frequently go to his house in Woodstock, upstate New York. What a cool and exclusive town it was, very organic. Adam had told me on a number of occasions that when he grew up he was going to be the manager of GM. I had never known such a young person to be thinking of what they wanted to do when they grew up, especially a career that held no glamour or fame. I was truly impressed. I have been tempted on occasion to try finding out if he ever did.

While back in the city, I would love to watch Peter work. He was an artist, and he had an assistant who also was a talented painter. It amazed me how he and Bernard worked together. Also fascinating was a trick I would find myself using, thanks to Peter. He would look in a mirror across the room at what he had painted and then make a telescope of his hands to look through in order to check for balance. Wow.

When Peter had another gathering at his home, I met a famous model and a guru Peter would "study" with—meditation and things. While he and the model were just talking, this hippie guru decided to take a swing at her, knocking her out cold. When she came to, he just stood over her and asked, "What was your last thought as I punched you?" I asked her if he broke her nose, and she said no, but she told him to get the hell away from her anyways. I would have had to hit him back. Oh, yeah.

Finally, the day came when I had to get back to making money and finding a place to live. The people in my apartment were not going to move out! I had nowhere to go! I did not know what I should do. I had planned to be gone for about four months, so I could not get back into my place.

It was at this time I had to go back to dancing. I decided I had better go back to Mambo to get some work. I had not danced for a couple of months and so was a little rusty. It didn't take long to get back into the routine, but soon I realized that the go-go dancing was getting a little to no-no dancing for me. The girls that were being booked now were getting a wee bit to raunchy for me. They would do their set, and then I would get onstage to do my real dancing, much to the disappointment of the men watching, as they realized I was not about to do the things the other girl was doing.

After I realized that this was the way it was changing into, I knew I would have to draw the line at some point. I had agreed to the pasties we all at one time had to wear, but now they had to come off because the audiences were getting bored with not seeing enough. Touching oneself and lying down on the floor or on a couch that had been set up on the stage was the norm, and if you did not do it, you were not getting hired back. I had even been sent home from some clubs because I would not do those things.

I finally had enough when I saw one of my good friends actually going the distance and removing all her costume and then lying on the floor of the stage and showing all her stuff to the men watching. I almost threw up. It was then I knew I had to quit once and for all.

At that time, I met Mike Linden. He was a friend of all the dancers and would come into the clubs to hang out with us. I never thought much of him. I thought he was full of himself and arrogant to boot, smoking his long, skinny, dark, exotic cigarettes. One day, while dancing at one of the tamer clubs, he had asked me to join him while on my break. I decided to see what he was all about. As we sat and talked, I thought he was actually nice. I had mentioned that I was looking to move out of the place where I was staying, and so Mike offered me to stay with him. I thought this could be a solution to my problems.

Mike Linden made life a little better for me, and I was actually starting to like him more and more. When I asked him how old he was, he said forty-two. I had a shock! I was only twenty-two, and the thought of being with someone that much older than me was repulsive. I did not say anything to him about that. I had to dig deep to find out how I really felt about the age difference. Had I not asked, I would have been fine, but I did ask and now had to live (or not) with that knowledge. It did not take me long to conclude I could handle it. The longer I stayed with him, the easier it became to ignore the age difference.

Mike and I would go out night clubbing at least four times a week. I would have a rum and Coke now and again, but one day Mike told me I should try some nice wine. At first, I did not like it, but to make him happy and stop insulting me, I would eventually become quite fond of the fruit of the vine. I was told to stop ordering kid's meals and order something grown-up, more adult. So I began ordering steaks and the like. The French red wines were my favorites. I eventually would be able to drink an entire bottle to myself in one evening. It had not occurred to me that I was drowning my sorrows. Mike was overbearing and bossy. His mother was Jewish and had migrated to America during the Second World War. Her husband, Mike's father, was an SS officer in the German Army, and because he was married to a Jewess, he had to either turn them in or get them out of the country. Mike never saw his father again. His mother, Edith, was a typical Jewish mama and was very controlling yet coddling. She was to create a successful business just for him where he would be the boss, overseeing dozens of Spanish women who expertly embroidered designs on baby clothes. It was a lucrative business, and Mike made plenty of money to enjoy life his way. His mother followed her love for antiques to become an antique dealer, leaving Mike in sole control of the embroidery factory.

I really think Mike had a desire to make women in his life cry. He got a charge out of getting them to grovel. It was while I was with Mike that I changed from being a dancer to becoming a waitress in one of the clubs. I never worked that club, so I came in fresh. I wanted to be a bartender so I could be behind the "stick." Rules are, you begin as a waitress serving drinks, then if there is an opening, then comes your chance. I humped drinks around the club Mike and Eddie Cvercko owned. They were really fun and funny, and I did enjoy working for them. They began to look at me like the little sister they never had. Even their mom and dad loved me. If Dad liked me, that was enough for them.

There was a rule that we pool all our tips at the end of the day. I thought everyone was being honest and showing all that they had made. Eva, who was my friend and also the daytime bartender, would try to tell me to hide my tips because the other girls were doing just that. I could not understand that they would do such a hateful and evil mean thing. I would show I had made about $90 or so, and they would always say they only made about $5 or less. I would have to give up most of my tips and go home with about $20 or $25, and they would be going home with over $100, thanks to my honesty.

Eva would try again and again to help me to not get taken advantage of. Day after day, she would slyly not charge me for a whole tray of drinks and tell me to hide it. Don't show the other girls. "I want you to make some money, Peparone," she would say to me. One night, while Mike was sitting at the bar he had in the house and while he arrogantly smoked his long skinny brown cigarette and sipped his drink, he called me stupid and naive plus other insulting things because I would not lie by saying I made less than I actually did. I could not bring myself to steal from Mike and Eddie by allow-ing myself to take those trays of drinks then pocket the proceeds. I had never been so insulted in my life. It was at this point that I broke down and started bawling only to be told to quit the crocodile tears. He went further to say, "You're an actress. You're not fooling me, so knock off the tears!" I was angry to have been so treated. To make matters worse, my younger sister was visiting from Massachusetts. She was scared to death. And like me, she had never seen or heard such language or heard anyone be called stupid and ignorant for being honest. Kim was so fearful of him, saying she wanted to go home. I had to calm her down, and soon, the evening resumed a more tranquil atmosphere.

The next day, I attempted my first robbery. As the days, weeks, and months passed, by I began to make good money, and I did not regret one bit hiding 98 percent of my tips. After the split, we *all* went home with equal amounts. Another lesson learned. Life went on for us, and the episode of "to steal or not to steal" was in the past. I actually believe Mike and Eddie knew what was going on. It was their desire to make a certain amount profit and anything more we could have. I have never met people like that ever again.

I was falling into a routine with Mike Linden and thought we were doing okay together. As I mentioned earlier, we would go out to dinner and afterwards lounge in the bar or, in some cases, remain at our table and visit with friends. It was on those occasions that Mike would make me sit on his lap and pet me for his friends to admire. What an ignoramus I was in those days. I did not heed my inner voice that told me there was something off with this scenario. One evening, he decided to take me to a club that he and his former wife would frequent. It was strange that there were no single folks there, only couples. As we sat at the bar, we ordered our drinks. As I had gotten quite used to drinking wine, I indulged in quite a few glasses. I was to meet a lot of "friendly" couples. One got so friendly that she began to caress my long ponytail. She was trying to hit on me. I figured that out myself and told her to get her hands off me. Mike was miffed at me for acting so rude to her. Once in a while, I would stand up for myself. Another couple we met, Rudy and Gerta, were nice people. They were a good-looking couple, and the fact that they spoke German fascinated me. Mike spoke German as well, but

I never asked him to teach me any. I would learn a phrase here and there but not much more.

We had made plans to go to a dude ranch in upstate New York. I was very excited about that as I had not been able to ride for years. I looked forward to getting reacquainted with riding horses.

The place was a good four-hour ride out of the city. It was nice to get out and into the country for a few days. The place was fantastic and rustic, nothing fancy. It was just like those places depicted in the movies. The barn was only a little way from the house, and I loved the atmosphere immediately. Mike had never ridden a horse in his life, which made me feel like a champ rider, until I realized I was not as accomplished as I believed I was. When we were asked about our horsemanship, Mike told them he had none, but I on the other hand said I was quite proficient. The owner and his head wrangler began pairing us all up with our horses for the weekend. I had told them I wanted a big horse and not a pony. Well, they said I was to ride the little gray named Mouse. I was so disappointed, but they informed me that because I was the smallest, I was indeed given a pony. I was really disappointed! I didn't blame the pony for his being small and so began to make friends with him. Mouse was a handsome little guy, and we decided we would have fun together. So now everyone was saddled up, and Holgar, the wrangler, said to his boss the traditional statement they exchanged every new group they had. Because so many people would claim to know how to handle horses (ponies) only to get dumped, the guys would have already started making bets between themselves. They would pay twenty-five cents for each one that fell, and if there was any bloodshed, it was fifty cents. I was to get a huge lesson in mollification. They must have realized how little I actually knew as I'm sure they noticed how I wore my waist-length hair up under a newsboy cap, and secondly, I did not check the stirrup length. As I mounted, I realized my stirrups were too short, but thought it was not a big deal. At this point, we had all mounted our horse and taken off for the trail. We were going at a fast trot already, and I was pretty confident, but that was soon to be shaken. As the horses went on just as they had been doing for so many rides before, they did what they were familiar with and *jumped* over a ravine hidden by tall grass. When Mouse launched himself over just as he always did, I flew off! I landed in a briar patch with my hat flying somewhere. With my survival instincts kicking in, I immediately rolled out of the way of the other horses. How the others stayed on while I got dumped was amazing and embarrassing to me. As everyone halted to wait while I assessed the possible damage done, I proceeded to let them all know that I was fine but needed to get the pickers out of myself. I also said I owed them twenty-five cents! Readjusting my stirrups and keeping my hat tucked in my belt, I proceeded to admit, "I guess I don't know that much." When riding a horse or pony, one must at all times be prepared for anything. My instruction on how to ride was nonexistent. I did not know there were so many things involved for a true and safe ride. I had always had someone else tack up my mounts, therefore never learning proper equitation either. My father just threw me on the horse or pony and said go. I figured that if I could stay aboard even though I was nearly knocked off by being run under a low-hanging branch, the fact that I stayed on made me think I was a natural and could handle any other steed.

My first experience at the ranch made me determined to keep riding. We would go up to that Dude Ranch frequently during that summer and the rest of the year. I still was not strong enough to handle a spirited horse, so when Mike decided to buy himself and me one, I was informed I needed a gentler, older one. Although Mike was the newbie at riding, he was allowed to buy the young three-year-old filly, Penny. She was such a pretty and fresh little lady. A lot of spirit. I was not able to make my mounts do what I wanted, but instead, I allowed them to do what they wanted, in a sense giving them control over me. When I was told I was not "mean" enough to handle a horse like her, I was insulted, yet I knew he was right. He did not infer that I had to beat or be cruel to them, but needed to make them do what they were asked to do. That meant not stopping whenever they wanted or wandering off the path to have a little snack of grass or whatever struck their fancy. I though it meant to force them to go where I wanted. I was aware of that fact, yet I could not change my ways.

At some point, while up at the ranch, I developed a crush on Holgar. He was so masculine, rugged, and handsome—all the things Mike was not. My crush would become so strong I would pine for just a look at him or to hear his voice. I had called him one day and asked if I could come up to work there for a summer. I was told it would not be a good idea because Mike spent a lot of money there, and he did not want to jeopardize that. It was then I knew I had no chance of getting closer to him. We continued going up there, and Mike would ride his red pony, and I would ride my Cleveland Bay named Hash. Hash and I had developed a wonderful relationship. I learned how to tack him up and make sure the stirrups were adjusted. I still was not taught proper equitation. One weekend, I had invited my younger brothers Jimmy (fifteen) and Ross (fourteen) to the ranch. Rudy and Gerta would also be there. By then, Mike and I had become really good friends with them even though I knew they were swingers. Even so, I would never participate in that lifestyle. They respected me in that. I think they were trying to wait me out. After we had been at the ranch for a couple of days, Gerta came to me and asked my permission to seduce Ross! My little brother! "Jimmy too?" I squeaked out, but she only wanted to cozy up to Ross. Ross was taller and good-looking for a prepubescent, but I could not get my head wrapped around this thirty-two-year-old woman wanting to be with a fourteen-year-old! Through gritted teeth, I told her, "Keep your hands off my brother!" I thought that was downright disgusting. Years later, I would tell Ross about it, and he said, "Why did you say no? I thought she was so sexy and beautiful! I would have loved that!" Well, I guess I learned another lesson in the world of the male species. We now joke about that. Gerta and Rudy decided months later that they wanted children, therefore halting their swing thing.

I had tried to break off from Mike and move out. I had been saving money so I could get into my own place. Mike would start to get teary-eyed and beg me not to go. I would give in reluctantly and would stay. I couldn't bear to see a man weep. Silly me, as it would not take long for him to return to the mean man he really was. We went on a vacation to Puerto Rico, where I recognized the keyboard player as being the one I knew from Virginia. As a matter of fact, the last time I worked that gig, he had asked me if I would join his band. I had to decline. Now I see him with a full-show band. Being the keyboard player, he would pick and arrange the songs they would do. As I sat in the audience, I told Mike I knew the keyboard player, and when the set was over, I went to say hey to him. It was such an amazing reunion, and I got to meet his wife and the other members and introduce them to Mike. We all became fast friends and planned on getting back together when they were to be in NYC in a couple of months.

Two months later as I was delivering some drinks to one of my favorite customers, he put his hand on my stomach and said, "I'd say about two months." I did not know what he was talking about. One thing I did notice about myself lately was my boobs had gotten much bigger, and they hurt a lot, which I attributed to the fact that I had not completed my growing up. Hmmm. Oh, and my waist was getting thicker. I had been thinking if I could lose weight but keep the boobs I'd be happy. One more thing happening to me was my hair was flat and lifeless, plus the black circles under my eyes. Later that day as I was making a Scotch and water, I suddenly got nauseous from the whiff of alcohol and had to make a mad dash for the bathroom where I erupted like a geyser. It was then I had the realization of why all the changes in my body were happening. I straight away called my doctor, and he said I should come right in. After my visit to the doctor, he said, "You called it kid. You're pregnant." I nearly fainted. Dr. Hassid told me that I should get an abortion as he knew the situation I was living in and he knew of Mike Linden and his reputation.

Now that abortions were finally legal in the state of New York, he was all set for me to have one. I agreed with him and sadly made plans for the procedure two days later. When I got home, I told Mike I was hoping in some remote area in my mind that he would want the baby, but he got an attitude, telling me he would pay half! I was shocked! Shouldn't he pay for the entire thing? But again, I thought, *It takes two*, so I figured it was the fair thing to do. The next day, Dr. Hassid called me to see how I was doing and that he did wish I could have the baby and that one in hand is better than two in the bush. I will always hear those words said by him. I was never to get pregnant again.

A few months later, I would develop another mad crush on someone. His name would be Terry, and Eva would instigate the mutual feelings we had. I would look forward to going to work so I could see him. We would flirt and touch (respectfully). Terry was a gentleman. He was fun and had a good sense of humor, adorable. This went on for months until one day Eva set up a tryst for us in her apartment. I was so excited to finally get to really kiss and hold him even if it was for only a little while. We sat in her tiny living room and talked, laughed, eventually moving right on into a little romance. It seemed that no sooner did we get cozy than he said he had to go. I was ready to cry. I really wanted to spend more time with him. Alas, Terry was a married man. As I tell these stories, I am truly ashamed of myself. Maybe it was that I had seen my mother do that, making it seem acceptable to me somehow. Still, it was wrong. Not much longer did we continue our flirting, and Terry gradually stopped coming into the club. All for the better, I knew. I still missed him though.

I would still be going to HB Studios, and therefore, I would continue to audition for acting jobs. One of the agents I had left my photo and résumé with called me to do a walk-through on a porn. I vehemently refused. I told him to throw my information in the trash and never call me again. It was at that point he went on to tell me about the casting couch. I responded with "If I fit a part, then they will hire me. If it takes the couch to prove my talent, then I don't want the job that badly." I would not stop auditioning and studying the art and method of acting. During the months living with Mike, we would be constantly arguing mostly over my naivety and ignorance of the world and its ways.

Mike had a special little steak house he liked to go for dinner. I loved it there as well. It was a small intimate club, and the clientele was exclusive. As we walked into the place, Malcolm would greet us (as he did for all) and addressing us. He would seat us at a table in a way making us feel special. Malcolm had a talent for remembering names, dates, and places, as well as personal details. He remembered you having told him at a previous visit about each one of his regular customers. The food to me was very good, and the steak sizzling on a pewter plate set on an oval board would make me drool as Malcolm himself would deliver it.

The knack of all this personalization is what made the business very successful. One of his regulars was a young John-John Kennedy Jr., who would come in and try to order drinks, but as he was underage, Malcolm would let him have soda. He told us that sometimes he had to reprimand the kid as he thought he was entitled to whatever he wanted, therefore forcing Malcolm act like a surrogate father. That is probably just what John wanted. Anyway, one evening, while Mike and I were just hanging out and getting a bit drunk, there was a cute young man there chatting me up. Mike was happy with the attention I was getting. As I got more and more into my cups, I was to the point where I did not care anymore, and as this young man was really good-looking, I decided that if he wanted that kind of action, well, I would give it a go. He was much better-looking than Mike and younger—all a prerequisite for me. We all took a cab back to Mike's place and proceeded to drink more at Mike's personal bar. No time at all went by before we were all in bed together. I just let myself go with it and hoped that now Mike would leave me alone when it came to such things in the future.

During the entire encounter, Mike wanted to just watch; I did not care. I was allowing myself to enjoy being with someone nice-looking and closer to my age. We frolicked for some time before falling asleep. The next morning, we all went for breakfast, then went to the beach for the day.

We had a nice day, and by the time we were to part ways, he wanted to see me again. I had to tell him no.

The next day, he called asking if he could see me again, at which point I had to get more adamant that it would not be a good thing and that he should forget about us. I plodded on even in the face of insulting comments from Mike. I would get to work background work on a Jules Dassin Malina McKori film *Rehearsal*, which was about the student protests against the military government. I played one of the students that got shot by the military when they opened fired on the students. We shot two scenes, which took all day and no pay, but that is one of the ways to get a foot in the door.

Not long after that, I would audition for an off-Broadway showcase. I would land a part in the chorus. We all got to do a little feature part; mine was a clock (representing time). I was to move like a mechanical doll as I said my lines and then to be absorbed back into the chorus. The theme of the play was about a young man while dreaming meets his life's love, only problem is that she is from the past and of Russian Royalty, but in the end, he was to find out he was the reincarnation of her. By the end of the second week of rehearsals, I was to have a shocking experience at home. Mike showed up with a Japanese woman, Keiko. She was obviously a dancer, but I had never seen her before. She was very thin but having huge boobs, obviously had to be fake. Still not knowing what was going on, I joined them in a glass of wine. I did not have more because I was going to bed soon; call time for rehearsals began early. So I would not be kept awake by them listening to music and their talking, laughing, etc., I decided to sleep in the spare bedroom.

I woke up suddenly not knowing why. I put on an oversized dress shirt and crept out of the room only to hear them in our bedroom! Shocked and angry, I shove the door open, and seeing them in bed together just sent me into a rage I did not know I was capable of. I called her a pig and Mike a son of a bitch! I turned and ran downstairs when I realized there was nothing I could really do at three o'clock in the morning, so I sat down and shaking so hard I could not get my cigarette lit. All the while, both of them came flying downstairs, acting all concerned about me. Keiko tried to put a hand on my shoulder, saying, "Come on, join us." I was infuriated to the point of grabbing her by the arm, and I said, "Get your fucking hands off me!" Still trying to put her arms around me, I pushed her back, saying real calm, "If you don't get away from me, I'll rip your fucking fake boobs off and shove them up your ass!" Mike, watching this (I'm sure enjoying the show), said, "I'd move away from her if I were you." That was the first time I would have the "all I could see was *red*" experience. With that, the two of them went right on back up the stairs to our bedroom, turning around to say, "If you change your mind come in." I could not believe my ears. I was so upset I could not stay in the house any longer. I put my clothes on and packed my stuff for the day before I left. I did not care about being safe as I walked down to the park on West End Avenue to sit on a park bench. I did not care if someone tried to mug me. I felt I would and could tear anyone apart at that point.

Finally, it was time to head to the Steinway building, where rehearsals were. Upon arriving, I was able to put the memory of the sick scene I had been through just a few hours earlier out of my mind for a while. Just before we were wrapped for the day, who should be standing there waiting for me but Mike. He had a sheepish look on his face (one of his tricks) and some flowers. He asked if I'd like to go for dinner and that he was so sorry. He promised not do that again, if I would forgive him. He seemed to really be sad and sorry, so I accepted. I would be back to square one again.

By then, Eva was tired of my constant complaining about living with Mike Linden. She stopped what she was doing and, looking at me dead in the eyes, said, "Peparone, I think you like your situation, so stop complaining to me. I don't want to hear the same shit day after day. I love you, but I can't make you do what I've been telling you to do for months. So you stay there with that man and stop complaining! You *love* it!" That was the best thing she could have done for me. It made me think. I would call my brother Donni to get some brotherly advice. He had some that sticks with me, and I find myself sharing it with others when needed. His advice was to "pretend you're old age, and looking back at your life, what would you change if you could? If you think the place you are in now is not satisfying, then do what you have to, to make it something you can be proud of." We talked a little more before hanging up. Those words backed up what Eva had caused me to think. I knew I had to get out of there. As I waited to get courage for making my move, Mike and I would still go out together and such.

Yet another crazy thing would happen because of him. Mike and I would hook up with our show-band friends. We would enjoy a weekend out in New Jersey at the Playboy Club. It was nice to be away from the city as Mike was much nicer at those times. I would get to meet the Bunnies and their Den Mother. I would learn that no matter what their waist size was, the costume was to be one whole size smaller. The stays in the Bunny corset would be of whalebone or something as stiff, which had to be cinched to that smaller size. They had to wear spiked heels that had pointy toes. Their feet would hurt along with sore torsos. If I even thought about being a Playboy Bunny, all I would have to do was think of those costumes to change my mind. We had a nice time though. The club was more elegant than the one in NYC. When we got back to New York, we went on with our life, back to the usual mental abuse.

Two of our friends from the band came into town, and we invited them to stay with us. I was feeling so happy to have them. That night, we would be drinking and having a nice time. I would go through a bottle of wine myself, and the others would be smoking pot, as well as drinking hard liquor and doing poppers (an ampule that when snapped under the nose causes an extreme rush to help heart attack victims). Finally, I had to go to bed. I had no problem with leaving them downstairs partying.

About two hours later, I woke up with that odd feeling—again. Mike was not in bed, and yet it was very quiet, so I tiptoed down the stairs not expecting to see what I saw. Mike and our two friends were in the middle of a threesome! It was gross. With the disgust I was feeling, I went back up to the room and cried. I did not know what to do. Still, I can't bring myself to leave.

The final straw would come when Mike threw another party and invited one of the other members of that band. Again, I would be plugging through bottles of wine, becoming quite drunk. Finally, I would head up to bed. How I remember this was that right in the middle of dreaming that Mike had come to bed and was in the middle of having sex when all of a sudden Mike was speaking Greek to me! That is when I realized I was not dreaming, but this was real. Coming to my senses, I looked up into the face of a stranger! Screaming and hitting him, I kicked him off me, and throwing something on him, I ran out the door, crying. I fell on my hands and knees; all I wanted to do was slam my head on the pavement, but self-preservation took hold, and I slammed my hands on the ground instead. The friend from the band followed me out and helped me get myself back under control. I was mortified. Finally, going back inside, it would take a while composing myself. That Greek guy came over to me, apologizing profusely, telling me that Mike said it was okay to do that and that I was waiting for him. I was now done; I had to get out.

The next day, I asked Eva to show me the apartment one block away. I would see this funky little studio and felt nervous about leaving the nice big place of Mike's, knowing I better take it before someone else does. Luckily, I had enough money to pay the first- and last-month rent, but I did not move in straight away.

Mike and I would go to see the play *The Wiz* when it was playing on Broadway. Mike was being his usual insulting mean self, and I was miserable. On the drive home in his white Cadillac convertible (I called it his pimp mobile), the song "Masquerade" by the Carpenters was playing. I could identify with the lyrics. That is all it took to bring back my brother's advice and Eva telling me I must love the abuse. I did not. I knew I was ready to get out from under his thumb. The next day, while Mike was at work, I packed up the remaining things I had there, mostly clothes and such. I took my things to the apartment, and I wrote a note to Mike, telling him I had moved out.

It was such a liberating feeling, but I had to reacclimatize to such a small place again. I did it before, and I can do it again. It would take only two weeks for me to get used to my surroundings.

Mike would try for a few weeks to get me to come back, but when I leave some place, I never go back. I was done, done, done with him. I would try warning other women he would bring to the club I was now bartending.

I had been given a card after the show Yestermorrow had its final curtain. It was from a couple of agents who wanted me to give them a call. I did and made a lunch date with them for the next day. As we ate, they told me what they intended for my career. They wanted to create a star. They would groom me, train me, mold me into a highly polished entertainer. We were talking big money invested in me. I was almost giddy with excitement! The worm that was towing my ship from Alaska had handed the lines over to a torpedo. My joy and happiness was dashed in less than five minutes. I was asked if there were any photographs of me out there that could possibly be in a magazine, newspaper, or film anything that would or could suddenly surface, proving that I was indeed already in the entertainment business when I was so called "discovered." Their plan was to say they found me shopping in the market or skating in the park somewhere. They went on to ask if there was anything out there at all. I could not say, besides the Jules Dassin film, but that porn I was tricked into doing. And I just knew there were other pictures out there like the ones done by Horst Ebersberg. It did not take me very long to weigh the consequences. After investing a lot of money in me, if they found out that I had not been truthful, dire consequences would ensue. They were very forceful to emphasize just how serious they were; it was then I knew there was no way. I kissed a vehicle to success goodbye. We finished lunch and parted ways. I felt I could cry for a year.

I learned too late the lesson of going against your gut feelings. If you sense some wrongness, don't hesitate to heed the instincts and conscience of a higher power that is trying to help you feel what is right. Back to bartending. No fame and fortune for me. Ah, well.

It was about this time the bar was to undergo a slight alteration in theme. We switched from looking like a common lounge into a Western style with peanuts in barrels along with the shells strewn throughout the club. The outfits we were to wear were short, short cutoff-jeans button-down cowgirl shirt, and cowboy hat and boots. I liked it. Mike and Eddie Cvercko had hired a manager for the club as well. His name was Dick Gordon. When he first came to the club, I thought he was a nice guy but nothing more. I was glad he was there, and we all became really close friends. Mike and Eddie would spend time between their other club on Canal Street and the one I worked in.

One night, some stranger walked into the club, sat down at the far end of the bar next to the door, and as he sat down, I noticed a gun in the gap of his coat. He did not know I saw it, but I did. Acting naturally, I asked what he was drinking, but all he said was, "Where are your bosses?" I said, "In the back." He told me to go get them. I knew not to argue, so I slipped out from behind the bar and proceeded to walk a zigzag pattern as I headed to the back. As I passed the dancer, I quickly told her to stay on the floor of her stage. If this guy was a nut and began to open fire, I did not want her to be a target. After I went into the office and told the guys about the situation. Thank God that nothing happened and we all finished off the evening nicely and uneventful.

One thing about that experience was that as I walked away from that guy, I felt like my back was the broadside of a barn. A walk that normally took only twenty seconds at best seemed to take two hours of feeling like I was wearing a bull's-eye.

My anxiety over seeing that gun was because the night club across the street had been robbed at gunpoint, which had the SWAT team in full, causing us to close early and leave by the back emergency exit. I did not want to be a repeat of that situation.

As time moved on and since Dick Gordon came on board to work with us, the job got more fun. After we closed, Mike and Eddie (whom we began to call Fast Eddie), along with Dick and me, would all meet up at one of the bars on the Upper East Side. JG Melon's or Churchill's would be our most frequented. Rusty's would be another one we would hit now and again, but for the most part, we alternated between Melon's and Churchill's.

At some point, Dick had mentioned that he and his wife had been separated for a couple of months and that she was out on the West Coast. Thinking he was separated, I considered him a free man, so I did not mind allowing myself to hang out with him. I always enjoyed his company, and he always protected me from weird people and situations. The fact was that all his friends seemed to approve of our friendship, again causing me to think Dick was a free man. Even if I was not thinking anything, it would develop romantically. Until one evening when the bar was slow, the guys were playing poker, and unbeknownst to me, they were using us girls as their wager. Dick chose me as his, and when he won, he came over to me to say he had won me. I thought that was so adorable that he liked me that much. What it did was push me over the fence of indecision as to how I really felt about him. That night after our hangouts closed, Dick took the cab with me (as he had been doing) to my little apartment. I asked him if he wanted to come in. I said, "After all, you won me."

Dick stayed with me for a few more hours, then went back to his apartment on the Upper East Side. We would begin to get very close. Then one day he told me his wife was coming back and she wanted to work on their marriage again. He assured me that he did not want to lose me and would tell her he did not want to. Classic, and I fell for it hook, line, and sinker. It is always the same universal story, and all of us gullible women think our situation is "the real thing" and therefore not like the rest. I was no different. Judy, Dick's wife, came to the club later that week to meet all of her husband's new coworkers. She went out of her way to get to be a part of us, but Dick did not encourage her. I found out they had three young children as well. Dick and I did not change our routine of hanging out at my place after leaving the clubs. He would head home around five o'clock in the morning, and as time went on, of course Judy knew, as women do, that we were not just playing Tiddledy Winks. She tried to be cool and pretend that all was well. That is unless she got drunk, and then she would come gunning for me, at which point Dick and I would have to barhop like fugitives, except all the bartenders would call the bar we would escape to and give us a heads-up that she was hunting us down. This would happen about once a month. Still, I believed Dick and I would be together in the near future. Sometimes I would feel a twang of guilt but not enough to back off. It is these times of my life that I am ashamed of and have prayed for forgiveness. I pray that somehow those whom I hurt can forgive me. At least now I feel so horrible about what I had done.

CHAPTER 17

On one of the occasions while we all were hanging out at Churchill's, we had seen a little toe-to-toe with the manager Osher, who was a large man and no-nonsense (but he was a big mush to me and always came in to sit at my bar in the noontime before he went to work). All of us bartenders would barhop to each other's places. It was a club of sorts. So this evening in particular, Osher had to deal with someone who said, "Put my tab on the band's tab," at which the band said no way. The customer was told to pay or the cops would be called in. Then the man paid. His bill was less than ten dollars. After he left, everything seemed to go back to normal. As Osher was telling us exactly what happened, the door opened and in walked that man again, at which point Osher told us he'd be right back. As he escorted the man out into the street, the man pulled out a butcher knife and plunged it into Osher's stomach! I was watching through the window and almost threw up and yelled to everyone that Osher just got stabbed. The guy stabbed Osher! Mike ran out first as the perpetrator ran back into the alley. Mike hailed a cab as Osher was lying on the ground with his blood running down the street. I wanted to go to him and help put him back together, but everyone was holding me back. The cabbie, when he saw the situation, tried to drive off, but Mike pulled out an honorary police badge, telling the cabbie he was a police officer and he needed to get this man to the hospital. I watched as Mike alone wrangled the big man into the cab, along with his blood still pouring out of his gut like a faucet.

Dick, at that point, took me to the apartment of my friend who was also Mike's girlfriend, Pam Finley, to have her watch me as I had gone catatonic. I had been drinking glass after glass of Drambuie. I was so drunk, and that is when I began to lose it. I cried and cried, and dear Pam held on to me. Even as I threw up, she held back my hair. She was wonderful.

It was a long time before I could get past that. Osher was DOA. We all contributed money for trees to be planted in Israel by his family as that is where he was from. I will say a prayer for him and his family forever. He was a good and kind man.

A couple of days later, I was able to return to the Ropewalk to work. Weeks became months, and I had moved on with my life, having graduated on to the next level in the University of Life. It was at this time that Dick and Judy were looking to move to New Hampshire and Dick would alternate between life in the city with me and his life in New Hampshire. It was on one of these occasions when Dick was in New Hampshire with his family, scoping out housing locations, that I was waiting on a customer and having a conversation with him. I asked him what he did for work, and he said he was a cop. He was doing transit at that time.

The next day, he showed up in uniform and driving a police car, telling me he would take me for a ride in it. After I finished work, I got into the backseat, and that is when he locked me in and took off! I was not scared, but I did mention that it felt odd to be locked in a police cruiser. He took me all the way to Queens, where he had an apartment. He invited me in, and I followed him. It did not take him long to throw the cuffs on me and say, "Try to get out of them." As I did, I noticed them getting tighter and tighter. I did not like the game. He then carried me to his bedroom, where he proceeded to go on with the game. I figured here we go again. I did not feel like he was going to hurt me; he just thought it was a kick to do things with me in cuffs. After he was done, we just got dressed, and he took me home. He still wanted to see me again and continued to come to the bar to do so. After not being successful in getting me back to his place, he gave up, and I never saw him again.

Naturally, as all those stories go, Dick and I were to eventually split up. I knew he did not intend to leave his wife no matter what he said or did. He truly had his cake and got to eat it too for over a year. I decided I was not going to stay with him.

During the time I was with Dick, Mike and Eddie decided they wanted to open a restaurant on the Upper East Side and eventually get out of the lower-class places of drunks and dancing girls. They wanted honest respect, not to mention that Mike was an awesome cook and wanted to own a five-star restaurant. It finally happened. They bought a place and began renovating and creating a fantastic seafood restaurant, calling it the Ropewalk. Only I was brought from the bar to work at the new place. Dick also was brought there as manager and head bartender. It was during this time Dick's and my relationship would be happening.

For the next year, the restaurant would flourish and get high ratings and comments on the evening news. Things were going so well, and the money was flowing in; the guys decided they wanted to open yet another bigger, better, more prestigious club in NYC. They began scouting out places where they could compete with the likes of the Hippopotamus, which was a very popular gigantic night club.

After finding the perfect spot, a building big enough to be competition to the other clubs, the guys managed to put together a night club with celebrity performers all lined up to be featured. They also hired beautiful girls to work and had them all fitted to some very elegant yet sexy outfits. During the entire time, the guys would find themselves going to some very questionable places for loans and string pulling.

As time went on, the Ropewalk was losing its standing in the ratings. The food was not as good, as there was no good money to keep the good chefs. The wine closets were getting depleted mostly by Fast Eddie as he interviewed the ladies or just wanted to impress some other lady. We had had some of the highest quality wines, but as the guys got deeper and deeper into debt trying to get the pachyderm, as it was to be called up and running. It was taking longer, much longer than anyone expected, causing the flow of money to dwindle. Deliveries were cancelled. Food was getting scarce. Wine was running out, as well as our bar stock. It was becoming an embarrassment to work there. We were not getting paid regularly, which was forcing us to have to take the money right out of the till just to pay our own bills. It was getting so out of control that I finally had to quit.

I found another bartending job on 46th between 8th and 9th Avenue. It was a Greek bar. All the customers spoke Greek and began to teach me. The more and better I got at it, the better my tips were. I was now making good money again. I worked long and hard for many months.

It was during this time that I moved into a small apartment on the edge of Harlem. It was a tiny place, but it was less expensive than where I had been and Dick was staying with me because Judy and the children moved up to New Hampshire and Dick would go up for the weekends. He even had a weekend bartending job while he was up there. When he would return, it was to my place.

I had met and became involved with a man who was from Greece, and he was working as a waiter in the restaurant next door. Nick would come in and hang for hours while I worked. We would then go out for breakfast then back to his place until the sun would begin to ascend. I would hail a taxi to head back uptown to my place. Dick would ask where I had been, and I don't remember what I would tell him. I knew I had to get Dick to just go stay in New Hampshire. I knew he loved his wife and that is the way it should be. I needed to move on with my life.

The more I saw of Nick, the more possessive he would become of me. It had gotten to the point of where he would threaten to confront Dick and tell him about us. I did not want that. I still had history with Dick and did not want to hurt him as I felt I was.

Nick was becoming more and more adamant, and I knew I would have to make some kind of confession to Dick or tell Nick to leave me be. Both scenarios did not appeal to me; I was having such anxiety fits I could not think straight. I was making such good money, and I did not want to leave the job, but I knew I had to make some kind of decision. Nick had asked me to marry him and move back to Greece with him. It was then I knew I had to do something now.

On one of the weekends, Dick had gone up to New Hampshire to be with his family. I was so depressed that I went out and bought a little Yorkshire Terrier puppy. I had saved exactly enough money to pay for him, and the next day, I brought him to work with me and kept him in an open box in the office where I could check on him. A couple of days later, Nick told me he was definitely going to find Dick and tell him of us and that he should stay away from me and go be with his family.

I knew that would lead to something terrible, and therefore, I would have to get Nick to leave town with me to go to my brother's place in Waterbury, where he lived with his lady, awaiting for the birth of their first child. I needed to make a decision and fast.

I went home and put together some things and grabbed my little Yorkie puppy, Ajax (AJ). I went back downtown to meet up with Nick. As the time for my shift in the Greek bar arrived, I could not call or go in as I had to make sure there was no way Dick could find me. I will never be able to feel good about the way I left my bosses in the lurch by not showing up. I really liked Dino and Angelo, so it bothered me a great deal. Nick, on the other hand, was not disappearing, so he had to go to his boss and beg off work for the rest of day.

I could not wait for him in his apartment for some reason, so he stuck me with a friend who owned and worked a sidewalk newsstand. I had to sit on a box while I held AJ and wait till Nick came and got me. I was so nervous scared and sad, and it felt as if I was in a very bad dream. What had I done, and how come I always make such bad choices in my life that end me up in such dire straits? This School of Hard Knocks was such a difficult education. I waited for hours in that cramped space. I held my little puppy and just listened to the chatter between the proprietor of the newsstand and his customers. I would hear the long conversations of his regulars and the quick question of a passerby or just the sound of the money exchange for a newspaper or magazine.

Finally, as evening was approaching, Nick finally showed up to take me to yet another friend for "safekeeping." We took a cab into Elizabeth, New Jersey, to a beautiful apartment building. We went upstairs and went inside, where we stayed the night. AJ had become quite sick, and I had to get him to a vet immediately. We found one in town where we got his problem addressed and medicine for getting better. My money was running out fast, but for my little guy, it was not an issue.

At the end of the day, I was on the bus to Waterbury, Connecticut, to stay with my brother Dave and Kathy, his girlfriend. They were expecting their first child, and so it was going to be good. I was with them to share in the wonderful occasion. Nick planned to meet up with me there on the weekend.

I stayed with them for about one month or so, and while I was there, Dick was calling, looking for me, but Dave and Kathy said I was not there. He kept calling and knew I was there and was going to drive out and look for me. I was so brokenhearted, as I really did still love him, only I knew this was the best thing for both of us, and I knew that by my being gone the odds of Nick confronting him were less. I finally decided to speak with Dick, telling him he had to go to his family and leave me to my future. He did leave me alone for a while after that.

As we went through the weeks, Kathy was getting weary being pregnant, so we would take long walks, and a couple of times, we would play some tennis. I don't know how she could bounce around like that with such a big belly. I would ask if she was scared, and she would reply "Not at all"—until she broke her water; that is when she began to cry. Now she was scared. It was becoming very real as the contractions began. Finally, we all piled into the car, and as Dave was driving, Kathy kept babbling things like "Dave, your herbals are choking me!" What she meant to say was the fragrance of his deodorant was making her sick. I will never forget that ride to the hospital, nor will I ever forget when we went up to the reception desk to check Kathy in (the nurse had already taken her away in a wheelchair), so it was just Dave and I. The receptionist looked at me and asked how far along I was! Man, did my brother and I laugh at that one. I was about 110 pounds and was wearing a very fitted jumpsuit; I was amazed at the absurdity of the question. We still get a good chuckle out of that one.

Dave and Kathy both asked the doctor if I could come into the delivery room but were told no. I had to wait in Pop's Corner. It was to be an all-nighter. Dave would come out and sit with me on occasion until it was getting imminent. Kathy would have the toughest time, and I thought it a miracle how she got through such a horrible experience. She broke every blood vessel in her face, neck, chest, and even her eyes were freckled with red blotches. Her doctor was brutal as well. The baby was born breech, and she had no anesthetizing at all. Finally, Duane David Thayer was born. The nurse brought him out to the viewing room, where I was allowed to see him before they even cleaned him up. All I could think about was how huge his hands were, and his scrotum was enormous! He was so tiny until I realized where he had come from and realized that he was pretty big in light of that revelation.

Duane (named after Duane Allman) was a beautiful baby, and we enjoyed him so much. I thought it would be funny to dress him in my stuffed Snoopy Dog's outfit. It fit him perfectly, but we howled at the hole for the tail and how you could see his little diaper through it. Because he was born breech, we all took turns making his legs go through the pedaling motion to get them to align with his hip sockets correctly.

During these weeks, Nick would come up to stay for a couple of days with me. Dave and Kathy would be amazed at his crazy beliefs and way of thinking or dealing with certain issues. I don't know if it was due to the fact he was old school Greek and obviously had a much different attitude toward things than we do. I wanted him out of my life but did not know how to do it nicely. He asked me to marry him on one of those weekends. I could not say yes or no, but he assumed it was a yes. He tried to boss me around, and I allowed it for a bit. Finally, the day came when I knew I had to make a move in one direction or another. I had to leave my brother and his new family to themselves, so I decided to go to my mother's house in Webster, Massachusetts, and from there, I could think clearer. Nick came with me, and we went to visit my Uncle George and Aunt Ginny. We were driving somewhere, and Nick and I were sitting in the back seat. Uncle George and I were joking about something, and I had in jest called Nick the Greek word for *homosexual,* at which point he yelled at me and said, "The next time you say that, I will slap you across the face. I don't care who we are with!" Well, that was the breaking point. I could not take his attitude one more minute and knew right then and there I was going to have to get rid of him too.

CHAPTER 18

During the time I was in Webster, I was in contact with my younger sister Kim, who was stationed in Ellsworth Air Force Base in Rapid City, South Dakota. Kim told me I should come out there to stay for the rest of the summer and be halfway across the country from all those crazy situations I had gotten myself into. Mom paid for my flight and took me to the airport. Upon landing at the Rapid City Airport, the weather turned from rain to huge hailstones the size of golf balls and baseballs that had never been seen before, causing a lot of car and trailer home damage, as well as killing some small animals. After that hail, insurance became mandatory. That was my welcome to the middle of the country. Seeing Kim was such a relief. I knew it was going to be a better summer than I had been looking at.

I moved right in with her in the barracks, bringing my puppy as well. No one cared back in those times so long as we were quiet and discreet. For the first couple of weeks, I was having nightmares about being one of the brides along with the other ladies on base. We were having a huge communal wedding, and we all were dressed in beautiful white wedding gowns and long flowing veils. As the time to get to the church got closer, I would begin to be scared out of my wits! I would find myself running as fast as possible to reach the main gate, all the while crying a storm of tears, desperately trying to reach the gate in time before they caught me. This was a nightly reoccurrence. Many times, I would wake up hitting my head on the top bunk and a tight scream caught in my throat.

My mother would tell me that Nick would keep calling, looking for me, and he would be crying. Mom took pity on him and told me to just write him a letter, letting him know that I had no intention of coming back. Finally, I did.

The days went on, and I was having such a great time with my sister and her pals. It was a long time coming in the desire for us to actually have fun just being together. I wanted that all my life with her, but we were four years apart, and she was never into the same things I was. Now we could relate on a higher level. I was in sister heaven. The fun we had every day and the adventures were nonstop. We would go swimming at Lake Pactola (skinny-dipping) or just hanging out there. We would go camping with the entire softball team and the coach. We went to Yosemite to camp and see the geysers. The master sergeant asked if any of us was having our period because of bear. If anyone did, then we had to sleep in a cabin. Bears can smell extremely well, and we were told that it would make a bear come after us. We stayed in a cabin anyway, just in case no one would admit it.

It was so awesome for me to be a part of the group. We roasted marshmallows over a campfire, and naturally, I would accidentally shake my flaming marshmallow right into Kim's hair! Twice! We all laughed so hard. I mean, what were the odds of doing that twice in a row?

I would accompany her and her pals to the chow hall, where we had to sign in. I would do as they all did using the last four digits of my SS number, and I would make up a rank every time we went there. Amazing how we were never busted. Not only that, but I would wear her uniform and get rides on military vehicles such as a chopper that had to fly over Mount Rushmore and back to base. We looked enough alike that everyone that did not know us thought we were twins stationed together. When I think of it, we were so lucky to not have been caught. We had so much fun. I got to go all over the place and see how the Air Force ticked. Kim was one of the star softball players on the Flyerettes team. I found it so exciting to watch her games. All those ladies really worked well together as a team, and they were the ones to beat. Not often. At one of the games, as I was kneeling down tying my shoes, a big yellow Lab lifted his leg on my back! Everyone was yelling for me to look out. Too late. I was so embarrassed I didn't know what to do. One of the ladies gave me a team shirt to wear for the rest of the evening. When the games were over, we would all go to Happy Joe's pizza parlor. That was always a highlight of any day. We would go there often. We were addicted to that place. I would find out later that there was a Happy Joe's in Egypt next to the pyramids!

My sister had many friends and to show how loyal she was (and still is), there was a young man John whom Kim had fallen for and he for her, but because he had a fiancée, my sister would not allow the relationship develop. Not long after, she met the young lady who was to become John's wife, and she liked her straight away, remaining a true friend to both of them. There was another friend Bill who hung out with Kim. I believe he had to be the substitute for our cousin Billy, whom she was more like a little sister to. They spent many years hanging out and even did some cross-country traveling, only this Bill I really don't think wanted that kind of relationship. He was happy just to be with her. Bill had a roommate Joseph Thompson (Jose) that would sometimes hang out with the two of them and, of course, met me as well. We all spent a carefree summer with a lot of laughs and experiences.

I got a real taste of barracks living and military base life in general. I went through the massive cleanup for the biggest inspection of the year. All the rooms had to be spotless and shining. For a week, we all scrubbed, buffed, and polished everything from the floor bathroom tile to the rubber lining in the refrigerator. Because Kim and her roommate Linda Branson were diligent in keeping their room and bath spotless at all times, it was not as butt-busting as the all the other ladies' rooms, and there were two floors of them! As we waited for the big guys to come and inspect, we were fortunate as the dorm guard brought them up to our room first. Upon inspection, they were very impressed and commended us (yeah, they thought I was one of them) and walked up to me as I too stood as best at attention as I could, just out of respect, when he put his face right up to mine and asked for my last four and rank, and as nonchalantly as possible, I said I was only visiting, at which point he just said, "Okay," and walked on to the next room.

Kim and Linda were allowed to leave the barracks for the rest of the afternoon. Upon returning, we found a barracks full of very unhappy women. Every single one of them had to pull apart their rooms and scrub, polish, rub, and spit-shine. It took them days to accomplish this task, and they were not trying to hide the stink eye we all got as we strolled through the place and came and went freely. Maybe they would learn a lesson in room care from Kim. I would like to say I did, but my husband would probably say I missed that class.

By the end of the summer, Kim had gotten a thirty-day leave due to the fact that she was being deployed to Turkey at the end of the month. We planned on me coming over later and live off-base. I had decided I wanted to join the Air Force and become a language and broadcasting (Morse code) expert. I was told I would have to do a year and a half of deep intense study. I was not worried as I loved languages (so long as there was no math). I never did follow through with that plan because I had no one to leave my little puppy with for the time I'd be in Monterey, California, where the school was. Not only that, but I did not have a diploma, although the decision-making factor was that I had nowhere to leave AJ.

When Kim was officially off, we headed out of town. In her little yellow Chevy, Nova, Kim, and Bill rode together while I rode with Jose in his deep-green Mustang. We drove straight through to New England and arrived in time to spend the weekend at our family reunion in Winchester, New Hampshire, where all the descendants of Amos Putnam gathered each year since 1935. It was a sacred holiday for us of the Putnam clan. We would reconnect with aunts, uncles, grandparents, cousins (first and second), and maybe there were third cousins, as well by the time we were born into the family.

Kim was to leave for Turkey at the end of the month and had many schoolmates and friends she wished to hang out with before she went overseas. I decided to return to South Dakota with Jose, where I would spend the rest of summer in hopes of getting a job to earn money for my trip to Turkey. I had to get traveling papers in order for me to bring AJ.

As we drove through St. Louis, we stopped to spend a few days with his grandparents. His mother was bipolar and was acting strange when we arrived, so I did not get a good impression of her. I felt bad for her.

We headed back to South Dakota, arriving on my twenty-fifth birthday. It will forever remain a frozen-in-time memory for me. I realized I was now a quarter of a century old, and here was the first day of a new existence for me. Jose had moved off-base and was sharing a house in town with two gay guys Gio and (yes) another Bill. Gio was openly gay while off-base, but when he was in uniform, he was straight acting for the most part. He would love to tell me how he would plan to get some of the young guys whom he deemed potential conquests and break them of their fear of coming out of the closet. Wow, I could not believe he actually did that. I was all ears just to be polite even though I thought that was awful. His partner did not seem to mind either. I had to share a room and bed with Jose, and of course, we would end up in a relationship.

Gio introduced me to his friends Neil (also gay) and Kyle (straight), who owned the local disco in Rapid City, telling them I needed a job and had tons of experience as a bartender and waitress. There was no need for a bartender at that time, but I could waitress until a spot opened. I began work immediately. After a month or so, they cosigned for me to get my first car. It was a gold Chevy Vega. I loved that thing. It was a stick shift, and I was savvy with that, thanks to my brothers Dave and Donni. Even so, I rarely drove since living in NYC.

During that time, I was living and working in Rapid City. I would call Kim on a special telephone line, and we would talk for a little while. We had made plans for me to fly to Greece and meet up with a friend of hers that was living there. I would be able to stay until I could get a train or something into Turkey. Everything was set for me to go. I even had papers all set to bring my four-pound Yorkie, AJ. All I needed was my ticket. I waited for Kim to let me know when I could come. I was to get a call from her, saying because the Greeks and Turks were fighting again all military personnel were ordered to move back on base, and that did not include American civilians. This meant I would have nowhere to stay, and it would be too dangerous for an American woman alone there. I would not be allowed on base at all. What a turnaround from Ellsworth!

So now I had to stay in South Dakota. I was not planning to stay very long there, but for the time being, I would remain, as I had a job a car and a place to stay. Besides, I had developed a crush on one of the bartenders that had come in from Brooklyn, New York. I was infatuated with him as he was tall and nice-looking. We became close and spent much time together. Then he broke the news to me that he was gay. I was so disappointed, but we remained good friends anyway.

While working at the disco, I met a woman who was also very gay. As a matter of fact, she looked quite butch with her short blond curly hair and rugged attire. We became close friends, and she was so respectful of my being straight. I trusted her. Because I spent so much time with her, people were beginning to think I was gay too. I didn't care what people thought. Anne was a wonderful person who had gone through a childhood of abuse, yet she was still able to be so caring and enjoyed life.

One evening, I noticed a man in a white suit. He had dark complexion, Asian eyes, black curly hair, and was little less than six feet tall, putting him bigger than I would expect of someone Chinese or Japanese—I wondered what he was. He was striking in the confident air he held himself. I was impressed. I thought he was quite handsome. I inquired as to who he might be. I was told he was good friends with Kyle, one of the owners of the disco. I asked if he was black Chinese but was told Filipino. "What is that?" I asked dumbfounded. I had never heard of a Filipino. I got a quick lesson on what, where, how, and who. I was fascinated.

Bob Fahey would come in and hang out with a group of four other people and affectionately called themselves the Quint Club. This elite group of people was Karen, a tall beautiful blonde (married) of Swedish decent, lady who was one of the bartenders; Jay Elwein, a photographer; Steve Menke, construction worker; Jeff Kearns, heir to Caterpillar Equipment, and Bob, making it an exclusive group of individuals. These guys would play tricks on one another, and Karen had such a great sense of humor and was just a fun person that she would be able to get them with some good ones. Her husband was out of town a lot, so she was happy for the distraction. All was above board. Everyone respected Karen and watched out for her.

By the time I came into the picture, I was not to become part of their little group, and that was okay with me, although I would feel sort of left out. No one made me feel unaccepted as a friend, and that was fine with me. One day, Bob would come to work as a bouncer in the disco, and we would talk sometimes. I did not realize I was getting to like seeing him. Never for an instant did I think we would ever become romantically involved, until one day as I was setting up my station to begin the evening shift when Bob walked over to me, and looking down into my eyes and smiling, he said, "I had a dream about you last night." All of a sudden, I became fascinated with the fact that this popular good-looking guy would dream about me! In that moment, I decided I really did like him. I asked him what I was doing in his dream, but he only grinned and said, "Oh, I can't tell you that." I was smitten. From that day on, I would look forward to getting to work so I could spend time getting to know more about this intriguing person.

One evening, he asked me if I could give him a ride home. We sat in the car and talked for hours.

I think we sat in the car just talking for quite some time. He told me about his family and how close they all were and how awesome his parents were. I learned how much he loved animals and the more he told me of his life, he got more and more into my heart.

Finally, one day, another one of his dear friends who was to become one of mine as well, Merlyn Magner, would invite us all to come over to her little cabin in an exclusive part of town, where we would hang out, and I would learn that Bob played guitar. I thought he played beautifully as I sat mesmerized at yet another reason to love being with him. After a fun evening, Merlyn said she was going to bed and that we could stay in her spare bedroom. I was so nervous as this would be the first time we would truly get to be all alone.

I had moved out of the guys' house and got my own apartment and took a roommate so I could be with Bob without hurting Jose more than I had done already. I did not realize how much he really did like me.

Bob would come over and spend the night sometimes until he broke the news to me that he was leaving town to stay in Wyoming and he didn't know for how long. I was heartbroken. He said he would call me every night, which he did. After a few weeks, he decided to return to Rapid. I was overjoyed. He was not back very long by the time we were having a big concert featuring Grace Jones at the disco. As the roadies that came with her equipment were setting up, I was surprised to realize at how much I missed hearing my own accent (sort of a language)—that being a Brooklyn accent. I was setting up my station and listening to the banter of these guys and looking forward to seeing Grace Jones perform, but that was not to be because one of our favorite customers came in and began buying us shots of tequila. I was doing the salt, drink, and lime so often that I lost count and got so wasted I spent the rest of the night puking in the restroom. I passed out leaning over the bowl. The other waitress had to cover for me. I was useless and totally missed the performance. When I was finally able to wake up, I realized my arm was totally numb and would remain that way for about six months! Never again did I take another shot of tequila. My bosses got a kick out of my shameful experience. I was lucky, because anyone else would have fired me.

I had noticed a young lady that had come into the club one evening, and Bob paid a lot of attention to her. I was told she was a girlfriend he used to go out with. Her name was Gretchen, and I was jealous. While he was with her, he paid me no mind. I decided I was going to forget about anything that I had hoped would develop and forget all the wonderful things we talked about. At the end of the night, Bob walked out with Gretchen, and I was trying not to cry. I realized I was falling in love with him, but seeing him with her made me think it was over before it really began. I had a shock when he came back inside alone and walked over to say something, and before he could open his mouth, I looked at him with all the resolve and anger that raged within me, saying, "Get away from me! Go to your girlfriend and leave me alone. I am moving back to NYC. I am outta here!"

He then proceeded to follow me as I was cleaning off tables, telling me about his relationship with her and that it was over; he had just told her he was not interested in their having a relationship anymore and that he loved me. At that, I stopped and turned around to face him, and then he grabbed hold of me and held me. All was right in my world now.

We went back to my apartment and had a beautiful night together. Bob would stay in town but begin to do construction work with Steve Menke. During the time he was doing construction (keeping him in town) he would come and stay with me. One day as we sat on my waterbed, Bob asked me to marry him. For the first time in my life, I really did want to marry the one asking me. I said yes straight away. I felt giddy as the realization set in that I was going to get married—at the age of twenty-six. I immediately called my father to let him know, but all he could say was, "That's nice, and I can't send you anything. I can't pay for it." I said don't worry about it and hung up. I was not going to let him ruin my happy feelings. I called my mother, and she was very happy for me. Then we went to tell his parents. They were excited for us. Bob did not date much at all, and Gretchen was the only one he ever got serious about, so when Bob and I planned on marrying, it was a blessing to them.

We were married by the Justice of the Peace in Rapid City, South Dakota. Merlyn gave us our wedding bands as a wedding gift. We had our tiny reception at his brother Mike's house with his wife Barbra and two children, Jennifer and little Mikey, along with some musician friends of Bob's. My roommate came as well. That night, Bob had a softball game, and because he was the pitcher, he did not want to bail on them. After the game, we went to Deadwood and stayed in a hotel for our one night of a honeymoon. I did not mind one bit. I had married the man I loved.

Bob continued to work construction, and I would continue working at the disco, only now as a bartender. Karen and her husband moved away, leaving the spot open.

We would continue like that for a few months. We, also along with his brother Mike, put together a band. At first, it was Mike and Bob on acoustic guitars and me on flute. We would be known as the Fahey Brothers. We would play small venues around the Black Hills, and as we got more material in our repertoire, we wanted to develop a bigger band and electric. Bob mostly played acoustic while Mike played lead electric. We added a bass player and drummer. Once in a while, we would have other musicians play with us. For the most part, it was us three and Robert Kellem Dana Chase and, once in a while, Mike MacDonald. We would decide to call ourselves the Badlands Blues Band. We did not play blues at all, but it never occurred to me. Eventually, we would chop it down to Badlands Band.

One night, while we were playing at the Howard Johnson's in Rapid City, John Denver and his band walked in, and during the course of the night, he would become very friendly with us, and one of his band mates got onstage to jam. What a compliment to say the least. John would come in every night to hang out. We were invited to join him at his concert that weekend at the Civic Center. On that night when we arrived, his guys sat us down at the table and waited on us! When it was time for the band to play, the road manager (who knew my friend Gerry Stickells as well) escorted us to the front row. What special treatment. We were so amazed at how kind they all were.

The next day, they left for who knows where, and we headed out to our next gig, which was in Spearfish, South Dakota. Dan's Back Porch was our most favorite club to play. Dan knew how to treat his bands as well as his everyday employees. All business should be run that way.

One night, as we were ending our last set of the evening, I noticed the young man who looked at lot like John Denver, only I was surprised to see him so far out of Rapid City. Anyway, this guy just stood in the back and watched us. As I was putting my microphone back into the stand, I was watching this John Denver lookalike start walking toward us, and I noticed that it was none other than John himself! He approached the stage, smiling and extending his hand to take mine, saying that he heard me singing from the restaurant part of the club and said to himself, "I know that voice," and so he had to come say hi. After which, he spent the rest of the night hanging out with the guys in our apartment above the club. I was so tired I went to bed. They were smoking pot, and I was not doing that anymore. I have to say it was such an incredible thing to get to know such a talented and kind man. It broke my heart to hear when he died.

We worked throughout the Black Hills as well as Wyoming Montana and Colorado. After we had played these gigs, we decided we wanted to head west. We got an agent and began our migration. First we played in Gillette, Wyoming, for a week, then off to Chico, California. We had to travel sixteen hundred miles (like the song) steady to make it there to play in less than forty-eight hours. We drove all day and all night, only stopping for gas. We made it in record time only to see another band's name on the marquee. 21 Jump Street had been booked at the last minute because the agency assumed we would not make it in time. We decided not to send the agency the commission from the Gillette gig. That was all the money we had to live on now that we had been bumped. So off went our bass player to get drunk and pass out under a bridge.

21 Jump Street never showed up, so the owner begged us to play, but we had no bass player now! Bob had to do the bass, and everyone else did their usual stuff. It was not our best, but we managed to play the evening even if we did have to repeat many of our songs. Bob could not do his stuff while playing bass.

We made money that night, and along with what we had, it gave us enough to drive down to San Jose, where Bob and Mike's sister and her boyfriend lived with their three-year-old son, Denny.

From there, we went on down to Santa Barbara, where we hooked up with Merlyn, who was now living in Montecito. We parked in her driveway for a few days and proceeded to hunt for a new booking agency. We found one in Santa Barbara.

Loved that town and wanted to make that our home base. While we waited for our next booking, we hung out and toured Los Angeles. While in LA, we caught up with an old friend of Bob's and Merlyn's who left South Dakota for the bright lights of Hollywood.

Cathy Bachman had landed the part of Daisy Duke on the television series *The Dukes of Hazzard*. We went to her apartment, where we helped her sign promo pictures for her fan club. I thought that was interesting that people would have Cathy's signature but in my handwriting. I understood it was impossible for her to sit there and sign them all. When we had signed about a hundred of the pictures, Cathy went to get ready for an appearance on *The Merv Griffin Show*, which she had gotten us passes for in the audience.

The other guest on the show was the actor who played Mr. Howell on *Gilligan's Island*. We met him after the show as we were in the studio parking lot. It was an interesting interaction. I think he was actually trying to flirt with Cathy, who was formerly married to the son of Angela Lansbury.

I had asked Cathy for a name of an agent she thought I could send my picture and résumé to if we were to not be working for a while, but I did not follow through with the information as we had gotten work that had us booked for quite a while.

The Santa Barbara music agency got us gigs around the Lompoc, California area, and Santa Maria, as well as in Santa Barbara. For a couple of months, we played around those areas and gradually worked our way back up the coast. When there was a dry spell of gigs for a while, we went back to San Jose, where we stayed again parked at Trisha and Neil's place. The rest of the band members went back to South Dakota to be with their families. It was there in San Jose where I felt my first earthquake. It was an incredible experience. The ground was literally moving under my feet. For native Californians, it was a rather small one, causing no damage, but because I had never experienced the very earth move under me, it was amazing. I would feel many more in the fifteen years I was to live on the West Coast.

I had to find some temporary work while we were waiting for the rest of the band to come back. I started with a company called Remedy, and it would send people to help the elderly in light housekeeping, shopping, bathing, and just an hour or so of company. I was not crazy about the job, but it was a mobile one, and I could take as much or as little work as I wanted. The pay was not much, but it was enough to keep us from sponging off our benefactors.

After a couple of months of working for Remedy, the company had all of us workers go to a weeklong seminar on the care and handling of the elderly and emergency response techniques. It was held at the San Jose Civic Center. I learned quite a bit of useful information as well as CPR, which I could not do if I had to anyway, even though I passed the exam. Thank God, I never needed it while working for that company.

CHAPTER 19

Finally, we were able to get some work, and the rest of the band came out. It was only a few gigs, and when they were done, we decided to do an open mike in Cupertino, where we were seen and approached by two agencies. One was looking for bands to play in a nudist camp, and the other was to book us first of all on a USO tour in Alaska. I absolutely refused to take the nudist colony gig but jumped on the other. Jim and Diane were to become our agent and manager. Before we knew it, we were getting coiffed and dressed for publicity pictures and advertisement shots. It was all so whirlwind and exciting to be treated with such kindness and respect, but what was the most exhilarating for me was the faith, belief, and trust they had in our ability to do them proud. We were one of two bands that Jim and Diane wanted to represent so they could give more attention and financial assistance to for equipment.

The USO gig we did was awesome, but the lead into the day we were to leave was so exciting. We had to leave out of Rapid City to Colorado, then to Washington onto Anchorage, Alaska. It was an experience I will treasure all my life. We were met by Sergeant Sanchez from the Elmendorf Air Base, which was to be our homey base while in Alaska. We all had a meeting with the captain before we did our first show. There were protocols we had to adhere to, but my personal instruction was not to have any personal interaction with any of the troops. I assured them I was a singer and flutist, not a hooker, plus the fact my husband was with me. The captain went on to tell me that there were many bands that had used that as a front, and there had been much trouble with that, so it was a point they had to make to all the bands with women in them. Okay, fair enough, I thought.

We were to set up and play for the troops at that base first so they could see what our style was. We were the only band that did not audition for the job. Diane and Jim were so trusted in their previous choices of which bands to send that we were hired sight unseen. We had passed with flying colors.

The next day, we were flown to a remote site. All the troops had, for company and entertainment at these sites, one another and a USO show once in a while. The length of time they had to stay there was about one and a half years.

The base was Sparrevohn, and it was truly remote. No joke. Besides one another for company, they had bears as well that tried to come into the buildings. Some sites had dogs for search and rescue.

While we were at Sparrevohn, we were taken out so Dana and RD could go fishing for Salmon. The water was frigid, and the hip boots they were given to wear leaked! RD got out of the water as soon as he felt the first leak of freezing water, but Dana knowing this to be the only time he would be experiencing this, just waited for his legs to go numb. He was determined to catch some salmon. Meanwhile, we hung out on in the field, listening to the officer in charge of us telling stories about the place until I had to go take a potty break. As I went off by myself into the wooded area and while squatting behind a tree, all of a sudden I got the horrific sensation that a bear could come lumbering out of nowhere, and I was truly in a vulnerable position. So forcing myself to be done with my business and scrambling to get my britches up and back to the guys, it did not take me but seconds to accomplish this, and as I was running down the little hill to where they were, they were all looking at me and laughing like hyenas! I was mortified as I knew before they told me why they were howling. Our fearless leader went on to tell me that they always take bets on how long it takes for someone doing that, and that everyone always comes running back with the thought that a bear might be on their tail.

Harrumph!

Finally, Dana had caught enough salmon and was now so cold he had to get out. I think he caught three of them. There was a smokehouse at that site so Dana's fish could be ready to take home to the Lower 48 when we were done with our tour. That night, we were to taste some previously smoked salmon, and it was the best ever! How nice that salmon happens to be good for you. One of the guys there asked if we did the song "Hit Me with Your Best Shot" by Pat Benatar, and of course, I did (he claimed that they could not get the latest music from the Lower 48).

The major told us that the guys sometimes would play tricks on the bands, and nobody ever knew what or when it was coming, so upon walking into the club, I looked around for anything falling on us (like a bucket of water). When nothing happened for the first hour or so, I felt pretty confident that we were in the clear until the moment I hit the verse "Hit me with your best shot" when all the guys turned around and yanked down their trousers, mooning us! I was afraid to begin the second line of "Fire away!" They become so stir crazy after being secluded in those remote sites that anything is possible as an escape. Luckily, nothing came flying out at us. I thought maybe they all were going to fart! I had to laugh so hard. I had been expecting that at some point in our trip, because of my experience with living among military young men. I had been mooned before. An entire recreational bus full of guys mooned out the windows at my sister, her roommate, and me, and we laughed then too. Plus, the fact that I grew up with so many brothers and hung out with many rowdy rock bands. A couple of my brother's co–band members lit a match as they farted and even got their butt scorched! So I can't see why I would be mortified by those young men mooning us in unison. RD insisted I was embarrassed. We finished the show and then just hung out with those wise guys and had a great time.

When it was time for lights out, I was given the room belonging to the captain, which was a deluxe accommodation, making the rest of the guys in the band very jealous and not very happy at the special treatment I was getting. I would have gladly stayed in the men's barracks (there were no women there) with the rest of the guys along with the troops. Well, that did not go down well, and I was

170

ordered to stay in that nice room with a private bathroom. Ah, well, the trials and tribulations of being the only girl around. Incidentally, the captain instructed me not to answer the phone if it rang, because it very likely would be his wife, who was expecting the birth of their first child and she would not understand that it was not what she would be thinking, so to be safe, I better not answer the phone. I was wondering why I would anyway, as no one would think to call me!

After we played and were done for the night, we all went off to our assigned sleeping quarters. I was so in awe of the view outside the bedroom window, which was of the top of the mountain with the clouds draping around it about a mile down! That is how high we were. I was told that the cloud that was always there was nicknamed George. A cloud named George. I loved it. Breathtaking to say the least.

The next day, we were off to the next site—King Salmon or someplace like that. We were to play there and many other remote places as well as the main oases around Alaska.

After we played in King Salmon, I think we might have played in one or two more. Sometimes we would play one gig and fly out to the next one the same day. The planes we took were everything possible, from a seaplane to one really skinny plane called the pencil. We flew in C-130s and prop planes. Some were rather scary. We had a bush pilot Cal, who was a crazy man, and we loved him. Sometimes Cal would do a quick maneuver so we could have a bird's eye view of some polar bear or fox or just a lone house on the vast expanse of snow. On one of those occasions, Dana, not buckled in, ended up smashing me against my window seat, at which point he held up the doughnut he was eating and offered me a bite. Laughing, I told him to get off me and go buckle himself into his own seat.

We went back to Elmendorf for a couple of days, in which time we were loaned out to a private mental institution to play for the kids living there. I always had paranoia of mentally handicapped people. I never knew when they would have a fit and come after me. That had happened to me when I was younger and had gone to work with my Aunt Harriet, whose job was cooking for the same kind of place, and one of the bigger kids came flying up to my face, making all kinds of crazy gestures and loud grunting noises. I nearly passed out from fright. Now there I was going to be in close proximity with that again. When I saw that the area we were to perform was not on a stage but on the floor with the audience of these folks, I was almost paralyzed with anxiety. I was assured that all the super physical ones would not be there. Well, that did not help much, as I knew anything could set any of them off.

Sure enough, as we were performing, a big kid came lunging out of a side room only a few feet from where we were, but thankfully, a hand shot out and grabbed him back in. For that second, I forgot to sing. My heart was pounding. Yes, I did get myself under control quickly. The rest of the show went on nicely, although I never took my eyes off that room. I felt so sad for those kids and was ultimately glad we were able to bring them some joy as well.

The next day, we were driven over to Fort Rich and Army base, where we were to play that evening. On the drive through the woods, we saw a mother moose and her baby eating some grub. Sergeant Sanchez stopped for us to take a look. I wanted to get a closer look because I could not see them. Getting out of the van, I crossed the dirt road and began to climb the mound, all the while the sergeant was telling me to watch out as mother moose could be aggressive. As I was almost to the top, the guys started yelling, "She's coming!" Well, I did not need to be told twice, and I turned around to run back to the van, and because the guys kept yelling, I panicked and fell down. It did not take but a nanosecond to regain my footing and leap back into the van only to find them all choking laughing at me, saying they were just kidding. I could have strangled them.

After Fort Rich, we went on from there for the long drive to Fairbanks to play at that base. We took a blue Air Force recreational bus which we had all to ourselves. We stopped at the North Pole, where Santa's house is. We took a tour of his home and workshop. We got to see the reindeer and sleigh as well. How apropos to be really in the North Pole and find that Santa's workshop is there for real.

We also got to stop and walk right up to the pipeline we had been riding parallel with. I had heard so much over the years about this thing, and here I was able to walk right up to it. I was surprised to see it was suspended above ground and was so huge.

Another thing that surprised me was how city like Fairbanks seemed. There was even a big indoor mall with all kinds of upscale shops. One of the stores was a Nordstroms. I had just acquired a credit card from the one in Hillsborough, California. Of course, I had to use it on something there. I still have it to his day. I still have the card as well.

After playing in Fairbanks, we were off to Sitka for a performance. We also went on to Fort Yukon, where we were not welcome by the local Athabascan natives. Fort Yukon was a very small place, and we actually did find some new friends there. After we finished our gig, we were invited by some of the native people to ride out onto the tundra with them and look at the Aurora Borealis even though it was not in its fullness at that time. Those new friends we made were really cool. We got to race around the tundra in the moonlight. I guess I don't need to put that on my bucket list.

We were scheduled to play in Tin City, which was way out there, but it had to be cancelled due to a major snowstorm. We did go to Point Barrow and played, and from there, we were flown in a C-130 to a site above the Arctic Circle. When we landed, we were given a certificate commemorating our achievement of doing that. From that site, we were flown to Indian Mountain, and I took a stroll into the cockpit, where I got to see some of the most beautiful and spectacular sights. The sun was so bright I could hardly keep my eyes open even though I had put my sunglasses on. Seeing all this through the giant windshield was breathtaking. Back in my seat, which was being strapped to the wall of the aircraft, I was able to look out the portholes and take some pictures. When it was time to land, we all had to be strapped back to the wall. RD had to take some antianxiety pills before he got on anything resembling a military plane (he was a former Green Beret in Vietnam) because he would get serious flashbacks of being in the helicopters and all that went with it.

I had noticed that all the fire trucks and other vehicles that were to drive us back to the base had backed off the runway, which incidentally was a slanted one. Well, that was quite the landing; we had banked a one-eighty to the right, then to the left, and when we landed, it was hard, but I was not worried. I just thought it was cool. When we had been picked up and escorted to the chow hall for some food and hot coffee, the major in charge of us at that site told us about our hot landing and went on to describe in great detail how everyone thought we were either going into the Chukchi Sea or into the mountain. Wow, great, so that was the reason why the landing was rough. And we were also informed that the pilot was a student. Well, all I could say was he did it, and we were all fine, thank God. RD was about to flip out, and I mean really have a meltdown. I was so glad he went to the VA office in Anchorage for those pills. We were there for two days. I was celebrating my twenty-eighth birthday forty miles off the coast of Russia. Wow. That sight was so long and wide; it was a city. It was so cold there; no one would want to go out anyway. We did get to walk outside to go to another building, and I couldn't help but notice the ravens were the size of a macaw. They had to be pretty hardy to withstand the elements. Those birds probably even flew back and forth from Russia as well.

So big was that site they even had a state-of-the-art theatre for the guys. We had a special viewing of none other than *Stripes*. We really had to laugh when Bill Murray was threatened to be sent above the Arctic Circle (right where we were). After the movie, we had one of the best meals we had ever had. The cook (chef) was one of the best sent up from a five-star restaurant. After dinner, I was presented with a big birthday cake. A cherished memory to this day. The only hitch to that day was that I was beginning to feel sick. By the next day, I was in full-blown misery.

We waited on the edges of the runway for the pilot and did a number of "touch and gos" (touch down and take off again) before we were allowed to board. The pilot was standing outside while equipment was being loaded onto the C-130, and as we stood there together, I was describing how we almost bit the dust coming in for the landing the other day; it was with a stink look that this pilot revealed to me that it was him. I could have sat on tissue paper, and my feet would have dangled; that is how small and mortified I was.

We were transported back to Anchorage and stayed there for a couple days before going on to our next site, which was to be the Aleutian Chain. These islands were very difficult to get clearance to enter. Many scientists were on a waiting list to be on any of them.

Adak was the one we were to do a couple of shows on. First, we had to land on a tiny island called the Rock so we could have ourselves and all our equipment sniffed out by dogs looking for drugs or anything dangerous. After passing inspection, we were flown on to Adak. We were given a tour of the little island and found it to be ever so quaint. I was told not to worry as there were no bears on that island. Glad to know. We played in the local theatre on the base, which felt like we were in the old West saloon. Nice big stage, and I used every foot of it. After the gig, we partied with the troops stationed there. Navy I believe they all were. One of the sights we were taken to see was the nesting ground of the bald eagles. There were so many eagles perched on abandoned Quonset huts, and the feathers on the ground were so plentiful I saw no reason why I could not have one, but as I reached to pick one up, I was yelled at by our tour guide that those are considered sacred and no one was allowed to even touch them unless presented in a ceremony by an authentic Native American ritual. I had to leave them as they lay on the ground. There were a lot of things in Alaska that were considered sacred and against the law for anyone other than a native to do, have, or take part in. Okay, I could respect that.

I think that was one of the most educational stops we made besides Indian Mountain.

There was one place we played that was atop a mountain, and the wind was so fierce that unless you weighed over 180 pounds you would be blown right off the mountain. It was that site that we had to be driven in some kind of giant machine. I had never seen anything like it before. It had to maneuver up the skinny snow-stormy mountainside, and I was scared out of my mind. If you looked out the massive windows, all you would see was down, down, down the mountainside for miles! I could not wait to be done with that place.

Our stage area was a partitioned-off part of the recreational hall, which was not very big to begin with, but I was not bothered by that. What did happen later during one of my songs was insulting and harmful. One of the boys in the crowd hauled off and whipped a bottle cap, which hit me in the face. It hurt, and I was so angry at such rudeness I walked right off the stage. RD was ready to go after him, but the other guys held him back. Immediately, an MP came and took him to the brig. I would not go back into the stage area until he was gone. I guess I was embarrassed at that as well.

I have to flash back to the gig we did right after Indian Mountain. We were flown to Point Barrow. I was really into the cold. I had been slammed with the day before, and by then, it was in full bloom. I did take some medication, and that helped me get through the toga party we played there. In spite of my misery, I had a really nice time. Watching those guys and girls having so much fun running around in their togas was hilarious. They wanted to do the Animal House thing. I could not stay and party with everyone, so I went off to bed while the guys stayed and partied.

Many of the places we played allowed the locals in to enjoy the music. I got to meet some interesting characters. One outstanding feature about the local women was that none of them had all their teeth and yet they still were as happy as ever—another part of the world, another attitude, another lifestyle. I felt privileged to get to know some of them. I'd even like to think that the surreal memory I have truly did happen, and that was I got to see one of the igloo huts one of the locals took us to see.

We also got to fly through many of the mountain passes and got to really see up close the crevices that were all over the place and some wildlife as well. Cam, our bush pilot, would do his crazy maneuvers to make seeing these things easier.

At one point, while we were flying over the tundra, I had to go to the bathroom, but we were not anywhere near a toilet, so by the time Cam came across a lone house in the middle of nowhere, he landed! I ran so fast and did not even stop to ask the two old gentlemen sitting on the porch if I could use the facilities. I just ran in and found it. The look I got was just like something out of a movie. Cam later told me that place was a rest stop for people flying around or dog sledding. That was good to know even if it was in hindsight for me. Cam was a trickster as well. He let me believe I was running into a private home. True is the saying "When you gotta go, you gotta go!"

Cam went on to take us to where the walrus would hang out at the edge of the Bering Strait. He stopped to let us walk through the squishy tundra grass to the edge of the cliff to see them in their habitat below. Most unreal was how the ground felt to me as I walked through what appears to be hard ground, until you step on it. It feels like the earth is made of sponge. Good thing I did not have to run from anything; it would feel like running in a nightmare. Instead, I will remember it as an experience I will most likely never have again. I also got to see seals as they lay around their ice float and slide right on into that frigid water.

The month ended, and we were headed back to the Lower 48, taking with us such memories. The last day, we were presented with certificates of appreciation from the USO.

CHAPTER 20

Now we were back in Rapid City and stayed there for a few weeks and enjoyed the holidays with family and friends before heading back out to the coast to where our gigs were being set up.

Upon the band's return to the coast, and while in Southern California, I decided to look up Neith and Gerry. I called first to find the time best to show up.

Their house was a cute one in Burbank, and in the backyard were her horse stalls. Among other critters, she had a parrot, which I fell in love with. On she went showing me her home and especially the curio of music boxes that Freddie Mercury had given her from all the places he went.

After spending the day with her and Gerry, I had to head back to Santa Barbara, where we were staying with Merlyn Magner. I have not seen either of them since, but it was nice to know we were friends again.

There was one place that the Santa Barbara agency set us up with in Salem, Oregon, where there is a huge insane asylum as well as prison. Sometimes a patient would be released and somehow end up at the club. One day, as we were beginning our first set, not too many people had arrived yet, but one of the few that came sat front and center of the stage, where he was engrossed in rolling the napkin that came with his drink into what appeared to be a giant spliff (a Jamaican joint). He lit it and wielded it all around his head just as I began to sing a Linda Ronstadt tune. When I had hit the highest note of the song, he let out a huge howl as if I was breaking his eardrums. It was actually quite funny. He fortunately left right after that.

In another incident, one of the regular customers, who happened to be electrician for the club, came tumbling in and rolled all the way from the door to the other end of the building. He truly looked like a pill bug. We had become the Peppertree's house band. At first, I was upset that the bass player, RD, had negotiated a contract that we would play there for six weeks straight. I was not used to staying anywhere that long. I wanted to keep moving on to the next gig. I had to learn to be okay with it, although we did have a job booked in Ontario, Oregon, during that six-week period, that being the desert part of the state bordering Idaho.

As we were getting ready to roll out of town, we were told that Ontario was full of cowboys who really do hitch their horses outside the saloons and that they only liked country music. Back in those days, it was Hank Williams, Johnny Cash, Loretta Lynn, and the like. I was really nervous knowing that I did not have much in the way of country music in my or the rest of the band's repertoire. How many times during the week could we play the one Johnny Cash song we knew. I could get away with some Linda Ronstadt songs, but I knew that would not be enough to keep an audience.

This situation put me back to the memory of getting booked at a club in Lemmon, South Dakota, where it was truly country. We nearly had a blues brothers experience until one of our guitar players broke into "Down the Line" by Johnny Cash. I sang every Ronstadt song I knew, twice. I got away with some Stevie Nicks tunes, and we managed to get through the night with those.

On another note about Lemmon, South Dakota, is that they have the absolute worst-tasting and worst-looking water I have ever smelled. I tried to brush my teeth and decided I would wait till the next town; I could not even bath in it. It smelled like two rotten eggs!

Back to Ontario. As we drove through the night into the wee hours of the morning, we found where we had to play for the next week (providing we were not run out of town before then). We found a hotel where the price was doable, and as we were checking in, the desk manager proceeded to tell us in a not-so-friendly tone of voice, "When you people get back from your show, be quiet because we have working people here trying to sleep!" I was incensed to say the least. Why did these people think we were not working folk either? If anything, every waking moment of our lives was a working moment. Ah, well, we did not argue. We just said no problem and they would not even know we were there.

After we checked in, we went on to set up for that evening. With great anxiety, we walked in, carrying our equipment and proceeded to set up (after checking in with management, of course), and someone sitting at the bar yelled out, "Hey! Do you play that loud rock and roll stuff?" At first we were not sure how to respond to that question but decided on the truth and get it over with saying, "Yes, we do." The gentleman at the bar hollered, "Yahoo!" Well, we were so amazed and relieved all we could do was join in his laugh. He had some beer brought over to the guys. I was not drinking during the afternoon. I would allow myself one glass of wine before playing. Any more than that would render me unable to hit my notes.

That night, when we began our first set, the club was already full. We were to find ourselves enjoying the most fun crowd we had had in a very long time—better than at the Peppertree, where we were the only successful group to get the crowd back.

When you know an audience really appreciates your music, the ability to play extra fine was in our performances. One of the nights, there was a drummer who loved to play Stevie Nicks songs, and Dana gracefully handed his sticks over to him to play those songs. I will never forget just how wonderful and exciting it was for me having the Mick Fleetwood's type of rudiments accompanying me. I was overwhelmed and nearly forgot where I was in the song. I was so amazed how much better I felt about singing them.

We were sad to be done with that gig as we headed back to Salem and the Peppertree. I don't remember how long we had been playing there. By the time, a lone gunman opened fire in one of the other rock and roll clubs in town, killing about five people. It could have been us instead as we found out it was a random choice. Every time the door opened, I was ready to duck and cover—not a very good feeling, like a sitting duck on the stage that had been moved to where the entrance was.

A few weeks later (yes, we extended our contract), I met a young man who appeared to be much older. As I was talking to him on one of our breaks, he went on to tell me why his hair was falling out. It was a patchy mess at that time, and he knew I was curious. He finally told me he was in the club that got shot up, and the persons on either side of him was shot and killed, but he somehow did not catch a bullet. Now he was a nervous wreck and under a doctor's care. This was the first outing to a club since then, and his coming in was part of the therapy. I always keep him in my prayers. He could not accept that his friends died while he lived. It was nothing short of a miracle. I often wonder what he is doing these days.

CHAPTER 21

The volcano Mount St. Helens was going to blow! It was all over the news for weeks. No one could predict exactly when it would finally go off, but all the authorities were working against a time bomb to evacuate anyone living in the vicinity of what would be hit. There was an old man who refused to leave, saying that he would be fine. All during that time, we were in Oregon, and the ashes that had already been spewing would dust everything, but when it finally blew, the ash became so heavy that our windshields would be thick with the gray stuff every day. What a mess—nature taking its course. It was an exciting time to say the least. The old man did die.

When we had completed our time at the Peppertree, we were sent on to the sister club in Albany, Oregon. The proprietor of the club also owned an airstrip, and that is where the club we were to play was. That stage was the skinniest, longest, and highest one I was ever to perform on. Being that I am afraid of heights made for a scary and nervous time for me.

Next stop was a club in Corvallis, Oregon. This was a college town. We were to play at an upscale hotel there, and I had to wear evening dresses onstage. We were given rooms in that hotel as well, and I quite enjoyed the luxury. I also had to hide my little Yorkie, AJ. He was my little road dog. When we would get invited to party after the show, I would always decline because I wanted to get back to be with him. I did not want to party anyway, so it always worked out. Many times I had been called a drag. Oh well!

Somehow we got booked in a club that wanted really heavy metal rock, and that we did not do nor could we improvise, so after we played one set, we were told we did not have to finish the night.

We got paid anyway, but the owner did not want to lose any customers because of us. I think that was one of the most embarrassing gigs we did. We could not even see the humor in it. When that week of playing was over, we went back one more time to perform at the Peppertree.

As we were getting ready to go onstage, we were getting a little worried that Mike, our lead guitarist, was not there yet, which was unusual. We had finished playing the first set when the manager got a call from the local police, saying they had Mike there and he was being held as a suspect in many crimes. We were dumbfounded as Mike most assuredly was one of the cleanest law-abiding persons, albeit he smoked pot all the time so had some on him when they arrested him. We immediately called Jim and Diane. Jim was a lawyer, so of course, we doubly needed him to take over the situation.

We played the rest of the night, repeating all of my songs and some of Bob's. The crowd knew what was going on, and they were very supportive of us in that time of need.

Later that night, the police drove Mike back to the hotel where we were staying. Jim had read them the riot act.

Mike told us that he had been stopped because of a broken headlight, and when they did a check on his license, up popped a criminal list as long as his arm, causing the cops to make Mike kneel in front of the cruiser for almost an hour in the rain. Cold and angry as well as knowing we had to play without him was bad enough, but that long excruciating wait on his knees in the rain and being thought a hardened criminal was too much to bear. But he had no other choice. Finally, they brought him to the station and shoved him in a holding cell. As it turned out, there was a guy from Rapid City who knew Mike and used his name when he got busted, so that is how it came about. They thought he was this horrible person. Thanks to Jim, Mike got out but not after withstanding the meanness of the local police. What a rotten way to end our time at that club.

Cathy Bach (formerly Bachman) called us at the hotel we were staying at and wanted us to come see her at the car trade show. She was booked to appear at during the months of hiatus from filming *Dukes*.

We joined up with her and spent the day looking at all kinds of muscle cars. Much to the disappointment of old and young men alike, Cathy wore blue jeans and a woolen sweater. They kept asking to her annoyance, "Where are your shorts?" It was maddening to think that they only liked her for her fabulous legs. After a fun day hanging out with our friend, we had to head back up to play that night. Cathy was saying how she wished she could come see us, but she had to do another day of that trade show and then on back to LA. We then packed up our equipment for our trek back to Modesto and got some more work.

During the time we were being handled by Jim and Diane, we were doing gigs all over mid California, like Modesto, which was where they lived, and handled business from Tracy, Sacramento, and around the Bay Area (San Francisco). We were also booked to work Bend, Oregon, which was a wonderful little town. Then we went on to play the in Seven Sisters Mountain Ski Resort. What a gorgeous place! Just spending the days walking around the grounds was wonderful. We were playing in the bar lounge, which was not very big, but it was intimate. At the end of the week, we were to head back to Modesto, but the guys had another idea. They all wanted to go back to Rapid City. They were tired of the road, missed their families, and last but not least, they were tired of the way we had to pay for the equipment Mike had bought until it was all paid for, and then he said he was not going to let us keep using it, which meant we would have to shell out for another mixing board and whatever else Mike decided to take home with him. That was the beginning of the end of the Badlands Blues Band.

Jim and Diane were putting together a USO South Pacific tour for us, but when only four of us returned to Modesto, that put an end to that. But what really put an end to our continuing on even though we could have replaced Mike was the incredible fact that upon our return, we could not find our agent/manager/lawyer! The office they worked out of was empty, and they were no longer at their condo. They and their two German shepherds were gone as well. We were dumbfounded. Where and what happened to cause them to leave so abruptly with not a single word of warning? One of my speculations was and still is that they were into some illegal activities and had to get out of town in a hurry. It was not that they were trying to ditch us because they had put a lot of their own money to get better equipment for us. They did not owe us any money; if anything, we owed them!

Our band was not too much longer in existence anyway because the guys were not happy that I was being promoted as the star of the band and all the radio advertisements were focusing on saying my name while referring to the rest of the guys as the band. They said they were not the Magarette band. I had nothing to do with any of those decisions. I never told any of them that it was me that they wanted and they had a band lined up for me to work with but I was to come alone. They did not want the other members, not even Bob. I could not ditch them to further myself. During that time, whenever Diane and Jim would come to watch us play, the guys would turn up their amps. The stronger I sang, the louder they cranked up the amps, until Diane came up and told them she saw what they were doing to me and to turn down the amps. She was angry. I was thinking I was imagining that the guitars were getting louder. I think that was the beginning of the end for us. So now the rest of the band went back to Rapid while Bob and I went back to stay with Trisha and Neil.

During the time we had gotten into California, I had been in touch with my brother Dave. I had told him that if he wanted his marriage to last, he needed to get out of Bellingham. So they sold their house, loaded up the old Caddy, then Dave, Kathy (she was pregnant with Ian), Duane, Jessica, Steve (Kathy's brother), and Edna (Kathy's mom) piled into the already packed car to make the southern route trek to Southern California. I had told Dave that was where we were planning to stay, but we ended up staying in Northern California in San Jose, always thinking we would end up getting back to Santa Barbara.

Dave and his entourage were to begin a new life there, and Dave had to start at the bottom again and take menial little truck jobs. At that time, they were living in a hotel when they had enough money; otherwise, they were to repeat what we had to do as kids when leaving

Bellingham, and that was having to live in a tent for a few months. Camping life in Southern California was much nicer, as there were not a whole lot of rainy days. When they did stay in hotels, Kathy could use the dresser drawers for Duane's and Jessie's beds. I thought that was classic.

After about a year went by, Dave and family had moved into a little house in Lawndale. It was not long after then that my brother Ross moved out to Lawndale, and a few months later, brother Jimmy followed.

Around this time, we were still playing gigs in the southern part of California, and when we got booked to play in Lompoc, which was relatively close to Lawndale, they came out to see us. Dana let Duane sit at his drum kit and bang out some Duane-style rhythms. To me, it was one of the highlights of my band days, having my family able to see us perform. When we finished up that job we went back up north.

All during the time we were staying with Trish and Neil, we would take work catering for Mybergs Kosher Deli. We would work with Neil, and that was actually an interesting job. It was never the same old, same old day in and day out. We would do bar mitzvahs and bat mitzvahs, as well as weddings and anniversaries. We did office parties during the day as well as Christmas parties in the exclusive parts of San Francisco.

During those months, I would go visit my Aunt Eunice and Uncle Bud (who happened to be my second cousin). I called him Cous-unk. I would sometimes spend the weekends with them and was so happy to be with family. My mother's sister and my mother's cousin lived in Redwood City, California, which is only twenty minutes south of San Francisco. I would attend church on Sunday with them, and after Sunday dinner, Bob would come and have supper with us before heading back to San Jose.

We would head back to South Dakota for a month or so and park our Open Road van in his parents' driveway. Bob and I would sometimes stay out in the hills with his friend Jeff Kerns and where another friend was also staying. Jeff was his most generous and kind friend I had ever met. The place was so big, and we all had nice-sized bedrooms. I felt the best when we were out there. Cody (Jeff's half-wolf, half-shepherd) would parole the grounds, keeping anyone thinking they could trespass at bay. I had the privilege of watching him in action once when some tourist (I guessed) drove up the long dirt road to where the house was, but Cody circled continuously, not allowing them to exit the car. Finally, they turned around and left. I had been hidden while I sunbathed naked deep in the tall wheat field, so I did not want them getting out and find me in my birthday suit! Cody was my hero.

Cody would sometimes bay at the moon, and when Jeff would say, "Cody! What are you doing?" he would actually get embarrassed and not bay for weeks at a time. I loved that dog. He was a good boy.

Cocaine was an evil drug—more so than heroin to my way of thinking. Heroin would cause extreme mellowness, whereas coke would cause everyone who touched the stuff turn into someone who could not stop. I had seen some very successful businesspeople lose everything, including dignity. I saw relationships fail, and I watched some ladies do what I knew was desperation to get the next line.

Bob had been dealing for quite some time, but only in small exchanges. Nonetheless, I would always get so paranoid every time I saw flashing red and blue lights—until I decided to try a line myself. I loved it. I loved the wonderful high it gave me. I loved everyone, everything, and life was more perfect than ever until I began to crash about an hour (if that long) later. At first, I would wait until I was offered another line or until everyone else was ready for the next one. Over the next couple of months, I began to get more and more aggressive in my nerve to ask before anyone was ready to set up the next row of the stuff.

Bob and I went to meet up at his supplier's house hidden deep into the hills. When we found the drive, which was overgrown with weeds and tall grass, we were met by a real full-on wolf named Wylie. We had to wait for the guy to come out and call him inside, where we would be properly introduced to him so he would know we were friends. I was so enthralled to be so close up and personal with one of the wildest and majestic animals God created. We hung out there for a couple of hours, and during that time, this supplier kept drawing out lines of some of the best cocaine I ever had. The high was awesome. I loved the world and beyond. After a while, I found myself unable to wait for the next line, so I outright asked for some more. It was then that I knew I had a problem and better get it under control and soon.

I would accept more and more as the evening went on. By the time we left, I was so high I knew I would be in for a big crash. I had such a terrible time the next day as I knew I had to refuse putting any more of that wicked stuff up my nose. I was feeling horrible for days as I waited for everything to clear out of my system. From then on, I would refuse to do any more cocaine. I have not touched any drugs (except prescriptions).

Bob and I used to work part-time at Budget Tapes & Records downtown Rapid City. It was there too where the cocaine flowed like water. I would find little balls of tinfoil all over the place, but because I had accidentally thrown out almost a thousand dollars' worth of cocaine, to this day I have a fear of throwing away what is obviously trash. So fiercely angry our boss Kevin was when he could not find the tiny ball of tinfoil that had been on his desk, which I had cleaned earlier.

Every now and again, we would stay at his house while he went out of town. While staying there, we took care of his Doberman pinscher, Zedrick (a.k.a. Zedhead Zeddie). He was such a beautiful dog and so funny. He loved to play with AJ as I held my breath. Zed would have to lie completely down to be level with my dog. Zed would ride with me in the van once in a while. He would look so royal, sitting there in the passenger seat, looking out the window. He was one of the biggest Dobbies I have ever seen. In the morning, he would come into the bedroom and just lay his head down next to mine until I woke up eye to eye with him. Zed had a chest expansion of forty-two inches, and when he would sit on the couch, he could place his front legs down on the floor. Zed would smile upon seeing anyone, but some who didn't know him thought he was growling and getting ready to bite. All he was doing was showing how happy he was to see you.

That was the year Reagan was elected president and the embassy hostage crisis ended.

Not too many days later, I would get a package from a lady who was a good friend to Jose Thompson, who, after Bob and I got married, left the Air Force and move back to St. Louis to become an engineer at a small recording studio. This woman sent Jose's silver necklace along with the local report of the autopsy, letting me know that Jose had died a few nights before and that no one knew from what or why. I called the number she gave me immediately, and she told me that they had gotten very close, even though Jose refused to get serious with anyone, and he always seemed sad. In the meantime, she was the one to go into his apartment where she found he had a shrine dedicated to me. My pictures were all over his walls. Her belief was that he died of a broken heart. It was then that I realized this person did not like speaking to me. She went on to tell me how his body was found slumped in the driver's seat of his beloved green Mustang. I was informed that his body was set to the CDC in Atlanta for further testing, as it was a mystery as to how he died. After hanging up, I was in somewhat of a shock that this person actually blamed me! I said a prayer for Jose and put his necklace away in a safe place. I still have it today.

I could not help recalling the time he brought me to his father and stepmother's house in Cheyenne, Wyoming. He was excited for me to meet his father and younger brother. When we got there and I met everyone, I could not help but notice that his stepmother did not seem to like me. This was a new experience for me. I would keep to the background while the family rallied around a BBQ. When it was time to go to bed, I was given the younger brother's bedroom. AJ and I woke up really early in the morning, around 5 a.m., to some not-so-subtle talking in the kitchen between Jose and his stepmother. She was telling him he had some nerve bringing me to the house. And she was really upset that I had a dog too. I don't remember what Jose said back to her, but I was not going to take a chance on running into her again. I snuck out to the car and slept the rest of the night there. I stayed in the car until later that afternoon. I refused to go in where she was.

On the way back to the base, he explained why his stepmother was so upset. She was jealous. Unbeknownst to his dad, she had molested both he and his brother. Jose was about fifteen when it began. He said she would wait until their dad was on a business trip and then start by having him undo her bra, and on from there, she taught him the ways of sex. When he left for the military, she turned to the younger brother. It was at this revelation that I figured out why the boy was always having migraines and odd behavior patterns. Jose knew he should tell his father about all this but was afraid for his kid brother and the result of letting someone know. There were no child protective services back then. I just knew I never wanted to go back there again. Another lesson in life. I wondered if hiding that demon all those years played a role in his sorrow. I hoped that woman paid in some manner, shape, or form for her disgusting self.

Kevin would come back home, and we would go back to his parents' house and sleep in the van, which was fine by me. The only time I had an issue was when Bob would go off for the entire night, selling and doing dope until the wee hours of the morning. I would be alone, waiting for him, and cry over the turn my life had taken.

We would hook up with the guys periodically to play a gig here and there, but soon, that was not enough to keep us in the cold months, and we would head back out to California.

We stayed there for a couple of months or so, and I would fly back and forth from Northern California to Southern California to be with Dave and the family. I always felt bad when I had to go back up to the Bay Area.

I would also stay with Aunt Eunice and Cous-unk more frequently. It was while staying with them that I had met the neighbor Hans. He was very much liked by my aunt and uncle, and so when he asked if he could take me out to breakfast with him and some friends, Aunt Eunice said I should go, as he was such a nice man even though he was more than twice my age. Hans was fifty-six and from Germany. He was knowledgeable in many of the things I was curious about, and having done research in the areas, he was supposedly wise, and it fascinated me. One of those things was doing horoscopes and the I Ching. I said I'd be over the next day with my information to do an in-depth personal horoscope. I came back to spend the next weekend with my aunt and uncle again and to get the results of my horoscope.

Hans had made plans for a dinner date, and then he would tell me what his findings were. After dinner at an authentic German restaurant, we headed for what I thought was his house, and there he would give me the results of my horoscope. Imagine my horror when he pulled up to a hotel, saying he would be right back as he was going to book a room for privacy in going over the information. I adamantly refused and said if he could not just give it to me, then never mind. I did not need the results that badly. Off we drove back to his house, where he finally gave me what I had not expected such drama over. Hans was very apologetic, and we parted still friends. I would yet again go visit him next door, and we did the I Ching then, all the while him telling me his life's story about how he was in the German side of WWII. I also would have him teach me the language as well. When I was back in San Jose, I would call him. We would just chat, and he would make me laugh.

During that time of my life, I was on a radical diet known as Nature's Aid. It was a thin broth-like soup and had to be done for seventeen days strictly. I went from 128 pounds to 92 pounds, and on the next weekend, when I was visiting my aunt and uncle, they told me I was too skinny and had to eat. I said I would on the outing Hans had invited me to. We were going to Napa Valley for some wine tasting. I had never done that before and looked forward to the experience.

Between orchards, we stopped to have a picnic of French bread, cheese, and wine, along with some fruit. As it was my first solid meal in over two weeks, I was ravenous. I got nice and tipsy. On we went to more wine tasting and getting drunk. I was feeling pretty good.

As we headed back to Redwood City, he pulled into a little motel where he said we could hang out for a few hours so I could sober up before him taking me back to my family. I did not think anything of it. I was too in my cups to care one way or the other.

As soon as we walked into the room, Hans took immediate advantage of the situation and tried to plant a big sloppy kiss on me. He tried to push his tongue into my mouth, where upon I bit it so hard he screamed and jumped back. I bit so hard that he was bleeding. I just looked at him as if to say, "Well, you deserved it." I also told him I don't kiss. Ever. I did at one time in my life but not anymore. It was too intimate, and I was not willing to go there, especially with an old man with only three teeth in his head. Not to mention he was bald on top with a Caesar's halo of white hair. But he did have the most beautiful blue eyes—very northern Germanic features. He was very handsome once upon a time in his life and probably could not believe he had aged into an old man.

I found I was intoxicated enough to allow him the liberty of having sex with me. I was so disillusioned with love life and happiness. I was now broke all the time as I had no gigs. The little money I did make was spent on basic necessities, and I had to pay for everything. Bob was not contributing. I was happy to be taken out for once and to be able to enjoy doing something fun. Bob was making me crazy, and I did not want to keep living the life we had. We were not playing out anymore, and Bob did not want to put together another band. My life was sucking.

So that is why I just closed my eyes and let this old man do his thing. I fell asleep to block out the memory of what I had allowed myself to become. When I woke up, I took a hot bath.

We left that place, and I was no different-looking, and I was still intact, so upon realizing I had survived that demoralizing act I had permitted to happen, I just went into a state of denial.

When I walked into my aunt and uncle's house, no one was the wiser. Back in San Jose, I decided I needed to get back down south. I enjoyed living with Dave and his family and contributed to all the household needs as well as babysitting for them once in a while. After a week or so, I knew I would have to find a job, as well as doing the round of auditions for bands.

I took a job in a Chinese restaurant for about two weeks but could not take the craziness of the way they treated me. I had decided it was time to look for a band to join, and Kathy took me around to auditions. I was not having much success because I had no tapes to send out for more auditions. When the band broke up, any and all the recorded tapings we had done disappeared with everything else.

CHAPTER 22

I was grateful to be living with family and being in Southern California, but the cramped living quarters had to be getting to them as well. I knew it was time to try something different, so I called my brother Donni's and my friend Chris Boutillette. He sent me a plane ticket to come back east. He picked me up, and we went straight away to his best friend Leo Cazault's thirtieth birthday party. From there, Chris drove me up to Pease Air Force base in Portsmouth, New Hampshire. Because it was so late by the time we got there, Chris and I spent the night sleeping on the floor of my sister's townhouse on base.

He left the next morning. I always felt good and safe when I was with Chris, but our time was not yet. Two weeks had passed, and Kathy had called to let me know that one of the show bands I had auditioned for wanted me to come do a gig with them in a Hollywood Howard Johnson. I couldn't believe it. This was my lot in life, I guess. I had to call them and explain that I was on the other coast.

While I was on the East Coast, I went on auditions for vocalists, but no one was interested. I had such a nice time staying with Kim and her little family. Tracy was about two and ever so tiny, and Corey was about six months old and as big as Tracy. Here I was again, living on a base with my sister. I was content. I got to see the rest of my family as well that summer.

Then came the Putnam family reunion, and I had an audition with another band in Boston and would be meeting up with Kim and Jeff at the old homestead on the mountain in Winchester, New Hampshire.

After the audition, I headed out for the long drive to Winchester. There was no GPS, and I had written down the directions given to me by my brother-in-law, Jeff. I kept getting lost, but eventually, I did make it to a mountain I thought looked familiar and proceeded up that dirt road. I drove to the top and realized it was the wrong one. That is when I realized that the locals I had asked were acting strange. Suddenly, I got so scared, believing I had been hoodwinked into thinking I was on the right path/road. The only thing that came to mind was that they had sent me up to be kidnapped and brought to a witch's coven. I broke into a cold sweat, and while fighting back tears, I struggled to get Kim's little Turkish pick up to turn around in what had become just wagon ruts in the road. It was so dark; only the headlights broke through the pitch blackness of the night. Finally, the trusty little pickup got back on the road, and I flew down to the bottom and onto the next town, which I saw was Winchester. This was the right one. So I was finally able to make it to the campsite, where we all pitched our tents or parked our little trailers. I was still shaking from the wild imaginings of the last town.

It was so nice to be with the East Coast original Putnam reunion. I stayed a little longer with Kim before I flew back to San Jose. I was there for a week or so when a friend of Neil's asked if I would stay at her house and take care of her cats in Los Gatos for the week. I was more than happy to have a nice place to be by myself. During the week, I found I wanted to talk to Hans. He had rather grown on me. I did like his company. After talking to him, he drove straight up to the house. When he came to the door, I was not feeling good about letting him in. I never knew if Bob was going to show up, and I did not want to get into a do-or-die match, so I told Hans I was not going to have him come in. He just looked at me and said if ever I needed anything to give him a call.

When my friend came home, I decided I needed to head back for Southern California to stay with Dave and the gang while I tried to get my head together and figure out what I was going to do with my life and how I could get away from Bob. We were headed nowhere. He would not let me pay bills, and we were in debt, thanks to him taking out loans in my name (I did not object when he took me to sign the loan), and now not being able to pay them back, we have creditors hunting us down. I was sick and tired of that life—not the road life, but the drug and debt life. I had to save myself.

I went back to my aunt and uncle's house, where, of course, I met back up with Hans. I told him I was going to move back down with Dave and Kathy. Hans said he would take me there.

I could not take AJ, and that broke my heart. I had to make a move forward somehow, and I did not have a whole lot of choices. Because there were kids in the house, I was afraid that one of them would let the dog out and he would get hit by a car or stolen. I knew I would not be able to keep an eye on him, nor would I be able to bring him to whatever job I could get. I had to leave him with Bob. I knew he would be safe there.

Hans and his friend Frank Door drove me down to Lawndale with as much of my things I could take. I did not have much anyway. Before they left to head back up north, Hans gave me one hundred dollars and said I should take Dave and Kathy out to dinner.

I felt like I had a thousand bucks and looked forward in resuming my band hunt. I went to bed that night, feeling like my luck had taken a good turn.

The next morning, I got up feeling great; I knew I could take my only upscale dress to the dry cleaners, finally. That night, I told Dave that I wanted to take him, Kathy, and the kids to the In-N-Out Burger, thinking it was within my budget. I thought it was good because it had much more quality and class than McDonalds or Jack in the Box. All was agreed on that, but when the time came to go, Dave had a better idea. He said, "Hey, Edna can watch the kids, and the three of us can go to someplace nicer." I said that was okay by me, not thinking he would be taking us to someplace hoity-toity.

Dave pulled into a really posh-looking Japanese restaurant, and I nearly chocked. I had only one hundred dollars to last me till I found a job. Well, I thought he would at least be conservative with what they ordered. Was I in for a surprise.

Not only did he order the most expensive drinks for himself and Kathy, but the most expensive appetizers and the most expensive entrée on the menu. I began to seriously worry, wondering if I had enough to pay for that now. The final blow to my budget was when Dave ordered the most expensive dessert for both of them. For myself, I stuck with the least expensive of everything.

When it was time to get the bill, I was devastated; it came to over seventy-five dollars, and that was not counting the tip! I walked out of that restaurant with a ten-dollar bill. I knew I had to have ten for my dry cleaning. What was I going to do? So on the way home, Dave wanted to stop at the liquor store. I went in with him and was so out of my mind upset (I did not show it) that I figured, "Oh hell, why not go all the way broke?" and bought a bottle of Baileys Irish Cream, which took the rest of the money I had. I was screwed anyway by now, so why not just drink and be merry? When we got home, I drank so much Baileys Irish Cream I actually got drunk. After Dave and Kathy went to bed, I was still up, and once I was alone, I broke down and cried and cried. I was so sad that my brother would have done that to me. I was so disillusioned with not only love being overrated, but even family love was apparently overrated as well. I could not believe my own brother would do such a selfish thing to me. I was paralyzed with shock as I wondered what I was going to do. No money, no tapes for my auditions, no nothing. I was disgusted with life and thought I might as well take advantage of being with someone who wanted to lend me a hand.

I felt that there was only one thing left for me to do. I had to call Hans and tell him I would come back up there and stay with him. I needed his help. Being intoxicated made it easier, and once I had thrown in the towel, I could not and would not change my mind.

All the rest of the day I was still so hurt that Dave would do that to me. This was to be one of the three biggest game changers of my life. I had gone to seek the advice of Edna Dave's mother-in-law, and I really needed to cry on someone's shoulder, and I was looking for some answers to the *why* of it all. When I had found her where she had a babysitting job on the next block, I went to her and just broke down crying and telling her of the past evening's events. After listening with the patience only an older citizen could give, she went on to tell me how my brother had done the same thing when he and Kathy went to visit my Uncle Howard and that he had done that to

Steve, his brother-in-law, as well. So I learned something I had never seen in Dave before. I still loved my brother and had to look at this behavior as a purpose in a bigger picture. This was a move I never could have foreseen in a million years. I was about to go live with an older man, something that had always disgusted me. I just couldn't stand the thought of an attractive young woman living with an old man. Never was my attitude toward these ladies flattering, and here I was on my way to do the exact same thing. I always thought it must be fate's big get even for my judging others.

After moving back up north and letting my aunt and uncle know that I was to be their neighbor, they were overjoyed. They thought Hans was the best neighbor they ever had and considered him a good way for me to get out of my gypsy ways.

I so very much wanted to continue with my road life, and if it were not for my little Yorkshire Terrier, Ajax, I would have begun looking for bands.

Ajax was like a child to me, and it was tearing me apart not being able to have him with me all the times I was escaping down south. I wanted him back, but that meant I had to be in a position where I could give him a stable home for once in his life. Being with Hans would give me that. Plus, there were other reasons previously mentioned that played a part in my decision, but the catalyst to the ultimate one was my dog.

Now I needed to get my AJ back, so I borrowed Han's car and drove to San Jose, where Bob was staying. I knew when he wouldn't be there so that was when I planned on stealing my little guy back. Since I still had a key to the place, I was able to open the door and just scoop him up. I left a note on the door, letting him know that I took him, but as I was getting back into the car, who should drive up but Bob. As I tried to drive off, he tried to stop me. He really gave a valiant attempt, but I managed to get away and never looked back.

After I had officially moved in with Hans, I began to wonder what I was going to do now for a job. I did not want to go back to bartending as I had done that before and wanted something new. I wanted a trade under my belt just in case I did go back to life on the road. The occupation I had always thought would be perfect was cosmetology.

Hans, my aunt, and I all put our heads together and decided that I should enroll in a private school of beauty, which I did immediately. I went for the next semester, beginning shortly. It was April when I signed up, and I think I started in June. I graduated eighteen hundred hours later. It was not easy. One would think it would be, but the fact that so much dangerous chemicals, odors, electric currents are used every day while touching people, as well as the vast differences each person has, makes for so much in the learning. Every class always has dropouts. I stuck it. I graduated, passed the rigid state bar exam (the toughest), and went on to take an apprenticeship with one of the top salons in the area. Terry De Marco was a master. He began as a barber but went on to become a master colorist, stylist, and all things chemical in the hair industry. I worked as an assistant to the stylist there until I was deemed accomplished enough to get a station where I was to become a true stylist. It took me longer that anyone because I was so afraid I was going to make a mistake with someone's hair. I advanced as a stylist very slowly and meticulously. Highlights and perms were my greatest talent, and I was requested a lot in those areas. I had stopped listening to my rock and roll music and stopped singing even in the shower for fear of facing that truth of wanting desperately to get on the road and stage.

As it happened, a band had returned a call I made a couple of months previous to my going to beauty college. The lady who phoned me asked if I was interested in joining her band and if I would be able to go back on the road. At first, I was very excited and almost said yes. Looking at my AJ as he contentedly slept on the floor by my feet, I went on to say I really would like to remain in the area so I could be home at night. She said that they already were planning on traveling. It really did cause me sadness to feel the need to decline the offer. So I would put my all into the new task I had committed to and only listen to classical music, which I had loved since discovery (in my teens). Oh, and German ballads and church choir music.

One day, Hans and I were going back up to Naps Valley for the day, and we stopped at a local deli in San Carlos to put together some snacks for the ride. While we were in the shop, the young lady behind the counter asked if I was his daughter, and without skipping a beat, Hans vehemently answered in his gruff German accent, "No, she's my girlfriend!" I immediately started laughing so hard, thinking that the look on the woman's face was so funny, as an angry Hans, without even looking up, growled out his response while going through the cheese bins. I must admit that there were more of this sort of reaction when it was obvious we were not father and daughter. I would always be so embarrassed. One day when my cousin Cathy Hatch came to visit our aunt and uncle next door, she came over to see me too. At one point during our visit, she said, "Can I ask you a personal question? You don't have to answer." I don't know how many times I was and would continue to be asked that exact question, and I knew exactly what the question was, and I had an answer for her too. I said, "Sure, you can ask, but you're right, I don't have to answer." Without looking at me, she asked me, "So what is it like being with someone older? I mean is he, you know, wrinkled and, well, you know..." Yup, that was the one I was expecting, but because she was a close cousin, I decided to let her in on a little secret. "No different than a younger man, and I was surprised to realize that myself. I too wondered whenever I saw a younger woman with an older man. To be honest, I am so drunk by the time he wants something I don't even see or care by that time. I just shut my eyes real tight and clamp my mouth shut!"

I knew what everyone thought anyway. I was getting weary of the jabs and comments and behind-my-back whispers, so then I realized in the end that love was not a real thing, at least in my life. Hell, even my own father did not love me, so how was anyone else going to? I decided that I would acquiesce to his request of marriage. Now Hans was overjoyed and became much nicer and softer-spoken. It was looking okay.

During my time living with Hans, things went smoothly as long as I did just as he commanded. I had been on a strict diet of low-calorie foods and drinks, but on the weekends and on special occasions, I would allow myself to eat what I wanted. That worked for me beautifully until one day (even after he agreed to that arrangement), only a week later, he made a lentil soup that was filled with all kinds of fattening ingredients. It was in the middle of the week, and I had been looking (drooling) for the diet pizza on my menu for the night. Well, when I told Hans to freeze it and I would have it on the weekend, he flipped out! He took the entire pot of soup and threw it down the toilet. Then he took the pie out of the refrigerator and threw it across the backyard, all the while screaming and yelling at me all kinds of mean things. I was so frightened I told him, fine, all right, I would do whatever he wanted, but to no avail.

From that day on, I decided to eat whatever I wanted, as well as whatever he made. Over the next year or so, I had gained more weight than I ever had. I then went on to bleach my hair out to as white as I could in an attempt to make myself look older. I was getting sick and tired of people commenting on how much younger I was.

I also wanted to see what it was like to not have guys hitting on me all the time and even chase me on the highways and local roads. One time, I was coming home from the shop I had just begun work at when a couple of men in a car had whistled at me along with some catcalls. Ignoring it, I drove on only to realize these individuals had followed me all the way to my exit. By the time I had noticed this, I knew I would have to do some fancy maneuvers in order to ditch them. Hans had just bought me a turbo-charged Pontiac Sunbird convertible, which had such a fast acceleration the front end would lift off the ground. I had wanted this feature for merging with California freeway entrances (you do not stop before merging). I was now doing some sudden turns, U-turns, and block weaving until I had truly lost them. That was the last bothersome situation I was to have for many years to come. I also noticed that many nice things come along with cuteness, like the extra mile someone (not just men) would go to give me a helping hand. No more lingering looks or heads turning, nor were there random conversations that had been a constant in my life happening anymore. Even babies were not inclined to keep eye contact with me. I never noticed these things until they were no more. I decided to live my life like an old German *hausfrau*. I spoke German, sang German songs, ate German cuisine, and danced German dances. Even when we built our house in La Honda, California, which was to be accomplished a year later, it was German style. This was especially evident in the kitchen with the eating corner, which was a booth built against the wall and a long table with chairs on the other side. German paintings adorned the walls as well as European-style furniture.

Before I made any real big decisions, I wanted to think many things through and weigh the options that were out there for me to choose. Looking back, I had thought of calling Chris Boutillette and asking him if he would come out to the West Coast so we could put a band together ourselves and I would be able to have AJ with me. I trusted Chris, and if I was with him, I could get happiness back in my life. What stopped me was when I honestly thought about it, I was afraid that I would hurt him if it were true that he liked me. I had to realize that if he did come out for me, it would not be because he felt like leaving life as he knew it to move out to the West Coast to play music; it would be because he really did like me. I loved and respected his friendship too much to do anything that could jeopardize any future relationship I might have with him. How did I know? My conscience would not allow me to be that cruel. So go figure. I decided that I should marry the old man.

By that time, Aunt Eunice and cousin/uncle Bud had moved back to the East Coast on Cape Cod. I had called her to see if she could help me arrange a winter Cape Cod wedding later that year. She was overjoyed. I picked December 1 for our wedding date because we were a May-December relationship. I felt that the first of December was the youngest part of the last month of the year, which represented me, and the month itself representing the oldest part of the year. Made sense to me, and it also made it possible for me to celebrate a New England Thanksgiving for the first time in years. Another important factor was that my aunt and uncle had introduced us, and the icing on the cake was that Aunt Eunice could do something she could never be a part of—a daughter's wedding. She had two sons and always talked of wanting a daughter. There was never a time when Aunt Eunice would not comment on that, even to this day. I was happy to have her act as my mother. Aunt Eunice was always my mom's closest sibling during her adult years. Aunt Eunice was always there if my mom needed her. I love her dearly and thank God for her.

Hans and I flew to Logan Airport in Boston, Massachusetts, rented a car, and then drove to South Yarmouth. Arriving a couple of days before the holiday gave us time to relax and then go to the town of Yarmouth Court for a wedding license. The look on the judge's face was just one more of the disapproving expressions we were to receive. For the next few days, we were to meet with the pastor of the Bass River Church for the mandatory discussions on the meaning of marriage. Finally, we were to enjoy a wonderful Thanksgiving.

The days following, we would be getting things ready. My mom and her husband and my youngest sister Heather (who was to be my bridesmaid) came up to the Cape from Spencer Mass.

We had our rehearsal and dinner at a wonderful local restaurant of Aunt Eunice's choosing, which went without a hitch. The next day was to be me (the bride) and my family. Hans was on his own. The next day, November 1, Heather spent the night with me at Aunt Eunice's while Mom and Mike stayed at a hotel. Hans went to the place where we were going to stay the night of our wedding. I wanted to keep to tradition as much as possible. I was not to see Hans for the entire day. I so enjoyed the time without him, instead having time and space with my family.

Now the day of the wedding. It was to be a candlelight service at 6 p.m. For the day, we had such a fun time getting ourselves ready. I for one was feeling rather ill. I felt lightheaded and warm and getting warmer by the hour. I managed to keep on going even so. We finally were to head out to the church. My uncle was to walk me down the aisle. It was coming together perfectly. When we arrived at the church, we went down to the finished basement where there were a couple of rooms to do our final preparations. It was fun to watch as my aunt flittered and fussed over all the fine details. I will forever love the memory of the fun I'm sure she had. She is such a perfectionist and saw to it in every way.

I put the final touches on my and my sister's makeup and hair. Finally, donning my wedding hat with a small veil, I was quite pleased with my choice in a Victorian-style dress from Jessica McClintock and the hat I found in a wedding boutique in San Francisco. Everything in bone white matched perfectly. The shoes and hose complemented the style exactly. I was not going to let my feeling rather ill and fever-ish keep me from enjoying what my Uncle George was to call "a nice party, at least." Not everyone thought that my choice of a husband was a good idea (I secretly was one of them).

When the time came for me to take the walk down the aisle and was being escorted by my beloved cousin/uncle Buddy, I was so enthralled with the ethereal atmosphere of this fabulous old New England church and the faux hanging candlelight fixtures, as well as real candles at the front of the church. My aunt would have made a great set designer with the ribbons and bows and flowers arranged in absolute perfection.

As we proceeded down the aisle, I knew there was no turning back. By the time we arrived at Hans's side, I just let myself enjoy the show.

Previously, I had requested that I have the reception in Christmas decoration. The place my aunt had chosen was an exclusive golf club banquet hall on the Bass River, so when we were being driven up the long winding tree-lined driveway, I was (by then really feverish) thinking we were driving into a fairy tale. The club did indeed put up all their Christmas decor as requested. I was not sure if they would, but they did, and it was spectacular.

The evening went beautifully with family and friends from both coasts, and we laughed and danced the night away. Even with my fever escalating by the hour and I becoming almost delirious, I still managed to enjoy myself. Due to my fever, I was flushed, giving me a nice glow, which incidentally gave the impression of the blush-ing bride. (Yeah, blushing all right—from embarrassment.) Before the evening ended, Hans and I sang "Silent Night" in German as requested by Aunt Eunice.

When all the festivities were over and everyone had taken their leave, Hans and I went on to the lovely old Cape Cod Hotel for the night. By the time we got to the room, I was beyond making any sense. I was burning up so badly and by now was shivering violently.

I took more drugs and passed out. The next day, I don't remember if we went to my mother's in Spencer or if we went straight to the airport.

Upon our return as a married couple, I was hoping the embarrassment of being called girlfriend would no longer be an issue. It was better to be called his wife even if the looks we would get were of shock and disbelief. I had thought that being his wife would cause him to be more willing to make himself dress better and do something about his teeth. I had asked if he would join a gym with me and we could work out together, but he never would. I went back to work at the salon in Foster City, and it was at that time I was given my first station as a full on hairstylist.

During that time, we were looking for a place to buy. We looked all over the Bay Area but found nothing that appealed to us. Finally, we decided to buy some property in La Honda and build to our specks. Hans was a brilliant carpenter, but he was a silent partner in a big construction company. He was the purchasing agent for Bay Area Construction out of San Carlos. He was so brilliant in what he did all the lumber companies were afraid of his skill in knowing exactly when to purchase; I never knew it was a minute-to-minute gamble on the cost of lumber. Just another interesting thing to learn, I thought.

Because Hans had hundreds of blueprints to choose from, he was able to pick some things from one and something else from another, and so it went until we had the house he thought would become the monument to his talents as a master builder.

I had found the property, and it was a nice-sized piece. We were only seven miles from the Pacific Ocean and about seventeen miles from Redwood City. La Honda used to be a hippie village back in the '60s and '70s, which also was the home of the acid king Timothy Leary among others. In the late '80s, La Honda began to get exclusive homes built as the old-timers were seeing a huge profit to be made in selling their little piece of land. One old hippie/biker hangout known to many bikers and hippies alike was Apple Jacks, right off Highway 84. People like Tracy Chapman and Neil Young have been known to hang out there on occasion.

It took about one year from start to occupancy—from getting all the proper permits to begin and commence, getting the property on Questa Real bladed and graded. With seventy-six pilings at thirty feet deep to anchor the basement so solidly due to the earthquake factor, to the hole being dug and the preparations for the concrete to be poured, to be followed by the walls all lifted into place, creating a skeleton of the floor plan to the first and top floors. Hans had hand-picked the entire crew from start to finish.

It was April by the time we gained occupancy and moved in. We spent the rest of the spring and summer months working on finishing the bathrooms and wall papering.

During that time, I had been trying to get pregnant. I always did believe I would have at least one child. By now, I was looking for my fulfillment in becoming a mother, hoping that would help Hans become kinder, more apt to keep himself in better shape and health (quit smoking), dress better, and get some new teeth. I honestly thought that a baby would make my life so much happier. I would put my whole heart and existence into being a mother. Having a family is an instinct so strong it can take over one's mind. I would find that getting pregnant was not happening, so I was forced to seek help. I went to a doctor at Kaiser Permanente that specialized in that area. I would undergo many tests and study my ovulation patterns, all to no avail. Month after month, I would pray for success, but not having any made for so much heartache.

The years went on, and most of my siblings were having babies right and left. Kim gave birth to three babies, all my sister-in-laws were having babies, and when my baby sister gave birth, three times, it was too much for me to bear—until one day when Hans and I had driven down to San Luis Obispo to meet up with my brothers for our West Coast contingency of the Putnam family reunion, which was going on in Winchester, New Hampshire. As we drove up to the campsite, five hours later, I would go through an epiphany so profound it would be the beginning of me getting my head in a whole new place—a place of peace and letting go. It happened so fast all it took was a mere second as I was getting out of the car and closing the door, all the while looking at two of my sisters-in-law as they both held onto their tiny new babies. I thought how wonderful for them to have handsome young husbands and beautiful babies as well. It was so excruciating that my mind and heart did that sudden flip of the switch. I no longer cared about having a baby, and all I wanted to do was get back into shape and look forward to a new beginning. I was tired of the relationship with a bossy, controlling, mean old man. Freedom became my goal.

Not only did I have this sudden epiphany of no longer needing to duplicate myself (or Hans), but I also lost a huge part of my appetite, therefore allowing me to begin my weight loss. That week was to have its other more noticeable drama, as every year there seems to be one. This year's drama was while we were down at the lake and we wanted to sit under a tree or bush, anything causing some shade. The only problem was that a family with a huge Rottweiler had taken the entire area. No one dared to go anywhere near that huge beast. I was glad to see that in this extremely hot weather that poor thing with his black coat did not have to be in the direct sun.

After getting settled into our spot, I decided it was high time I made my way to the water and take a dip with my family. I had such a good time cooling down and basking in the sun while we all sat on the raft anchored in the lake. I thought Hans would enjoy the cool water as well, so I proceeded to go back to shore and walk up the slight incline to where we had parked our things and Hans was just relaxing. As I was about halfway up to where Hans was, I saw out of the corner of my eye something coming very fast toward me. As I turned to look, I saw it was that Rottweiler coming full tilt and looking right at me. First, I thought he wanted to play, but I then could hear his growling, and his teeth were bared. As he got closer, I was thinking and hoping his tether would hold him back, but it was clear to see that there was plenty of more leash to go, enough to reach me and then some. A whirlwind of thoughts flew through my mind in a nanosecond—the first being the fact that this huge crazed dog was coming at me at a great speed with the jaws of death salivating to get a hold of my throat. I had less than a nanosecond to respond correctly. He would have gotten the back of my leg by the time I had turned around to run, so my only option was to make like a gymnast, punching off my feet, popping me straight up and over, enough to clear that death machine heading toward me. I managed to land a smidgen further than his leash reached. I looked up to jaws snapping and a growl that seemed to come from the depths of hell itself. While all this was going on, the owners were leisurely pulling the leash back, saying, "You invaded his space!" "Ahhh, excuse me!" I was shocked these idiots were blaming me for being in *his space*! "This is a public beach, and your dog was dozens of feet away from me! I was in no way in *his* space!" Next, I look up from my safe haven in the sand to see Hans standing in front of me, saying in his German accent, "He would not have done anything to you if you stood there!" I begged to differ, telling him he was not staring into the jaws of hell. He was out to kill! My brother Jim, who is a respiratory therapist, came running to me and took my pulse, because I was pretty shook up. As we walked down to the water's edge to cool off, my other brother Lorne suddenly said, "Oh my god! Hans just got bit!" Turning around, just in time to see him dropping to the ground, convulsing while my sister-in-law who is a nurse, holding his arm in the air. All the while, the dog owners were saying Hans instigated the dog. If ever there was anything decent I could say about the man, it would be that all animals loved him. I have seen agitated horses stop pawing the ground to quietly watch him as he walked by; others will attest to the fact that a water buffalo followed him back and forth in its water trough. Dogs, cats, birds, and I wager an aardvark would fall in love with Hans. So no, I did not buy that news for a second. Plus, Kathy said he did nothing that warranted getting half of his arm ripped off! The lifeguards called the ambulance and the police animal control, all the while Hans was still in convulsions and turning gray. Both Kathy and I think he had a small heart attack. He was taken to the hospital emergency by ambulance and went into surgery. All this time we were at the hospital, those crazy people were fighting with my family. We finally made it back to the campground and began to make the best with the rest of the day. Hans handled his situation with so much humor that we all began to lighten up.

The next evening when we were getting the campfire going, Hans decided to spray lighter fluid on the wood in order to help a little spark to ignite. Well, when the spray hit it, an arm of fire shot up the stream of lighter fluid, and when he dropped the can, the fire jumped onto Hans's foot, setting it on fire. It was like the Keystone Cops comedy of errors with everyone trying to throw water, salt, flour, all running in circles, banging into one another, when finally Jimmy threw sand on him, dousing the flames. So now he had a burnt foot and a torn-up arm. That story will be told in my family for generations to come.

When we got back up north, I continued with my decision to further my quest of losing weight and getting back into shape. I no longer was going to allow Hans to bully me into eating all the fat-loaded food he loved to make all the time. I was letting him stuff me like a Christmas goose for years because I was afraid of his temper and his yelling like a banshee whenever things did not go his way.

At some point during this time, my brother Lorne would move in with us to help with the finish work, which Lorne was a master at. Hans and Lorne would become pretty close, and they fought a lot like a father and son would, but Lorne would learn much from him in the end.

Throughout the years that I was married to Hans, I was to realize I was being treated as if I were his daughter. He would yell at me in public, and people would comment on how bossy and loud my father was, and my reply would be, "I know."

Hans was into cults and rituals, while I was a very active Christian, attending church regularly and singing in the Redwood City Baptist Church Choir. I would do some cantatas during the holidays. I was always trying to learn about God and Jesus. I studied the scriptures regularly, although that was nothing new. For my entire life, I searched for God's truth. The more Hans would try to insult me in my beliefs, the more I would get divine assistance in finding the perfect reply to every insult or lie he would throw at me.

One day, I found a booklet that was written (supposedly) by Henry Ford, and it was all anti-Semitic, with all kinds of neo-Nazi ravings. I took that filth and hid it well in case I needed proof of his hatred. Later I was to find more books on Satan and his demons with spells and chants. My sister Kim and I took them in a box, hiding them in the dirt basement. I did not want to be in the same rooms as those evil writings.

I went to work for Maggie, who was a friend of mine, and she had a shop in Half Moon Bay. I would work with her for a few months and all the while trying to get myself ready for anything that would help me to have a more meaningful life.

I also began getting chiropractic adjustments, and when my doctor told me how he ran every day on the beach (which was only seven miles away from my house), I made plans on running with him and his dog.

The first day I went out to San Gregorio Beach for a run. I waited for Kyle and his dog to show up, but when an hour and a half went by, I decided to go for the run myself. I could not run for very long, so I walked for a while, then ran for a second or two until after weeks of doing this routine, I was eventually able to run the entire way and back the length of the beach. I was losing weight and feeling really good about my progress.

I was beginning to feel the urge on getting back into playing music again. I began to go down to Apple Jack's whenever a band would be playing. It was while I was hanging out there one evening when I saw Tom. All it took was a second for me to become smitten when we both saw each other, and in that second, my first thought was, "It's him!" There was this feeling of "This is the one I have really been waiting for." In hindsight, I was just desperate for a tall hand-some well-built man to rescue me from wasting more of my life. I was sick of being with an old man with no teeth or hair. I wanted to live an American life and listen to American music, dancing American style and eating American food again. I would continue to hook up with Tom for a run around the wooded areas in La Honda or to see him at Apple Jack's and dance all evening with him. We began to meet up in the surrounding towns to spend afternoons together in a hotel or motel. Those were wonderful times for me, and once, Tom paid for a plane ticket to fly me to Reno, Nevada, where his brother lived with his wife and two boys. This was truly a risky thing to do. I got up early, and after Hans went to work, I took off for the airport and flew into Reno. Tom picked me up, and we went to a hotel and spent the better part of the day there, but I had to catch a mid-afternoon flight back to the Bay Area. I made it home before Hans did, and I was amazed at how I pulled it off. I was not going to try that again though and push the envelope too far too fast.

I am not proud of the choices I made during that time in my life, but I must tell them and hope my sorry mistakes will help someone else to think about some of the decisions they make.

One of the biggest things I have prayed for forgiveness about is the fact that Tom was married at the time we met. I knew he had not gotten separated and had not planned on a divorce, but I was selfish in the meanest way. All I cared about was that I had finally met someone that I could enjoy who shared many of the things I did. I was desperate and did not even think about how this man was a husband and a father with two little girls. Tom would tell me how he would look through binoculars for me across the pond from his house.

I thought that was so sweet and romantic. He would also tell me how he would drive past my house and try to see me through the windows. I should have thought that was creepy, but instead, I thought it was awesome that he liked me that much.

For the next few months, I would meet up with Tom in a variety of places. Sometimes we would take drives for the day. We would head south for Santa Cruz or north of San Francisco. So many things to do, and we took full advantage of the time we had.

I met all his siblings, and they liked me and I them. None of them cared for Tom's wife, saying she was this or that, and of course, I wanted to believe them. It helped me in justifying my falling for this married man. Oh, the lies we told our spouses for a lot of months. I know Tom never really intended on leaving his family, but we became too entwined to not have caused any upset. Hans began to suspect something was up, and so he had our phone tapped. Oh, when I think of the conversations we would have, completely unaware of someone listening in and taping them! Finally, the day came when Tom told me I was being followed; Hans must have put a tail on me. Tom was very savvy in being observant, and he spotted the dark-blue Buick making every turn I was. The second time he noticed the same car again following me was when he told me about it. Oh man, I was so happy to just look at Tom that I never gave it a thought that I would be followed. When I think about it, I can't believe this character used such an obvious vehicle for Tom to recognize.

Finally, Hans asked me who Tom was, and the scenario could not have played out more typical. Every movie or novel had to have had the same dialogue. It was then that I was informed of the tape and that he had it delivered to Tom's wife; it was left in an envelope on their doorstep. All life turned upside down then, and a whirlwind of fighting and accusations, name-calling, and everything else a novel would have in it was all of our lives after that.

Hans tried to get me to go to a counselor, but I told him it would do no good because I knew what my issues were in our marriage. I was not happy for a very long time, and I knew I could never be happy with an old man, but I did not want to hurt his feelings by telling him that, so I just omitted saying any of it.

Hans would bring home books on how it is okay to enjoy being intimate (he just could not see himself), and I told him I would never be able to like being intimate with him. I had by now decided that I needed to tell him the absolute truth about how repulsive he was to me. I wanted out of his life.

Tom and his family had gotten to the point of no return, and they divorced. I moved out of La Honda and down to Atherton to a small one-bedroom apartment. I brought my three birds (a Catalina Macaw, an umbrella cockatoo, and a cockatiel), plus Ajax, who was now very old. It was a very traumatic time in my life, for I was truly scared. I just had to do it. I had been sad and miserable for too many years. Never knowing if there was a bead on my or Tom's back for the next couple of years was nerve-wracking to say the least.

During that time, I would either stay in Tom's apartment in Redwood City, or he would stay with me until the time we decided to move in together. Finding a cute house on Magdalena Avenue in Menlo Park, we moved in, and I was starting to feel better having what I had hoped was the true beginning of my new life with the man of my dreams. It was then that the red flags were beginning to become more and more vibrant. Tom had begun to do to me the same things he had done to his wife. Almost to the letter, he would repeat the actions of driving past a certain house in a specific neighborhood, taking me with him as he did these drive-bys, I'm sure not giving it a second thought whether I was savvy to what he was up to. He would take weekend trips to stay in Reno with his brother or somewhere else, telling me some bogus story or other.

I could not stop myself in loving him and forgiving all those times he was obviously hanging out with other women. It would not be long when we would be moving to Hawaii. Tom and his brother, along with his family, had planned the move, so of course, I was on board myself. Where we would move to just happened to be where I had spent time with my sister Kim, who had lived on Oahu for many years before leaving only the year before. My Macaw would be returning with me to where he originally came from and to the same vet. I couldn't get out of California fast enough.

CHAPTER 23

I got a job at the Windward Mall in Kaneohe on the island of Oahu in a Regis hair salon.

I was to meet the best friend of my life there. Ingvild Garmo was from Norway, and we became best friends almost immediately. Ingvild is back in Norway now and married to Petter Bergeise, a wonderful, kind, and very talented man.

Ingvild Garmo, everyone should experience a friend such as her. The first time I saw this intriguing lady, I felt a bond straight away. I think we both connected in that first moment. My first impression was of how she made me think of a fairy pixie elf. Being of average height and not a tiny person was the striking part. I knew this individual was full of mischief yet possessing an ancient wisdom. While I was speaking with the woman I was being interviewed by, she swung a quick look at me, and in that instant, I saw the twinkle of a friend. Being from Norway, Ingvild has the face and similar accent to one of the most talented beautiful actresses, Swedish-born Ingrid Bergman. Both possessed the classic chiseled Nordic features and gorgeous skin. I would get the job and begin work the next week. Ingvild was one of the master stylists there, and as we became close in our friendship, she would teach me many of her skills, albeit I could never duplicate her work. Yet she never gave up on me. Ingvild was married to a sergeant in the Marine Corp when I first met her, and they shared an apartment with Sergeant Michael "Mac" McDonald. We became such good friends as I'd not known before.

After getting divorced, Ingvild would eventually need to return to Norway, much to our grief, but I knew in my heart she would return. I was right. Mac went after her, and they returned to Hawaii together. Mac and Ingvild would get married, but to qualify for a green card, they had to prove themselves truly a couple. I, among others, was to write a letter of why and how we knew the couple to be legit and the relationship was true. Things were going well until her dad passed away, and again, my friend would have to fly back to her homeland. Ingvild knew that delegating her clients to the stylists would be satisfactory to her picky people. We all were afraid she would be gone a long time, as most of the folks only cared about their hair being done the Ingvild way. Upon hearing of Ingvild's father passing away and that she would be leaving for a few weeks, one lady's could only whine, "But she has to do my hair!" I was speechless with shock. The next thing I had to tell her was that it would be me. Oh heaven smiled on me; she was okay with that, and we went on to become a good match-up. A funny thing about this lady is she did care; it was just some people panic. Ingvild would return about a month later, and life went back to normal. Now this lady would be able to alternate between us. She was always covered. We even at times went to her house on some special occasions.

One day, we got a phone call from her husband telling us Ruthie had passed away from a reaction to an aspirin she took for a headache, but because she had severe asthma, the brand of aspirin was a deadly combo to her other medications. Ingvild and I were heartbroken over this dear friend's sudden passing. The two of us would go to her funeral, of course, and as we sat in the Buddhists temple for her service, we could not keep from weeping and sniffling—that is until the monk began the ceremony. Neither one of us had any idea of how that was to play out, but it was not long before we were trying to keep from laughing! We did not want to appear rude, but when the monk began to throw giant feathers up in the air as if they were the soul of Ruthie (we assumed), Ingvild and I were no longer feeling such a loss, instead we felt a lightness and carefree. I have to admit being ignorant of such proceedings and feeling ridiculous as we both had to work at keeping a stoic face. We were bursting inside. We think about Ruthie and her husband and daughter with love and affection even still. We will always remember.

Mac, Ingvild, and I were heading to a wrap party being held at Duke's in Waikiki for the *90210* episode I had worked on for the last two days. While driving down the Pali Highway, Mac broke the news that they were having a baby. I was shocked as that was not in their plans. Ingvild was adamant in that she did not want any, yet here I found out that had changed. Because they were happy, so was I.

Over the months, I witnessed Ingvild's belly growing, yet other than quitting smoking and drinking, her activities never altered. Well, before she got too big, she still played softball. I will forever call her Inger-ville in the manner the announcer for the games had done whenever I have something funny to share with her.

On the months trolled, and bigger she got. Mac would be away on TDY for a couple of months, so Ingvild and I would hang out and watch TV (while I imbibed). One evening during her later months, we would find ourselves doing the polka all around the rec room. Laughing and sweating from the exertion of the way polka is really danced, I was amazed at how agile and energetic she still was.

It was around this time I finally broke it off with Tom. That meant I had to get a roommate. I was okay with that, and I continued on with my life. Ingvild and Mac were heading off to a work-pleasure trip on Maui so asked me to stay in their home on base so I could take care of the animals. My first night was quite eventful. As I had begun to feed the critters, I had to go outside for something, but unbeknownst to me, the door automatically locked! There I was only in my underwear. I was a hair's breadth of panic. I had no key, and there was no way to get in through the windows either. I did not want to be picked up by the base police while only in my undies. I suddenly remembered her neighbor Kim and ran over to her house and banged on her door, waking that household. She did think it was a funny scene, and she had me safely back in the house where I finished feeding the dogs, bird, and Guinea pigs.

One day Ingvild would come to me with an idea that we needed to leave Regis and go work for ourselves. It was a scary venture to contemplate, but she and Mac convinced me I could do it too. I gritted my teeth and ventured into this new territory. Being self-employed meant many things had to be done. I was to have one of my breakdowns and holed up in my townhouse for many days where I would watch my feel-good movie *It's a Wonderful Life* with Jimmy Stewart. I watched that movie over and over and over while I made out notices of my move from Regis to Salon Mirabella. If it were not for the intense faith my dear friend had in my ability to be successful in this venture, I would never have attempted such an endeavor.

Returning early from a date with a young man I had met the week before, I went to hang out with Ingvild and Mac. I would have a few drinks while there, enough to make me sleepy. I was to wake up with a chunk of tinfoil in my hair! Guiding me to the bathroom sink, I let both of those guys wash out whatever was in that chunk of foil. After shampooing and conditioning then looking in the mirror, I saw a three-inch-wide swath of bright-orange hair! Such a contrast to my light blonde! Thing is that I liked it. I kept it that way for months, touching it up as needed.

Sometime later, Mac would get orders to ship out for a tour. Ingvild and I would spend much time trying not to get into trouble. With Ingvild, it was easy to do. So full of harmless yet hilarious mischief she was and still is. Finally, Mac returned from tour of duty. I would be juggling my acting and salon job as life rolled onward. I had quit hanging out with that young man mentioned earlier, making my life less complicated. Ingvild had a few weeks to go before her due date, so while I was sitting with some friends down at the Aloha Tower Market Place at Fat Tuesday's, someone came over to me, saying my agent Margret Dovasolla and the other agents were searching for me. I was so amazed at that, and I immediately called to find out Ingvild had gone into labor prematurely and was looking for me. Wow! That was a surprise.

Everyone took the birth of a baby so seriously on the island as it is such a blessed occasion, culminating in what locals have a baby luau on the first birthday. The baby boy Erik came into the world at a whopping four pounds, but because he was so strong, he was able to go home a couple of days later. Upon placing this tiny new bundle in my arms, Ingvild reminds me of how I burst out in tears, not because I could not have one but because it scared me to be responsible for not dropping him.

For the next two years, I would be so amazed at this little boy—smart, athletic, and so strong. He was my little love. Ingvild, Mac, and Erik would become my roommates, and that was a bunch of hilarious episodes worthy of a book in itself!

I will never forget the time when I was home with Erik while Mac was out to sea and Ingvild had gone out with some friends. She came home at about four in the morning, banging on the door. While still in a dream state and Erik sound asleep next to me, I crept up the stairs to see what the commotion was about. Opening the door, who do I see standing there *naked* was my friend, and all she had of her clothing was a pair of shoes in her hand, and she laughing. I had to laugh as well while she explained to me that all the gang had gone skinny-dipping in the ocean and she did not remember where she left her clothes. At least she had her shoes in hand. I think later she recalled her clothes were in her friend's car.

It would be a couple of years later when Ingvild, along with Scarlette Dunn, a manicurist, would go into business for themselves, inviting me to come rent a station from them. I thought that would be the best thing for me, working right there next to my best friend. We would do fairly well as we built up our clientele, but it would be only a couple of years of this before Ingvild and Mac decided to move back to Norway. I was crushed. On the day they were to leave for the airport, I accompanied them to wait for the plane. It was truly a very sad day for me, as I knew they would not be back. This time it was for good. It was hard saying good-bye to the friend who had taught me to believe in myself. I would not hear from her for the remainder of my time in Hawaii. It would be a couple more years before I was to leave the island myself.

Looking back to Tom, there are many things I have to say I am grateful to him for, but it was the deceit and hurt he caused me that keep me from feeling any warm fuzzes toward him. I have forgiven him in my heart, but I don't ever want to see, know, or hear of anything concerning him.

Another thing that keeps me in forgiveness is that I really did not deserve better treatment. What I did to Rebecca, Anna, Marie, and Monica was despicable to say the least, and in hindsight, I feel happy to know I was put through the exact same thing I put her through. I am actually happy for her. She is free of his lying, cheating, crusty butt and has now moved onto someone more deserving, although I will spend my life saying I'm sorry to her and the girls even if they don't hear me. I got my just desserts.

Over the years we first got to Oahu, Tom got a job on the American Hawaii Cruises as an able-bodied seaman even though he was a licensed third mate. He managed to scope out the layout of the vessel and its passengers. He was able to sniff around, keeping to the background, literally videotaping whatever attractive women he saw. Planning. Planning on his moves when he finally did get the call to third mate, which came in a few short months. Now that he was an officer on the cruise liner, he was able to interact with the passengers. His plan was coming to fruition.

During his off-time between rotations, after taking an exclusive vacation with some woman he met on the ship, he would go on to upgrade his seaman ranking through the training school for mariners in Dania, Florida. He would do this every time he was off the ship, going from ABs all the way up to captains and harbor pilots. During these times, he was not only going after all the rich women that fancied him, but any woman he took a shine to, including fellow employees. I would have my deep-down woman's intuition but not to the degree of what was truly happening. I was considered his fiancée by the captain and the crew, as the officers had to be wholesome and honest. He treated me very nicely (so I thought) and never made any acts, plays toward anyone while I was onboard, which was only Saturday morning to about four in the afternoon.

Twice I was allowed to sail for the week with him. Tom had told me it was only when the captain said it was all right. Later I discovered I could have sailed with him as many times and for as long as we wanted; I know now why he lied. I would have put a whammy on his anthill of trolling for the perfect rich lady to seduce.

But during that time, I convinced myself life was normal. At that time, my family and I were to get the most magnificent gift of our lives. The baby sister that my mother had given up all those years ago had now been found! It was such an emotional time for all of us. I could not wait to meet her.

CHAPTER 24

Sheila, who had been renamed Ellen, would be coming out to stay with me for a week, and I was beyond excited. Everyone was asking how I felt about meeting her for the first time. I knew I was beyond over the moon, but I did not know if it would be like meeting a new friend or if it would feel like meeting an actual blood relative, like a cousin maybe. I did not know.

The day I was to pick her up from the airport, Tom (still in his second mate's uniform, which was quite impressive) and I waited at the gate she was to come through. As people were streaming by, I watched and waited, holding the two leis (which is the tradition in Hawaii) to put on her as she came out. Feeling calm and nervous at the same time, I laser-focused on each and every face exiting the plane. For the longest time, I saw no one looking like the photograph I had to go on. Finally, as the last few were passing us, I was getting worried that she had missed her flight when all of a sudden this tiny woman appeared. I noticed right away she held her head the exact same way that her father did. What finally convinced me that this was my baby sister was the light that seemed to frame her eyes. Those were her brother Lorne's eyes! I worked my way over to her, and suddenly unable to say anything (as I was so choked up), I pulled her into my arms, putting my hands behind her head, holding her tightly to me. I began to sob as I had never done before. All I could manage to say was, "I have waited thirty-two years for this moment just to hold you! And you're not much bigger than you were when I saw you through that window so many years ago." My family was complete now. I am amazed at the fact that you can tell when someone is a part of your family. It's in the DNA. Ellen is truly our sister, and we will never let her go. Never.

After the wonderful time with Ellen and life had gone back to the norm, it would take Tom about two years to gigolo his way to the one most desirable and wealthiest woman. It was then that he began to get more distant and strange-acting. He would come home wearing clothes and colors he hated, as well as styling himself in a completely different manner than he ever had done before. Not only that, but when I would now be on the ship with him, he would not be as attentive or nice anymore. I had seen him on the bridge at night with his binoculars, telling me he was keeping an eye on one of the crew members (of course a woman) as she was running in the dark of the area we were docked at and that he did not think it safe, but she went anyway. Yeah, right, I bought that. Did he really think I had forgotten how he had done that with me?

The next year, he was in full-blown doing whatever whenever he wanted without regard not only for me but for his daughters either. He would forfeit precious time with them to be with these women, but when it came to the one he really wanted, he just went full steam ahead to achieve his goal. Finally, his new woman was tired of waiting for him to leave me and gave him an ultimatum, so when he made his first attempt to break off with me, I was devastated. I had never had this happen to me before. I tried to ignore the signs, only to come to the realization that my intuition was spot-on.

We would go through these breakups a few more times with him coming back, saying he could not leave me because he loved me and if it were not for the wealth of this other woman, he would not be doing this to us. It would take about six more months for Tom to finally make up his mind and choose. I should have told him to get away from me, but he was a bad habit, and I could not break it. I would see him again as he drove up to Kaneohe to our townhouse to see me. He drove up in a beautiful gold Jaguar Convertible, my favorite car. He gave me the keys and told me I could drive it. So like an idiot, I did and quite enjoyed it. I knew it was his rich woman paying for it, and I loved that Tom was screwing with her as well. Later that evening, he went off to the downstairs to make a call to her, and when I walked in on him as he was sweet-talking to her, I lost it and screamed at him to get out! He did, but not quietly, as he called me some of the foulest names, just like he had done to Rebecca when she screamed at him while seeing me. Full circle. Now it was my turn.

Tom left to take the ship up to Portland, Oregon, for dry dock, where it was to undergo a complete refurbishing. This was going to be for a few months. All during this time, I had the feeling he was with someone, but I chose to put the feelings away. When he came back to the island, I noticed he had telltale signs of the other woman. I knew then that she had spent the time there with him. It was while I was spending the day with him when he decided he was going to leave the phone off the hook. I immediately knew why. I called him on that move, and he had to admit to the truth. He had been with her, and she brought her teenage son out there to meet him. So that is when I knew we were done. I picked up my things and just walked out and off the ship and drove back home. I was so hurt, angry, disillusioned, and so very sad.

Tom left to sail about a week later, and I would begin to bring his things over to his brother's house. Oh, how I wanted to rip his tailored uniforms and put them in a garbage bag full of dog poop, but I was not going to sink to the classless level he will never crawl out of.

It was a few weeks later that Tom would call me and say he really missed me and needed to be with me. He said he told Cindy (plah!) he really wanted to come back to me. I believed him. I wanted to believe him.

He was due home in about a week and gave me his flight information for me to pick him up at Honolulu at 9 a.m. the following Saturday. I went shopping to fill the refrigerator and did all the things ladies do to make sure we look ravishing when we pick up our men whom we have not seen in a long time. I was looking to make sure he would be pleased with his decision to come back to me.

Leading up to Saturday, I was in such good spirits. I thought I had won, until that Saturday when I was all dressed and ready to pick him up in the next couple of hours that I got the phone call that he did not board the plane because *she* wanted to try to work things out with him and he felt he owed her that. He said he was going to catch a flight out of Texas or somewhere out that way. I told him in no uncertain terms that I was done. He could stay with her. She could have him. I was now definitely done, done, done. I told him to never ever call me or come by again.

About a week later, I was really truly over him, and it felt good. The millstone was finally off my neck. I was free from the agony of him. I no longer cared. Cindy could have him. One day, I got a letter telling me how sorry he was, and if I could change my mind and let him see me and be with her as well, he would love it. I was laughing at the absurdity! No way would I even honor him with a reply. What an arrogant bastard. Oh yeah, Cindy could have him, and he could enjoy her money, because that was what he really wanted. Ha! She did not have to wait long because I know the phone call I got a few weeks later (under a ruse of something having to do with his daughter's dentist) was her phone number! I wanted to mess with that person for a little, but I decided it might bring that creep back into my life for more confrontations, so I decided to just let her have a taste of life with that liar and have done with that part of what was now my past. I moved on quite nicely and never looked back.

I had a brief interlude with a younger man who looked like one of the models from a harlequin romance novel. He had the long flowing hair and chiseled jawline as well as a buff body. He was not long for my life; he had too many mental issues. I wished him well and said adios.

I would have more roommates over the next few months, mostly Marines from the Marine Corps base down the road. One evening, while in my master acting class, our teacher asked if any of us wanted to take kickboxing lessons with a student of his that was coming back to the island from LA and was signing people up for them. I was a huge boxing fan, thinking it would be a great exercise and a way to understand the skill.

The evening, when I met Hugh, I thought he must be so full of himself as he was quite handsome, tall, strong, and had the deepest dark-brown eyes and black hair. So this would be my kickboxing instructor. Hmmmm.

At the end of the class, we were introduced, and from there, we began to talk boxing. I was happy to learn I now had a comrade in enjoying the sport with. My fellow actor Jean Simon also signed up for his classes. It was not long before the three of us became a trio of pals.

Eventually, he would come stay with me. I had given him his own room in the hopes that we would eventually develop our relationship further. For four years, we would go on like this, and even my roommates would tell me to get rid of him as he was just using me. One roommate I had went so far as to even ask him what his intentions were about me, and his reply was that he was not interested in me for a relationship. Her next question put to him was, "Do you think one day you will wake up and realize you wanted to be with her?" His reply was an emphatic "No! I would know by now if she was the one." I was later informed of this little conversation and was highly advised to tell him to go find another place to live. It seemed no one understood; no one knew as I did that he would eventually come to realize that we should be together.

Hugh's mom was to come out for a visit and stay with us for the Thanksgiving week. We had a wonderful time together. His mom really liked me, and I her. We would talk about her son's seeming lack of interest in wanting me as his other half. Andrea and I would laugh and scheme all in a fun way how to win his affection. By the time she left, we were still in the same place as when we started. Oh well, I was willing to wait. I knew he would one day realize we were meant to be.

Jean Simon, Hugh, and I were like the three musketeers. Jean and I were like competing sisters, and we were still good friends to this day.

There were many times I suspected I was being a blind fool and chose to cast a blind eye in that direction. I would say a prayer to the Almighty God every night, asking for some kind of sign as to whether I was wasting my time or should I hang on. I would not see anything that would indicate either way, so I kept going as usual. That is until one day I decided to go see the most popular psychic on the island. I know it said in the scriptures (which I tried to live my life by) we should not seek the counsel of soothsayers, numerologists, or live by astrology, but I prayed about getting a sign that this particular woman would be all right. When I did not receive any kind of feeling or image that would indicate wrongness in seeking her out, I was excited to think that it would be fine to go. When I saw a friend whom I believed to be a New Age Christian, I couldn't wait to tell her about my decision to see Von for a reading, even if it meant waiting all day long for someone to cancel. No sooner had I told her this, she went straight into telling me what I had already known. Her words were the exact same words I had used on others who wanted to seek out psychics or any of that stuff. I was so amazed at her reaction that I knew beyond a shadow of a doubt that this was from the Almighty himself! Wow! This is what I meant that Jehovah will step in if he is permitted to. My free will was to seek his counsel first. I never did go see Von. I knew in time the truth would be revealed. I was willing to wait.

So on I went for a few more months, waiting and looking for something to change. I had his mom on my side, which included his dad. I could not get a better support system. All the while, the people around me on the island wanted me to get him out of my life.

Finally, I put a prayer up to the Almighty God to please give me something to let me know if I should keep patience up. I prayed that it would not be too hurtful.

CHAPTER 25

It was not even two weeks after that prayer when that exact situation happened. It was nothing short of a miracle of how things worked out. I had told him he would have to find another place to live, seeing as he found it fine to lie to me and think I should not care. He knew how I felt about him but felt he had every right to take advantage of my love for him and deny to everyone we knew that he cared not a whit for me and how I waited all those past four years. They all thought I was crazy for hanging on. Well, when my prayer was answered to the letter, I knew there was no doubt left as to what my next move had to be. I had found out he had been seeing a twenty-three-year-old woman. It was then I realized it was time for him to go. He wrote me a letter telling me that he could not love me the way I needed to be. I was not happy—no, not by a long shot—but I will never grovel for any man. I told him he could stay long enough to find another place to move to.

After a few weeks, he stopped looking and just settled in thinking I was not going to make him move. In the corner of my heart, I thought he might be reconsidering his feelings, but he made no move to show me anything but indifference.

Shortly after my taxes were due my accountant had been able to make it, so I owed nothing when I thought I was going to owe over two thousand dollars. So I was crying with relief. After I got my emotions under control, I decided to use that money to take a much-needed vacation. As I was contemplating on where to go, I had the thought that if I went back to visit my mom I would give Chris Boutillette a call and see what he had been up to and if he was still single.

I made a reservation for the 6th through the 14th of May to go to Boston, Massachusetts, where my mom and sister Kim picked me up. It was so wonderful to see them and know that I would be able to spend some quality time with my mom.

A couple of days later, I had a surprise phone call from Chris. I was amazed to hear his voice, especially as I was going to call him within the next few days, but he beat me to it. My former sister-in-law (whom I still consider a sister) told him I was going to be in town. We made a date to spend a day at Martha's Vineyard. That was all it took to get me to say yes to an all-day affair. I had never been to Martha's Vineyard, and it was something I had told all of my friends in Oahu I was planning on doing, so yeah, I jumped on that. I feel that was sort of miraculous in itself. After talking to him, I felt that the time was right to rediscover our feelings for each other. I had always felt at peace with Chris and was now open for anything a future with him might hold.

We had not seen each other for at least eighteen years but had talked on the phone now and then throughout that time. Now we were going to see each other on an equal playing field, both of our hearts finally in the same place.

When the day came for him to pick me up in the morning early, he was late. I wondered if he forgot, but when he drove up in his black Ford 150 pickup, I felt really excited to see him. When I opened the door and we looked at each other, it was such a wonderful feeling. I knew I was going to be all right with him. His whole countenance was of strength and self-assuredness. That was something I had not seen in a man in a very long time.

It was so cool how we had to take a ferry out to the island. We spent the day walking around the town and dined in a local cafe (I was bummed that town was dry), but no worries, I was enjoying myself and Chris's awesome company, and he was a great tour guide.

We made the final ferry back to the mainland, and by the time we got close home, it was nearly midnight. Chris asked if I wanted to see his house, and realizing how late it was, I thought I might as well stay over till morning and he could take me back to my mom's.

As he pulled into the driveway, I noticed we did not go to where he used to live in Webster, but where he grew up in Oxford. I was also surprised to see there was a cabin-type house attached to the original house that I remembered as a younger person. Oxford always was a town I felt a comfort in.

Chris walked me in the house, and as I stepped in it, I felt like the house was giving me a hug with the honey-colored pinewood that had such a wonderful warmth from the lights. We sat on the couch and shared some wine. Finally, we decided to go to bed. It was all she wrote. I knew this was where I should be. I had slept with him many times in the past but only once before on an intimate level. This would be the second. It felt so good to be really loved and feel cherished. This is what I had been missing all my life. I was going to enjoy his company for a long time to come.

My mom was a little miffed for not coming home, but she knew I was with Chris, so she wasn't really worried.

The next day, Mom and I went to visit her sisters on the Cape. We planned on spending three days there. By the end of the first day, I was missing Chris so much that I could not wait to head back. I was actually very happy when my mom said she wanted to head home sooner than planned. So off we drove back to Spencer. On the way back, I called Chris to see if he wanted to come over that evening, as I missed him.

On the eve of heading back to Hawaii, Chris had invited my mom and me to the movies. Somewhere along the line, my mom bailed, so we decided to just have a BBQ at his house alone. We went to the market and picked up the fixings, and when we got back to his house, he fired up the grill and put the vegetables on the stove. While we waited for the food to cook, Chris put his arms around me and proceeded to ask me to marry him. I began to shake, and the tears burst out of my eyes, as I knew deep in my heart that I was going to say yes. I wanted to say yes immediately, but I felt it was not the right time. I needed a few days to absorb the idea to know my feelings at that moment were true and would hold true for the rest our lives, not to mention the horrifying thought of leaving my beloved islands and so much more to consider.

I decided to enjoy the rest of the evening sharing the beautiful feelings we had. Then we realized the broccoli was burned and the chicken fell through the grill! It was one of the best meals I ever had.

Chris took me to the airport, and my mom came along to see me off. It wasn't until I was climbing out of the truck that I told my mother Chris asked me to marry him. My mom's eyes popped wide open, and she whispered, "Say yes." I nodded to her that I probably would.

As I left my bags with the outside concierge, Mom watched me, and as they drove away, I almost cried.

During the entire flight, I was literally in the clouds. I knew exactly what I had to do, and that was to see how Hugh reacted after my being gone for two weeks. Did he miss me? Would he say he realized how much I meant to him? Did he have deeper feelings for me than he ever realized? I really did not expect him to, but I needed to have 100 percent closure to my feelings for him. There had to be no doubts.

It didn't take me long to make up my mind. The fact that Hugh showed up half an hour late to meet me at the baggage claim would be the first sign. The second would be that when he did arrive, he smiled but just stood there with his arms crossed as per usual, and this would be the first time I did not rush over to him. I knew for sure I did not want him either, not any more. It felt amazing to realize the gift Jehovah had given me, and I was going to seize the wonderful opportunity that had presented itself. I called Chris that evening to tell him yes. I could say yes, yes, yes!

I had already been studying with a friend from the Kailua Kingdom Hall in learning what the Bible actually is teaching us. I had the heart and desire to learn more than I was on my own. I pray and have prayed to the Almighty God, creator of heaven and earth, for knowledge in his ways and my desire in seeking him. He sent Judy to me.

Because I had asked him to lead me to where I should be, when I had gotten together with Chris, I knew it was divine intervention that moved all situations to pave the way. I just had to trust his guidance in knowing that being with Chris was where my life would be fulfilled. I knew he would never hurt me or lie to me. Now I know where those gut feelings had come from. It was nothing short of a miracle that Chris was still single and never had any children and that he still wanted me!

For the next few weeks, I was "glowing," according to all of my friends. That is something I have never been told before, and I truly felt like I was. Chris and I set our wedding date for the 10th of August that year, which was 2002. The plans we were making were so much fun. It felt very different from my other past two marriages. This was the real thing. It gave me the feeling that this was the only one. I had known Chris longer than anybody I had ever been with in my life; I guess I had to learn the true meaning of love before I was able to commit the rest of my life.

Chris and I would talk on the phone every day, planning for our future. I did not want my happiness to be stomped on by anyone who was anti-marriage, so I did not mention it to Hugh, whom I knew would ruin my joy. But I did tell him I was going back to New England for a couple weeks in August and asked if he could take care of my little miniature pinscher Bruiser. Of course, he said he would. Bruiser was more his than mine, because all the while I was working, Hugh was home with him.

Days had passed, and life went on smoothly as I began to tell clients and friends about my upcoming nuptials. There was not one person who thought I was making a mistake, even Jean, who, if anyone, would know if it was the wrong thing to do. Her belief was that Hugh would be glad to be free of the entanglement of our lives. We were sure he would breathe a sigh of relief, knowing he could do as he pleased without hurting me.

The time came to tell him. We were watching a boxing match on TV, and I lying at the foot of the bed while he sat at the top (that was where we always watched boxing matches so as not to bother my roommate). Well, when I went to lean back and put my arm behind my head in absolute innocence, my fingers accidentally brushed his thigh (he always wore shorts). I, trying being funny, wiggled my fingers, at which point he said, "Quit it, or I'll spray you like I do Bruiser when he is misbehaving!" Continuing the jest, I wiggled my fingers again, at which point I got a sharp spray of cold water on the top of my head and Hugh telling me to stop or he'd do it again. Okay, let's see if he could really be so rude. Well, he was indeed and commenced spraying that single stream right at the top of my head, at which point I got really angry. I was finished with his taking advantage of my good nature and decided I did not care one hoot anymore as to how he might feel about my getting married. As a matter of fact, I thought he would be ever so pleased to know he would not be plagued with my affections anymore. Turning to look at him, I said, "You'll be glad to know that you will not have to worry about me messing with you anymore because I am getting married to a longtime dear friend and love of mine." I was shocked at how he just turned around and went into his room and closed the door.

I said through the door that he did not have to worry about moving right now as I had no intention of leaving the island for quite a while—at least until the next year. No reply. I said I knew how he hated the institution of marriage and that was his right, but I would appreciate his accepting my choices. Still no answer, so I just said when he was ready to talk about his attitude toward my decision, I would be happy to set this mind at ease.

I decided to just leave him alone for the time being. I had not realized how anti-marriage he was to be having this kind of reaction. I went back into my room and got ready for bed. A couple of hours later, I heard him rattling around between the bathroom and his room, but I didn't think too much of it.

The next morning when I went into the bathroom, I noticed signs of his anger with all kinds of aspirins and sleeping aid wrappers strewn all over the counter. I was blown away at his reaction to my news.

I called Chris and explained to him what was going on. As a man, he immediately knew what was going on in Hugh's head. I was sure he was wrong. Then I called Jean, and she was thinking like me in the fact that he was just so anti-marriage, therefore not wanting to see his dear friend go through with this dastardly deed!

As the days wore on, I was to discover that Chris was right; Hugh suddenly realized (or thought) that he loved me and did not want me to leave and marry someone else. He went out and bought an engagement ring, which he had engraved, and took me out to dinner one evening at the Turtle Bay Resort. Our table was right in front of the stage, and in full view of everyone, he got down on his knees and proposed to me while handing me the ring. Of course, the crowd and the band just went silly, clapping and ooing and ahhhing. I know the band had something to say, but I cannot remember what. I was so taken off guard, not to mention I did not want to embarrass him by saying no in front of everyone, so I just smiled and tried to remain calm. Then he tried to get me to dance, but I could not. I did not feel like having so many eyes on just the two of us. All the while, I thought about all those past years I had prayed for him to want me, never even daring to dream he would ask me to marry him! He went on to tell me he had told his parents of his plan. I knew they would be happy with his decision. Only now it was too late.

If it were not my faith and constant prayer, I would not have been able to see clearly into my own heart. I probably would have given in solely because I had wanted him to feel this way for so long. In light of all this, I was thoroughly confused and a wee bit nervous as to what would happen next. How do I tell him you don't gamble with someone's heart, taking advantage of the kindness and generosity given over the years?

Chris and I had set a date for me to tie things up and get back to the mainland. We planned the wedding for August 10, but in light of the recent developments, I suddenly had only a month to wrap things up in Oahu. Chris sent my mom to come help me. That was a blessing. With all that had to be done in less than thirty days, I had great anxiety. There was no time to realize I was leaving for good. I was having a hard time, so my mother being there was all that kept me sane and focused. When it finally hit me that I was leaving for real, I collapsed to the floor. If it weren't for my mom's strength, I might not have gone through with the move. My mom held me up in more ways than one.

Finally, everything was in place, and it was the day to leave. I will never forget driving off and waving good-bye to my friends and taking that last drive down to the Honolulu International Airport.

The next day and a half were spent traveling, my mom, my cockatiel, and me. When we arrived at the airport in Hartford, Connecticut, Chris was there to meet us. There he stood at the bottom of the escalator, holding a bouquet of beautiful American beauty roses. He was a sight for sore eyes after the last month I had. Looking at him standing there, I knew I had not made a mistake. I could finally trust someone. I could feel happy and proud to walk hand in hand with this man for the rest of my life.

After returning home, I enjoyed a day with Kim as she showed me around the quaint little towns and some historical houses that looked like they could have been made by a wedding cake decorator. Afterward, we headed back to Kim's house in Putnam, Connecticut, and ordered my perfect cake. It was beautiful. On the morning of the wedding, Kim picked it up and, with the help of Aunt Eunice Putnam, got it all set up and ready for the reception.

The walk down the rice paper was a comedy in itself. As my dear older brother and I were getting ready to take that enchanted walk, the first glitch happened. My six-year-old niece Lexie decided she did not want to walk down and toss the rose petals; she started to cry and blubber that she wanted to take a nap! My perfect little hula flower girl absolutely refused to go, so the next best thing was to tell her older brother Jordan to do it, but he most definitely refused. Okay, so now what? Zak, the other brother, was the only one we trusted to carry the pillow with the rings leaving him off the hook. Now with everyone looking and laughing, I was getting upset. Donni kept saying with a grin, "Keep smiling, we will laugh at this someday." Last resort, we turn to the dad of the kids and said "You're up, Sandman!" With that, he sighed and took the basket of rose petals, proceeding to walk ahead, tossing them all over the place. It was the funniest thing ever. That in itself made the situation tolerable. We still fall over laughing at petal boy, as he was called for the rest of the day and then some.

When our vows had been made and I was finally Chris Boutillette's wife, I felt a confidence and security that overwhelmed me with happiness. We both laughed as we walked back down the aisle to our guests for the real party. It was magnificent. My mom's backyard proved to be the perfect venue, with all of her gorgeous flowers blooming and the picturesque lake framing the entire scene. I especially took notice of all of the white flowers that had seemingly popped up overnight; they gave me the pure feeling that God was indeed showing his approval.

Chris and I wanted our dear friend Diane Paradise to be with us that day. Diane (Spooky), as mentioned earlier, had been a part of our lives forever, and it would not be right if she didn't share this day with us. Also, Donni's ex-wife Janet Lawsen had been a part of our family since the mid-seventies, so of course, we had to have her there as well. As it happens, my brother had brought his present wife and mother of his three children along, and we were happy for that, but what it did was put all the women that my brother had been deeply involved with in the same place. There was no tension at all; as a matter of fact, by the middle of the night, all three women ganged up on him, and they all fell into the pool. That was the highlight of the evening.

All had a fabulous time, and it was after 3 a.m. that Chris loaded me into his 1967 blue Cadillac, and we headed home. We only got a couple hours of sleep because we needed to catch our flight to Orlando, where we would spend the next ten days in Mickey Heaven!

CHAPTER 26

As the years passed, I would come to be very close with my mom. We still had those terrible arguments that happen in mother-daughter relationships, but it made all the times (which were many) when we would laugh till we nearly wet our pants. When Kim was with us, it was even better.

Mom and I used to drive down to Florida, where she would spend February and March with her lifelong friend Janet Cramm Wilson. During her visits, Mom would also spend time with her cousins that lived down there. I would fly back to New England until it was time for her to return home; then I would fly into Tampa, where Mom would pick me up and we would then head out for the trip back up north. Over the years, it became a tradition for us. We had our little habits that we created while on our trips, and till this day, I recall them with endearing memories. My favorites were when she would exhibit her mother bear personality.

I need to tell one story that will make you howl laughing. It was on our first adventure, and as it happened, we drove right into the heart of a huge snowstorm. Mom was a brilliant driver, and we were able to go quite a distance as we passed so many spun-out cars, jackknifed eighteen-wheelers, and such.

Folks in North Carolina were not used to snow, much less a blizzard! Finally, as we passed yet another stuck vehicle, Mom decided it was time to get off the road for the night. We pulled into a funky little motel, and they had one room left. We did not dare get picky and grabbed it. As I was trudging in with something, a couple of young men asked me where the nearest club was. I of course had no idea and assumed they were looking to get me to party with them, at which point Mom stuck her head out the door as I was coming in and in a fierce voice asked, "What is going on out here?" With that, those two knuckleheads turned back into their own rooms. Mom and I just laughed. I thought she was wonderful coming to my defense.

Later on, as we watched the junky television while laughing and snorting, she sat on the bed, and the headboard fell down with a crash on the floor behind it. That was hilarious beyond description. Because it was rather late at this point, we got aloud knock on the wall or door (it was hard to distinguish), at which point Mom immediately yelled, "Go to bed!" Oh, now that just sent us into another hysterical fit of laughter, realizing that it could have been just the next room, we quietened down. But just in case it was something not kosher, we decided to create our own safety precautions. As we were on the ground floor and there were no bars on the bathroom window, it would be easy for someone to slip in.

I took the plastic advertisement that was on the counter and placed it so if the window was moved in any way, the plastic would clatter to the tile, giving us a heads-up. Next, we wedged a chair under the front doorknob. For the final touch of safety, I gave Mom the long-handled snowbrush, telling her to put that next to her. Looking at my mother as she held her weapon was another round of snorting and laughing till our sides hurt.

Finally, we fell asleep. In the morning, we found ourselves snowed in tight. Mom, being the survivalist she was, knew how to get out of it. As I tried to move snow away from the tires, Mom would rock the Tahoe back and forth. Because the snow was so deep, it would prove impossible even with her skills and knowledge; then along came a payloader with George Clooney's twin! I did the proverbial double take. With Mom's knowledge, she instructed this gentleman on how to time her rocking the truck back and forth as to when he should pull. Within moments, she had that Chevy Tahoe clear and ready to travel. I was so proud of her. She gave the gentleman twenty-dollar tip. He was grateful and happy to be of assistance. Mom and I concurred. With that face, it was our pleasure. As the years flew by, I would have so many blessed memories made for cherishing.

Chris and I would go to Disney World as often as we could. It was, and still is, our favorite place to go as it is good and clean with kindness in abundance. That to me is a holiday we all need.

We brought Mom there with us once, not too long before we lost her. It was surely one of her favorite vacations. I will always get emotional when I think of all the fun we had. Chris is yet again to bring on the perfect moments in life.

One day, I got a phone call from my mother saying she had been to the doctor because she was suddenly seriously short of breath, scaring her pretty badly. The doctor made her come straight away and had X-rays taken of her lungs. Upon looking at them, he could see a dark mass of fluid halfway up her right lung. After testing the fluid and finding it to be cancerous, the doctor set up an appointment for her to get scoped and possibly retard its spreading. On the day of her surgery, I sat in the waiting room for hours. Finally, the doctor came to tell me his discovery and the actions he had taken. He began by saying that she had tumors all over her right lung and there was no way they could all be removed. He said he was so very sorry as he gently patted me on the back then slowly turned to leave. He was very kind, and I did not feel like he did not care. I cried and cried. All during this time, I had been in contact with my brother Jim, who is a neonatal respiratory therapist in Torrance, California. He was my rock.

Kim and I made a pact with Mom in that she would not go through this alone; we would be with her every step of the way as she went through all the chemotherapy blood tests and any procedures she might need. We kept our promise right to the end.

I have to give mention to all my family as they did their best to make the last two years of her life as comfortable possible, never letting her feel alone. All the brothers and the sister that live in other States made the effort to come be with her in her final hours. Most of all, I have to thank my husband for his unwavering support. He was such a help to her in making and would see to it her wishes were fulfilled in certain matters. He welcomed everyone into our home, which went on for over two months.

From the time we discovered the sad news, we kept all the siblings up to date from that point on. I have to say that because my mother was so adamant in her health regime over her life she was able to fight harder than most. Kim and I did as we promised and went everywhere with her. When it came to any and every doctor's appointment, procedure, or surgery, we were both by her side. Kim-Laurie was my champion, and I will forever be grateful for her strength and fortitude.

We got through the first year with as much fun and togetherness as we could. Not that we did not before, but it was extra bittersweet knowing we were on borrowed time. Mom took her usual vacation, which usually consisted from February through March (the least fun time in New England).

My mother's side of the family, the Putnams, has always been and still are a close-knit bunch, so when they were informed of her cancer and the length of time left, they were there for her.

Two more Putnam family reunions left for us with Mom so my brothers Donni, David, Ross, and Lorne, along with their families, made the long trip from the West Coast. What a blessing it was for her to have this wonderful time with her children. We were the original family to camp before the gathering, which was always held on the Sunday before Labor Day. Honoring the request made by my great-grandfather George Henry Putnam, we have been gathering yearly ever since, right in the very same building as back in 1935 when Mom was only five years old.

Now being in the triple digits from that one ancestor, it is an amazing sight to see how the camping grew from being only my mother and us six kids in 1961 to the tradition it has become today. It would take a few years for it to really take off, but the second year Mom's sister Ginny and her two kids, Jeff and Cathy, would become our yearly companions. Those cousins Jeff and Cathy Hatch were as close as siblings to us growing up, and the adventures everyone had could be a book in itself!

The Putnam family is now heading into its eightieth reunion. What a blessing. Now on the Thayer side of my family, we were not so close but close as cousins usually are. We shared many fun times with Bobby, Dickey, and Dianne, the children of our Uncle Howard and Aunt Bess. Howard was my father's older brother, and I loved him dearly. My dad's sister Jean and her family were also close to us until my mom and dad got divorced, causing us to be an embarrassment to them. We have since become close again, especially with Scott Kempton and his wife Carol. It's a good feeling.

Weeks before we found out about Mom's cancer, Chris had suggested that we have a big eightieth birthday bash for her and invite everybody, at which I had said they won't come all the way from California for a birthday party! Chris disagreed wholeheartedly. Chris has known my family for most of my life and so knew what their answer would be. So I went ahead and made the phone calls, and lo and behold, they all said yes, they would come. All but Jimmy.

We had a year to prepare, and they too had as much time to arrange travel plans. It would be about three or four months later that we would discover we only had a short time left with her, making the birthday bash that much more special.

Jim would come out for one-on-one time with her instead of coming to her party. It turned out to be a smash hit, and we were able to keep her in the dark all the way up to when everyone revealed themselves. She actually thought it was a Halloween party that the neighbors threw and invited her as well, which made her feel special in itself, but when it was time to reveal the true nature of the gathering, she was blown away!

Chris arranged for his friend Ernie, the DJ, to have the children do a walk about so we could see all of their costumes. Mom and I were to be judges, along with my brother Don, who wore an old-man mask and didn't speak the whole time. Mom was sitting next to him and trying to engage him in conversation with no luck. When Ernie gave him the microphone, he stood up and said in a mean drunkard kind of way, "I did not come to judge kid's costumes," but then (in a gentle voice) said, "I came here to celebrate my mother's birthday!" He removed his mask and reached for her hand to stand her up next to him. All the while, Dave and Ross rolled out a gigantic cake, followed by Lorne, Ellen Heather, Kim, and all the grandchildren, as well as many nieces and nephews with their children. They had all made the huge effort to be there for her special day. She cried.

During the next year we would live life as normally as possible. Mom would not look sick all the way to the last few months. Mom and I would take one last trip to Ohio to see my sister Ellen and her son Bryce. It was now late spring. We would not make the drive straight through as we used to do, instead stopping when Mom could not take any more travel. We would stay the night in a motel. We would resume the remainder of the trip to Huber Heights the next day.

It was a wonderful time with Ellen and Bryce, and I got some priceless pictures. I was noticing Mom not eating much, looking more gaunt and her skin darkening. She was also unable to camouflage her discomfort. She became increasingly snappy as the days went on. At first, I was hurt by her meanness only to catch myself and remembering the cause of it.

The weekend was over, and we headed back to Massachusetts. Mom slept while I drove for the most part until we got to the halfway point, where we checked into a motel. This would be our last one. After resuming our trip home the next day, Mom slept again most of the way. At one point, we had to stop for gas where a Krispy Kreme just happened to be (I love KK). I had to buy one. While standing there, waiting for the waitress, I decided I had to buy two of the KK coffee cups, which were old-fashioned-looking but with a tiny doughnut lying at the bottom of the cup. I had the coffee put into them and served one to Mom. When she got to the end of her coffee and noticing the little doughnut on the bottom, she thought it was something stuck that did not come out when washed, if it even got washed. I think that was the biggest laugh we had that weekend.

By summer, a couple of weeks into warm weather, the doctor said Mom was not getting any nourishment and said he wanted her to have a G-tube put in. The date was set, and I could not go with her because a freakish back spasm happened to me and I spent the next three days on the couch, but Kim was there. When the spasm hit me, I was out on the deck; I went down like a sack of potatoes and could not move even an inch. By the time Kim drove up and hearing my little dog Myla barking, she came up to find me laid out. She went inside to get Mom to help her pick me up, but upon seeing me, the first thing she (always the nurse) said was, "Wait! I'll get the blood pressure kit!" Kim was so funny as she told her to forget the BP kit and help get me inside first. I couldn't even laugh because it just hurt too much, but I laugh about it now, even still.

Kim told me later that while Mom was sitting on the hospital bed, still dressed and swinging her feet back and forth, the doctor to come in to tell her about the procedure (being an RN for so many years, she knew the information) came in, expecting to see a wrinkled and bald eighty-year-old in stage 4 cancer. What they found was that Mom had not lost her looks or youthful attitude, nor was she bald, but had hair that was full, fluffy, and curly. The doctor was amazed at how good she looked. He did not think she was the patient he was there to see.

As it turned out, she had not been getting any food at all. It was building up in her esophagus. We were unaware that she was getting no nourishment whatsoever.

The surgeons placed a tube into her belly that connected to a bag that would deliver liquid nourishment. Even though she wasn't masticating it, she could still taste it, and she felt like she was ingesting motor oil. By now, she is really starving and had been for so long. It broke my heart, and still the memory is painful for us. The hardest times were when she would insist on being at the table with us while we ate our meals so she could enjoy the food as we ate. It was not making us feel any better. Lorne left the table as she sat watching us eat. It was too much for him. Chris and I did not enjoy it either, but she insisted. We were able to ease into these things, but Lorne and the others did not and were shocked by all that was happening.

Over the next few weeks, many of the siblings would come to spend a few days with her, and seeing that she was feeling okay, they were quality visits. At one point, Kim and I were going out to Chicago for Codi's graduation from Navy boot camp, which happened to be over the Mother's Day weekend. We did not want to leave her alone, especially on Mother's Day. We knew Chris and all the other kids would be there for her but wanted to make what was likely her last Mother's Day special. What a treat it would be to spend it with as many other children as possible. Ross flew in from Southern California to be with her. God bless him.

Kim and I drove out to the graduation, and Justin (a dear friend of Codi's from high school) made the trip with us. The three of us had a long but fun drive out there.

When we arrived, we checked into our hotel and proceeded to the event, which was wonderful, knowing she was done with that ordeal. Later we went out to eat and celebrate. In the evening, we all went to our hotel room and just hung out and listened to the most hilarious stories about the things that transpired between Codi and her mates and/or the drill instructors or other powers that be. We laughed so hard my stomach hurt for days. The next day, we left for the trip back but without Justin, as he stayed to take a road trip with Codi for her break before getting her orders.

Kim and I had a good time just being together as we talked, laughed, and just contemplated things—just being sisters on a road trip. There would be fewer trips for me now. Kim does not like to travel, but she will, and I will tag along whenever I can.

We made it back to Massachusetts, but not in time to see Ross. It was wonderful knowing he was able to come for Mom on what was to be her and our last Mother's Day with her.

As the days passed, Mom was getting more and more discouraged with the quality of her life. She could not even drink water other than tiny sips. Eventually, she could not even tolerate that. Kim and I both knew she was not going to last much longer. Mom had lost the fierce desire she always had for life. It was hard for her to keep her breath, so she was hooked up to a machine to help her. She could not look forward to having her favorite dessert of strawberries and whipped cream anymore, which was heartbreaking.

When it seemed as though she was not going to make it another week, I did as Donni requested and let him know that the end was near. He arrived from San Antonio, Texas, just two days later. In addition, Ross and his two adult children, Jowelle and Ryan, came in from LA and our little sister Ellen from Ohio.

Upon seeing everybody by her, she was overjoyed with the chance to say one final good-bye, yet she seemed to gather strength from the angels as she basked (albeit in bed and unable to really speak with any force). She managed to stay with us for another month and a half. All of us took shifts in twos as we kept watch over her, and we had baby monitors in her room with extensions all over the house. We were giving her morphine every couple of hours, but had to increase the frequency as the days wore on and her pain was becoming more and more unbearable. Still, she held on. Even the hospice nurse had told us that she would not last the night and began preparing us.

We sat like schoolchildren as she instructed us what to expect. Mom hung on for one more month and six days! The hospice nurse was amazed at her tenacity and went on to say we were the best hospice family she had ever met. We were that attentive, not to mention that among us all, there was enough knowledge in the care of the elderly—one sister Karen being an RN and another sister Heather, a CNA. My dear friend Becky Powell, also a CNA, came to assist as needed. Along with her came her little dog, Crouton, who loved Grammie.

Our amazing mother stayed with us, we believe, for so much longer due to the fact that she had almost every one of her children with her under one roof. She did not want to leave just yet in spite of the immense pain she was in. We came to know every grimace and wrinkle of pain and kept a diligent eye out for that. Finally, one day we all came to the conclusion that she was hanging on so dearly to what was left of her well-lived life because we were still hanging on to her. We realized that we had not left her alone for one second. I had slept with her, but she complained to Heather that I kicked her all night, so our niece Tessie slept next to her all nice and peaceful on some of the evenings. There was big brother Donni, who seemed indefatigable as he administered her meds, keeping a running chart of each and every one. My niece and nephew, two of Kim-Laurie's children, would spend as much time with her as possible. Tessie, my sweet girl, would stay by her Grammie's side. It was so precious to see how much Tessie would act as her protector. We both had similar experiences with being under her rule, so I think we had our reasons for wanting to be as close to her as possible. I think the two of us, in our own ways, wanted her to know how much we loved her, and there were no more hard feelings. Corey, my nephew, would come over after spending all day bartending at Foxwoods Casino in Ledyard, Connecticut, which was over an hour's drive for him. He made quality time to be with her as well. In many occasions, they both would stay overnight and be part of the vigil keepers. These two precious grandchildren showed their Grammie so much love, which was what she could take with her. Ross's daughter and son, Jowelle and Ryan, were no less indefatigable in their diligent care of their beloved Grammie. It was all these precious ones that Mom got to see in her final hours.

Younger sister Kim-Laurie was no less diligent in her being by Mom's side, even sleeping with her head on the bed as she sat on a chair. Kim was continuously swabbing her mouth with a sponge on a stick full of water as she could not even take a sip of water or even an ice cube, leaving her with a cotton-dry mouth. Younger brother Ross, along with his daughter Jowelle, would do the toilet duty up until it was no longer possible. We came to the decision that we should give her a respite from all of us hovering around her 24/7, so in the wee hours of the morning of June 6, 2012, Mom quietly slipped away.

She now sleeps waiting to be raised up when God Almighty makes all things new. Hallelujah! I still miss her, and it is hard to believe she is gone, but to quote my husband, "Now you have to turn the page." A profound statement in so many ways.

CHAPTER 27

Donni had a reunion gig with the band he was a member of in the '80s, Mad Angel, along with Jimmy and Joey De Angelo was Joey Zaccarro, and of course, my brother. Being a very popular band, they decided months ago that Donni come back for that which was to be played at the Hanover Theatre in Worcester, Massachusetts, a prestigious place to be seen.

As it happened, the show was for the week following, which allowed Donni to stay for a bit longer. I was so glad to have him here, as being the family patriarch we needed his big-brother strength. Still do.

On the evening of his show and all the family was together again, we all went off to celebrate our brother's performance. All our seats had been purchased and reserved for months already, so in Mom's seat, Donni put a single rose along with a program. That was the only empty seat in the house. What a great bittersweet time we had that night. An evening to remember.

Life commenced, and we had much to do. A difficult task to say the least, but it had to be done and not put off so that we could begin the healing process. As Mom once said to me, "Time doesn't always heal the wound, but it will soften the edges some." Those were one of the most profound statements I have ever heard, and I have quoted her on numerous occasions.

I miss her so much. Another June approaches since she has been gone, and time has softened the edges some, a little.

Almost two years to the date of Mom's passing, we lost our brother David. He had just one month before he celebrated his sixtieth birthday and two years to the date of Mom. He now sleeps too.

I look forward to that time when we will see them again. Until then, we will laugh and cry over the memories. He is dearly missed as well.

On August of 2014, on our twelfth anniversary, Chris and I went up to Bethel, New York, where the Woodstock Festival was held on Yasgur's property, which is now a site dedicated to the original one back in '69. I had not been back since I was fifteen years old. The land was just as it was back then, except for a museum that was dedicated to those three days of love, peace, and music. We drove our RV to a site for camping. After setting in, Chris decided he wanted to check out the farm. After about an hour or so, he returned to tell me who was playing that night, but the best he left for last. He asked if I had any idea who was scheduled to play the next night. Of course, I said no, and then he went on to tell me an old friend was to perform in the concert hall of the museum, and that being Dickey Betts. I was so amazed. What are the odds of that happening? I knew I had to try to go see him. I had every confidence that he would remember me as little Peggie or little one from "Worcestah."

The next day was beautiful and sunny. It was the tenth of August, our twelfth anniversary. What could go wrong? Actually nothing went wrong, but trying to get to say even hello to an old friend turned out to be a sad failure. A couple of really nice things did occur, and that was we met the bus driver Larry Lorenzen, who owned the huge Prevost RV that I knew for a fact would be the one Dickey would be using. I inquired as to where I might find the man himself but to no avail as the driver did not know when he would get there from the hotel he was booked at for the night.

Okay, so we would hang out as was the plan all along to walk about and my telling Chris exactly what, where, and when things went on during those three amazingly dirty fun days. I showed him all the places where we sat over the course of those days. We went out to sit in one of the spots where I had sat so many years before. It was the night ten years after they played, and the Who and Sly and the Family Stone played as well. It was an awesome evening with friends. We still celebrate the anniversaries of that historic time.

While there, I was amazed at all of the people who never attended the concerts but still visited the museum nonetheless.

As we walked through the place, we would run into Larry on occasion but only nodded in each other's direction. Have you ever met someone you immediately felt a kinship with? Anyway, as the day wore on and we watched for the arrival of my friend, we would be meeting some of the band members as they arrived, and I had gone over to them one by one and asked if they could help me out. They tried but to no avail. I went over to the bus when I saw him pull up in a people mover van from the hotel and went to get someone to go tell him I was here at the same place he was for the first time in years. No one had any luck. The keyboard player tried but told me Dickey was eating and did not want to be disturbed yet but that he would try later for me. I thanked him and went back to my vigil.

At one point, I noticed Larry sitting on the wall and went to talk to him. I had mentioned how I was having so much trouble, so he said, "Why don't you go ask his son over there?" I was dumbstruck as I had been seeing him all afternoon and could have been talking to him. Well, I went over and introduced myself and asked what his name was. No sooner than he said Duane I felt a little shock, and (I guess he gets this all the time) I asked, "Were you named…" Before I could finish my question, he said, "Yes." At that point, I knew I did not need to expound on that subject—painful for me, redundant for him. I had mentioned being with the Brothers when they played Buffalo and Twiggs (the original road manager) and the tragic times that followed. I only got to relate a small account of the incident due to the fact they had to go onstage then.

Well, I know how it is with playing a gig that when you are done all you want to do is go somewhere else, and there would be no opportunity to get an audience with Dickey. Not even his son could manage that for me.

Chris kept telling me not to give up, but I did not want to look and sound like a groupie. For him, I kept trying. I will not challenge my self-respect for anyone, but because it seemed to be so important to Chris, I had to continue my attempts. God love Larry for keeping Chris company all this time, as they both sat hanging out and chatting.

When the concert was over, Duane came out and hung out with his beautiful lady, and I was able to chat with him a little more. He said he was sorry that his father did not remember me at all, going on to say that his memory was just about shot. I understood completely. Duane knows I realized the reason for this. I thanked him for trying anyway. A short while later, they all left. Chris and I then drove back to the campsite. We were together so that was a successful day no matter what, and we made a new friend in Larry.

Since that time, I have been seeing posts on Duane's Facebook page, and somehow Devon Allman began to pop up. I have since been learning of Butch's nephew Derik Trucks, who is a monster guitar player, and I love listening to him and Susan Tedeschi. All those sons of the Allman Brothers Band have grown into wonderful musicians in their own rights. I wish them the best.

Over this past year, we have been keeping busy with the record number of snow that fell by shoveling, snow-blowing, plowing, and everything else that comes with all that snow. I can just imagine how little kids will remember the mountain-high snow piles all over the place. I thought they were high when I was a kid, and we had nothing close to what this past winter brought. It was below freezing all over the country. We kept tabs on where Larry was, asking how his rig was handling the extreme weather and how he was doing with the hardship of navigating such a big rig in terrible weather. He managed. We might someday have to ask him for tips if we ever get caught in nasty cold weather, although I do not plan on a trip to Alaska anytime soon!

There was a time before the heavy snow began to fly when Larry had to take a band to Mohegan Sun Casino, and of course, we being only an hour away made plans to hook up with him for the afternoon. It was so nice to see our friend again. Someday we will make it out to San Antonio, where we will be able to visit him and my brother Donni, who lives out there with his family as well.

It snowed in May of 2015. Dramatic change in the weather is upsetting to most people today. Change in our lives usually is. There is one thing we can be assured of—God is the same now as he was in the beginning. I would like to end my story by including my wonderful friend Becky Powell, whom I mentioned earlier on. Becky is the champion of lost hurt or downright broken animals. She is the one we all bring these unfortunate creatures to for healing or a safe haven to pass away. Becky also has a special gift of finding people who long to know the God of the Bible. We met by chance—or was it? With her help, I search, study, and apply what the scriptures teach for remaining on the narrow path of righteousness—faith in the forgiveness of our many mistakes, faith in the mightiest gift all, the loving ransom sacrifice of God's only begotten son, Jesus.

There is one thing I pray you take away from reading my life's experiences. Keep in your heart that Almighty God Jehovah or however you refer to the Supreme Being is a hope we all have, superseding any fear we may feel in unforeseen circumstances that may cause us harm.

I have my life to show for it. I lived to tell.

ACKNOWLEDGEMENTS

I would not have been able to get this far if it were not for the boundless encouragement of my husband Chris.

I would like to thank my sister Kim-Laurie Thayer for helping me remember time sequences in certain areas.

My niece Tracy De Veaux for helping me organize my thoughts whenever I was writing while visiting her in DC.

One more person I need to give a huge thank you to is my Publication Coordinator, Stacy Tatters, who without her patience and incredible ability to restructure my maze of words this work would not have made much sense to anyone but me.

ABOUT THE AUTHOR

Magarette was born in a state of confusion. She went on to attend the School of Hard Knocks. She graduated with honors from the University of Diversity and earned her BA in the Community College of Heartbreak and Healing. Later on, Magarette would go on to become a professor of intrigue while studying with the masters of survival. Now she lives with her husband, Chris, whom she had known back in the '60s and married in later years. Together, they enjoy life with their Maltese, Myla-Jane, and two cats, Grumpy and Smitty Kitty Smudge-man.